Materiality and the Study of Religion

Material culture has emerged in recent decades as a significant theoretical concern for the study of religion. This book contributes to and evaluates this material turn, presenting thirteen chapters of new empirical research and theoretical reflection from some of the leading international scholars of material religion. Following a model for material analysis proposed in the first chapter by David Morgan, the contributors trace the life cycle of religious materiality through three phases: the production of religious objects, their classification as religious (or non-religious), and their circulation and use in material culture.

The chapters in this volume consider how objects become and cease to be sacred, how materiality can be used to contest access to public space and resources, and how religion is embodied and performed by individuals in their everyday lives. Contributors discuss the significance of the materiality of religion across different religious traditions and diverse geographical regions, paying close attention to gender, age, ethnicity, memory and politics. The volume closes with an afterword by Manuel Vásquez.

Tim Hutchings is a postdoctoral researcher in the Institute for Media Studies at Stockholm University, Sweden. He is a sociologist of digital religion, and his research has included studies of online churches, digital Bibles, evangelism and pilgrimage. His current work focuses on death, grief and memory in digital environments, as part of the Existential Terrains research program (et.ims.su.se) funded by the Knut and Alice Wallenberg Foundation, the Marcus and Amalia Wallenberg Foundation and Stockholm University. He is the editor of the *Journal of Religion, Media and Digital Culture* (jrmdc.com).

Joanne McKenzie is currently undertaking doctoral research in the Department of Theology and Religion at Durham University, UK. The project is focused on how social class shapes contemporary English evangelicalism and is funded by the Arts and Humanities Research Council.

Theology and Religion in Interdisciplinary Perspective Series in association with the BSA Sociology of Religion Study Group

For a full list of titles in this series, please visit www.routledge.com

The British Sociological Association Sociology of Religion Study Group began in 1975 and provides the primary forum in Britain for scholarship in the sociology of religion. The nature of religion remains of key academic interest and this series draws on the latest worldwide scholarship in compelling and coherent collections on critical themes. Secularisation and the future of religion; gender; the negotiation and presentation of religious identities, beliefs and values; and the interplay between group and individual in religious settings are some of the areas addressed. Ultimately, these books reflect not just on religious life but also on how wider society is affected by the enduring religious framing of human relationships, morality and the nature of society itself. This series is part of the broader Theology and Religion in Interdisciplinary Perspective Series, edited by Douglas Davies and Richard Fenn.

Recent titles in the series include:

Religion and Knowledge
Sociological Perspectives
Edited by Mathew Guest and Elisabeth Arweck

Religion and Youth
Edited by Sylvia Collins-Mayo and Pink Dandelion

A Sociology of Spirituality
Edited by Kieran Flanagan and Peter C. Jupp

Materiality and the Study of Religion
The Stuff of the Sacred
Edited by Tim Hutchings and Joanne McKenzie

Materiality and the Study of Religion

The Stuff of the Sacred

Edited by Tim Hutchings
and Joanne McKenzie

LONDON AND NEW YORK

First published 2017
by Routledge
2 Park Square, Milton Park, Abingdon, Oxon OX14 4RN

and by Routledge
711 Third Avenue, New York, NY 10017

Routledge is an imprint of the Taylor & Francis Group, an informa business

© 2017 selection and editorial matter, Tim Hutchings and Joanne McKenzie; individual chapters, the contributors

The right of Tim Hutchings and Joanne McKenzie to be identified as the authors of the editorial material, and of the authors for their individual chapters, has been asserted in accordance with sections 77 and 78 of the Copyright, Designs and Patents Act 1988.

All rights reserved. No part of this book may be reprinted or reproduced or utilised in any form or by any electronic, mechanical, or other means, now known or hereafter invented, including photocopying and recording, or in any information storage or retrieval system, without permission in writing from the publishers.

Trademark notice: Product or corporate names may be trademarks or registered trademarks, and are used only for identification and explanation without intent to infringe.

British Library Cataloguing in Publication Data
A catalogue record for this book is available from the British Library

Library of Congress Cataloging in Publication Data
Names: Hutchings, Tim (Sociologist of digital religion), editor.
Title: Materiality and the study of religion : the stuff of the sacred / edited by Tim Hutchings and Joanne McKenzie.
Description: New York : Routledge, 2016. | Series: Theology and religion in interdisciplinary perspective series in association with the BSA Sociology of Religion Study Group | Includes bibliographical references and index.
Identifiers: LCCN 2016034082 | ISBN 9781472477835 (hardback : alk. paper) | ISBN 9781315604787 (ebook)
Subjects: LCSH: Religious articles. | Religion and culture. | Material culture—Religious aspects. | Materialism—Religious aspects.
Classification: LCC BL603 .M38 2016 | DDC 203—dc23
LC record available at https://lccn.loc.gov/2016034082

ISBN: 978-1-4724-7783-5 (hbk)
ISBN: 978-1-315-60478-7 (ebk)

Typeset in Bembo
by Apex CoVantage, LLC

This book is dedicated to Rachel Hanemann, for her careful work as copy-editor; to Paul McKenzie, for his constant encouragement throughout the project; to our editors at Ashgate and Routledge; and to the committee and members of the BSA Sociology of Religion Study Group, for supporting the conference at which it all began.

Contents

List of contributors   ix

Introduction: The body of St Cuthbert   1
TIM HUTCHINGS AND JOANNE MCKENZIE

1 **Material analysis and the study of religion**   14
DAVID MORGAN

PART 1
Production   33

2 **From production to performance: Candles, creativity and connectivity**   35
MARION BOWMAN

3 **Blessed food from Jalarām's kitchen: Narrative, continuity and service among Jalarām Bāpā devotees in London**   52
MARTIN WOOD

4 **Music and materialism: The emergence of alternative Muslim lifestyle cultures in Britain**   67
CARL MORRIS

5 **Augmented graves and virtual Bibles: Digital media and material religion**   85
TIM HUTCHINGS

PART 2
Classification 101

6 Art works: A relational rather than representational understanding of art and buildings 103
GRAHAM HARVEY

7 Im/material objects: Relics, gestured signs and the substance of the immaterial 119
TIMOTHY CARROLL

8 'An altar inside a circle': A relational model for investigating green Christians' experiments with sacred space 133
MARIA NITA

9 The significance of secular sacred space in the formation of British atheist identities 151
JANET ECCLES AND REBECCA CATTO

PART 3
Circulation 167

10 Death in material and mental culture 169
DOUGLAS J. DAVIES

11 Religion materialised in the everyday: Young people's attitudes towards material expressions of religion 185
ELISABETH ARWECK

12 Mobilising Mecca: Reassembling blessings at the museum 203
STEPH BERNS

13 Matter challenging words: From 'angel talisman' to 'prayer ornament' 219
TERHI UTRIAINEN

Afterword: Materiality, lived religion, and the challenges of "going back to the things themselves" 235
MANUEL VÁSQUEZ

Index 242

Contributors

Elisabeth Arweck is a principal research fellow in the Warwick Religions and Education Research Unit (WRERU), Centre for Education Studies, University of Warwick, and editor of the *Journal of Contemporary Religion*. Her recent research has focused on young people's attitudes to religious diversity and the religious socialisation and nurture of young people. Recent publications include a number of chapters, co-authored articles and (co-edited) books, including the edited volume *Young People's Attitudes to Religious Diversity* (Ashgate, 2017).

Steph Berns is a researcher working within the fields of museum studies and the sociology of religion. She previously worked on a postdoctoral ethnographic study with Lancaster University, about urban rituals and religious events in London. Prior to this, she completed a collaborative doctorate with the University of Kent and the British Museum on visitors performing religious practices in museums.

Marion Bowman is based in the Religious Studies department at the Open University, UK. She is currently Visiting Professor in the department of Culture Studies and Oriental Languages, University of Oslo, co-investigator on the AHRC-funded project Pilgrimage and England's Cathedrals, Past and Present (2014–2017) (http://www.pilgrimageandcathedrals.ac.uk/about) and, vice-president of the European Association for the Study of Religions. Her research is fieldwork-based, focused on vernacular religion, contemporary manifestations/renegotiations of pilgrimage, and material culture. She has conducted long-term ethnological research in Glastonbury and in Newfoundland, Canada. She co-edited Vernacular Religion in Everyday Life: Expressions of Belief (Routledge 2012) with Ulo Valk.

Rebecca Catto is an assistant professor in the Department of Sociology at Kent State University, USA. She is a former convenor of the British Sociology of Religion Study Group, co-investigator on the £1.9 million grant 'Science and Religion: Exploring the Spectrum', and co-editor of *Religion and Change in Modern Britain* (Routledge, 2012, with Linda Woodhead). Her publications include work on Christian mission, atheism, youth and religion, law, policy and religion and belief, and interfaith dialogue.

Timothy Carroll is a teaching fellow in social anthropology and material culture at the University College London. His work addresses the use of materials in Eastern Orthodox Christian worshipful practice, focusing on the art-like production of the self. Currently he is working on preliminary research investigating the ethical and aesthetic implications around the body in end-of-life care, through death, mortuary and memorial practices in Orthodox Christianity. He is co-editing a volume entitled *Material Culture of Failure: When Things Do Wrong*, due to be published with Bloomsbury in 2017.

Douglas J. Davies is a professor in the study of religion and director of the Centre for Death and Life Studies at Durham University. He trained in anthropology and theology, and his death- and funeral-related work on ritual-symbolism, belief, emotion and identity is complemented by studies of Mormons and Anglicans. He is a fellow of the Academy of Social Sciences and of The Learned Society of Wales, an Oxford doctor of letters and an honorary doctor of theology of Sweden's Uppsala University. His most recent book is *Mors Britannica: Lifestyle and Death-style in Britain Today* (OUP, 2015).

Janet Eccles gained her PhD on Christian and disaffiliated women in 2010, as a mature student at Lancaster University UK, followed by a period as research associate on the Young Atheists Project. Now an independent researcher, she has published journal articles and/or book chapters on topics ranging from Christian women affiliates and disaffiliates and forms of non-religion to multifaith chaplaincy, Anglican monasticism and insider/outsider issues.

Graham Harvey is a professor of religious studies at the Open University. His research has largely involved engagement with the performance and material cultures of Pagans and Indigenous peoples, mostly recently contributing to the reconsideration of animism in diverse cultural contexts. His publications include *The Handbook of Contemporary Animism* (2013) and *Food, Sex and Strangers: Understanding Religion as Everyday Life* (2013).

Tim Hutchings is a postdoctoral researcher in the Institute for Media Studies at Stockholm University, Sweden. He is a sociologist of digital religion, and his research has included studies of online churches, digital Bibles, evangelism and pilgrimage. His current work focuses on death, grief and memory in digital environments, as part of the Existential Terrains research program (et.ims.su.se) funded by the Knut and Alice Wallenberg Foundation, the Marcus and Amalia Wallenberg Foundation and Stockholm University. He is the editor of the *Journal of Religion, Media and Digital Culture* (jrmdc.com).

Contributors xi

Joanne McKenzie is currently undertaking doctoral research in the Department of Theology and Religion at Durham University, funded by the AHRC. The project is focused on how social class shapes contemporary English evangelicalism and is supervised by Dr Mathew Guest and Professor Robert Song. In 2013, Joanne was a research fellow at the John W. Kluge Centre at the Library of Congress, Washington DC, on the AHRC International Placement Scheme.

David Morgan is a professor of religious studies and chair of the Department of Religious Studies at Duke University. Author of *The Forge of Vision: A Visual History of Modern Christianity* (2015), *The Embodied Eye: Making Visibility in Religious Visual Culture* (2012), *The Lure of Images* (2007), *The Sacred Gaze* (2005), *Protestants and Pictures* (1999), and *Visual Piety* (1998), he is also an editor of the journal *Material Religion* and co-editor of a book series at Routledge entitled 'Religion, Media, Culture.' He is currently working on a book entitled *Images at Work: The Material Culture of Enchantment*.

Carl Morris is a lecturer in religion, culture and society at the University of Central Lancashire. His research has focused on Muslims and popular culture in Britain, with publications on music, spirituality and young Muslims. He served as general secretary for the Muslims in Britain Research Network (MBRN) during 2014–17.

Maria Nita is an associate lecturer at the University of South Wales. Her research interests include contemporary spirituality, religious identity and green rituals. She is the author of *Praying and Campaigning with Environmental Christians: Green Religion and the Climate Movement* (Palgrave McMillan, 2016), an ethnographic study of green Christian activism.

Terhi Utriainen is acting professor in the study of religions at the University of Helsinki as well as adjunct professor (docent) in gender studies. Her research and teaching interests include ethnography of lived religion, gender and embodiment, ritual studies, death, dying and suffering. She is co-editor of *Post-Secular Society* (Transaction, 2012), *Between Ancestors and Angels: Finnish Women Making Religion* (Palgrave McMillan, 2014) and the forthcoming volume *The Relational Dynamics of Enchantment and Sacralization: Changing the Terms of the Religion versus Secularity Debate* (Equinox).

Manuel Vásquez is the author of *More than Belief: A Materialist Theory of Religion* (Oxford, 2011). He is currently working with Vasudha Narayanan (University of Florida) on *The Wiley-Blackwell Companion to Religion and Materiality*.

Martin Wood teaches Hinduism and Buddhism at the University of Gloucestershire and contributes to the Study of Religions programme at Bath Spa University. His doctoral thesis (University of Bristol, 2009) examined the relationship between ritual food and issues of authority, identity and vernacular traditions among Gujarātī Hindus in the UK and New Zealand. He has subsequently conducted ethnographic research with the Jalarām Bāpā tradition, considering the role of universal service, miraculous blessings and narrative in the beliefs, practices and development of the tradition in the UK diaspora (Leicester and London) and India. His current work focuses on the way that specific religious and cultural identities are negotiated between generations and promoted through media applications, wider social inclusion and charity and social service through the distribution of food.

Introduction
The body of St Cuthbert

Tim Hutchings and Joanne McKenzie

The idea for this book emerged from "Material Religion", a conference of the BSA's Sociology of Religion Study Group (Socrel) hosted at Durham University in the spring of 2013. It seems appropriate, then, to begin our introduction with one of Durham's most famous and disputed examples of the materiality of religion: the body of St Cuthbert, the relic that the city's vast cathedral was built to contain.

St Cuthbert himself lived as a monk, bishop and legendary miracle-worker in the seventh century, and is associated most closely with the "Holy Island" of Lindisfarne. His monks fled the island in the ninth century, to escape Viking raids, and travelled across their extensive lands in what is now the border region between England and Scotland. They took with them the body of Cuthbert, which was said to have continued to perform miracles along the way; in particular, the body refused to decay.

By the eleventh century, the body had reached its final resting place: Durham. The hilltop site is a strong defensive location, but legend insists that it was chosen through another miracle. During their travels Cuthbert's coffin suddenly became too heavy to lift, and the saint appeared in a dream to explain the meaning of this strange predicament. Cuthbert had chosen his future resting place, called "Dunholme", and now the monks had to find it. No one had heard of a place called "Dunholme" until the monks overheard a conversation between two passing women. One was searching for a lost cow, and the other suggested looking for it – at "Dunholme". Local knowledge had solved the mystery. The monks followed them, carrying the now-compliant coffin, and discovered the site that would become Durham. The story of the cow is remembered today in a prominent sculpture on the cathedral, and also in the name of a pub.

St Cuthbert's corpse continued to attract attention in the following centuries. The Normans constructed a new cathedral for the saint, and opened his coffin again to prove that his body was still flexible. Cuthbert's shrine became richer and more lavish, competing nationally with newer centres of pilgrimage, like Canterbury. Eventually the cult was closed down by officers of Henry VIII in 1539, who smashed open the grave. One persistent rumour suggested that the body uncovered by the officers was still miraculously undecayed; another claimed that the body they found was not St Cuthbert at all, because the faithful monks had hidden him just in time.

In 1827, Cuthbert's grave was opened again by the cathedral librarian, James Raine. This time, the excavation would be undertaken with all the care and attention required of scientific history. Raine's book, *Saint Cuthbert*, describes a carefully planned antiquarian exploration attended by a crowd of senior clergy and workmen. The conditions of the grave, coffin and human remains were all meticulously measured and recorded. Inscriptions, carvings, fabrics and treasures are described in detail, including a small golden cross, buried in the saint's robes, which no previous observer had reported.

Nothing remained of St Cuthbert but bones, without 'any other trace of human flesh' (Raine 1828: 213). In fact, Raine argued, there was clear evidence that the whole legend of miraculous non-decay was a fraud all along. Careful observation of the skull led Raine to conclude that when the body was wrapped in cloth it was already 'nothing more than a bare dry bone' (Raine 1828: 214). The empty eye-holes had been stuffed with something white, to mislead viewers by giving 'the projecting appearance of eyes in their proper places'. In a moment of disconcerting violence, Raine reports that he poked one out: the white substance, 'upon being removed from its place, was easily pressed into a powder by the finger and thumb.' *Saint Cuthbert* includes an engraving of the skull resting upon a book, like a paperweight in an antiquarian's study. 'In the language of books once to be found in nurseries', Raine writes with a proud flourish, '*see here it is*' (Raine 1828: 214).

Cuthbert's bones were housed in a new coffin and returned to the tomb, but Raine's own description acknowledges the limits of his interest. Some items were removed for study, but the remaining 'mass of broken wood, iron rings, and iron bars' were rather casually 'thrown into the grave' (Raine 1828: 216). When Cuthbert was excavated again, in 1899, in the presence of Catholic witnesses, Raine's "coffin" was discovered to have been a cheap packing crate (Willem 2013: 83).

As historian Richard Bailey points out, *Saint Cuthbert* must be read 'as a partisan document', despite its 'very real academic achievement' (1989: 232). Raine's excavation took place at a moment of great local, national, political and religious significance. The process of Catholic emancipation was underway, removing many of the historic restrictions on Catholic rights. In Durham, a large new Catholic church was under construction, dedicated to St Cuthbert. Raine timed his investigation of the tomb just two weeks before the opening. His text revels in uncovering evidence of Catholic superstition, greed and fraud, the folly of relics and the luxurious lives of wealthy monks. When Raine positions himself as the representative of reason, science and the future, uncovering the deceptions of the (Catholic) past, he is also trying to discredit the new atmosphere of religious tolerance.

The accuracy of Raine's account has been challenged, as well as his motives. According to John Lingard, a prominent local Catholic at the time, one of Raine's supposed witnesses denied any part in the investigation. In fact, Lingard's source claims, Raine and two workmen were discovered 'standing within the coffin and trampling on the contents' while a service was going on elsewhere in the church (Willem 2013: 79). Their excavation was chaotic and hurried, because they were desperate to finish before a crowd could gather. Another of Raine's listed collaborators later accused him of a 'wicked spoliation of the dead', for which 'I wish no evil may befall you' (Willem 2013: 78). No mention of Raine's plans can be found in cathedral records, suggesting that he may indeed have been acting without authorisation.

Durham Cathedral was rededicated to St Cuthbert in 2005, and the saint is now a key part of the building's distinctive branding and its appeal to visitors. The gold cross Raine found in Cuthbert's coffin has been adopted as the cathedral's symbol, and the shrine has been decorated to recapture some of its vibrant colour. Two contemporary banners by the artist Thetis Blacker hang on either side, each produced using wax taken from candles burned in the church. St Cuthbert's Day is celebrated every year with processions, services and special events. Regular pilgrimages travel between Durham and Lindisfarne.

The contemporary return to Cuthbert avoids the problem of his miraculous corpse altogether and instead reimagines the historical saint as a symbol of the distinctive heritage of north-east England. This adjustment allows the cathedral to package Christian spirituality as an integral part of regional identity and distinctiveness. The cathedral's dean delivered a sermon for St Cuthbert's Day in 2007, emphasising this theme with particular clarity:

> Cuthbert connects us to the world of Saxon Christianity . . . a Christianity of wild, remote places . . . rooted in the experience and traditions of islands that knew they belonged to the outer edge of the civilised world. His northern English Christianity stands for what is indigenous, forged and shaped among particular people in a particular place.
>
> (Sadgrove 2007)

According to this sermon, 'today's issues are not dissimilar': Cuthbert's seventh-century regionalism was echoed in contemporary tensions between England's north and south and in nationalist concerns about European government. St Cuthbert is still the focus for discourses in which religion is intertwined with politics, power and identity, just as he always has been.

St Cuthbert and the materiality of religion

These tales of St Cuthbert are stories of material religion. The connection between humanity and God is constructed, enacted, encountered and performed through material objects, including bodies, bones, rich treasures and stone buildings. At the same time, each of these stories also shows the complex interconnections between religion, nationality, money and boundaries. A material object, like the body of a saint, can be used to access divine power, to demonstrate authority and continuity, to claim an identity or to discredit an opponent. Attention to how people respond to and interact with material culture allows us to study their values, relationships, fears and aspirations. 'Religion happens materially' (Meyer et al. 2010: 209), but society also happens materially, and often through material religion.

The comic tale of the encounter between the Saxon monks and the cow of Durham, for example, is first recorded by the Norman monks who replaced them (Willem 2013: 28). The story reimagines the Saxons not as wealthy landowners and adept politicians but as lost, confused, helpless wanderers. By locating the source of their power entirely within the body of Cuthbert, the tale – and the public opening of the tomb in 1104 – eased the transition of authority to the new Norman owners of that body.

The subsequent reopenings of Cuthbert's tomb in 1539 and 1827 were also symbolic performances of ownership and power, designed to discredit the past and reinforce a new system. The role of the body was now reversed: post-Reformation, the transfer of authority required the destruction of Cuthbert's stubborn materiality, to prove that divine power had never been located within it.

Attention to materiality can also open up the question of "religion" itself. Cuthbert's body has transitioned repeatedly between degrees of sacredness, sometimes displayed as a site and channel of divine power and sometimes broken into a pile of bones. As we have seen, those transitions were accomplished through physical actions upon the body, accompanied by mediated discourses disseminated through reports and rumours. In the case of Raine's excavation of 1827, we also see the inflection of early archaeology and antiquarian history by theological commitments, religious prejudice and political anxieties, expressed through a determined effort to defend perceived boundaries between modern/rational/Anglican and superstitious/fraudulent/Catholic attitudes. Studies of material culture allow us to explore how religion happens, but also how it *ceases* to happen, and how the boundary between those conditions is established.

Defining the field: what is "material religion"?

According to S. Brent Plate, 'religious traditions . . . originate and survive through bodily engagement with the material elements of the world' (2015: 3). For Elisabeth Arweck and William Keenan, 'the idea of religion itself is largely unintelligible outside its incarnation in material expressions' (2006: 2–3). Matthew Engelke goes even further, arguing that 'all religion is material religion', to be understood 'in relation to the media of its materiality' (2012: 209). But what are these "material elements" or "expressions"? When we study material religion, what is it that we are looking at?

Introductions to material religion tend to begin with lists. According to the editors of the journal *Material Religion*, the terms "religion" and "materiality" can be understood only through 'a network of interrelated concepts', such as "body," "sensation," "thing" and "touch" (Meyer et al. 2011: 5). David Morgan introduces material religion in terms of 'ritual, daily practice, imagery, objects, spaces, and bodies' (2010: xiii), or 'sensations, things, spaces and performance'

(2010: 8), while S. Brent Plate mentions 'symbolic objects', sacred texts, special foods, buildings and human-made landscapes (2015: 3). These sets of terms outline a field concerned with human encounters with materiality, studying religion as it is lived and practised.

According to Plate, the key point of "material religion" is the primacy of materiality. Things are not just expressions or manifestations of ideas; on the contrary, 'ideas, beliefs, and doctrines begin in material reality' (2015: 4). As Morgan points out, objects do not always have a definable meaning, because 'human beings do not translate everything significant or compelling into words' (2010: xiii). The study of material religion begins with things and encounters, without expecting that their religious significance can be fully explained in verbal expressions of doctrine or symbolism.

Plate systematises these ideas to propose a five-part summary of the interests of "material religion", defined as:

(1) an investigation of the interactions between human bodies and physical objects, both natural and human-made; (2) with much of the interaction taking place through sense perception; (3) in special and specified spaces and times; (4) in order to orient, and sometimes disorient, communities and individuals; (5) toward the formal strictures and structures of religious traditions.

(2015: 4)

According to this definition, one of the functions of material religion is to mediate between individuals, communities and traditions, defining and penetrating the boundaries between them. Arweck and Keenan make a similar point, emphasising the role of materiality in the classic sociological issues of identity construction and social differentiation: 'materializing "their religion" is what different faith communities... *do* to put their cultural "distinction" on the map. By their material expressions shall they be known' (2006: 1–2).

Applying these ideas to St Cuthbert, a "material religion" approach would seek to explore the details of individual encounters with the body of the saint, looking for historical and contemporary records that might help us to imagine the emotions, experiences and sensations of his petitioners. A material approach would also look at the different constructions of space around St Cuthbert, analysing the use of architecture, decoration, sound and ritual to focus attention on his shrine. In the present day, the rebranding of Durham Cathedral as "St Cuthbert's shrine" is a perfect example of the materialisation of 'cultural distinction' (2006: 2).

Plate's summary also reminds us that embodied interactions with Cuthbert have societal consequences. As we have seen, material interactions with the corpse have been used to discredit rival traditions, orienting and disorienting communities with mixed success. Appreciating that meaning is not inherent in an object, we should consider the intentions of the different actors in these projects of 'orientation' or 'disorientation' alongside the distinctive qualities of the materials used and any evidence of responses from wider publics. In some cases, for example, materiality has become a source for unexpected resistance. Raine must have hoped that his use of cheap materials to rebury Cuthbert would go undiscovered, but that decision eventually helped to discredit his excavations (Willem 2013: 83).

These lists and summaries suggest important themes and approaches for the study of "material religion", but offer very little assistance in defining what "materiality" actually is. Plate's definition mentions "physical objects", but what counts as a "physical object", and what does not?

Material religion and belief

Discussions of material religion have tended to address this question negatively, clarifying the focus of "materiality" by framing it in opposition to something else. Dick Houtman and Birgit Meyer, for example, argue that 'matter and materiality are – and only make sense as – relational terms that thrive on contrast' (Houtman and Meyer 2012: 5).

Most commonly, the opposite against which the field is defined is the study of "belief". According to Jeremy Stolow, for example, 'the study of material religion has served as a powerful vehicle for exploring a range of ways that "religion" extends beyond the seemingly abstract world of symbols and propositional claims about knowledge and belief' (Stolow et al. 2015). S. Brent Plate claims that the study of religion was 'once commonly perceived to be a companion to that of philosophy' (2015: 3), and Gregory Grieve suggests that this might still be the case: 'scholars of religion often operate as if people engage the divine primarily through printed scripture' (2015: 55).

Of course, belief itself can be studied from a materialist perspective. Even when a particular religious group does try to promote a 'project of immateriality' (Engelke 2005: 118), seeking to create 'a religion in which things do not matter' (Engelke 2005: 119), their work can never be completely successful. Beliefs are learned, experienced and adapted through embodied engagement in rituals, relationships and practices, as Anna Strhan has demonstrated in her recent study of evangelical Christian embodiment (2015). Beliefs are lost through embodied encounters, too. David Morgan describes belief as a 'slowly sedimentary practice', built up over a lifetime of repetition and inflected with emotion. When listening to someone speak about their belief,

> we must learn to hear his sighs, his gritted teeth, the murmur of nostalgia, the distant gaze of eyes searching the memory of folded hands, sore knees, and the lingering memory of the Eucharist liturgy. He says he believes, but what he really does is feel, smell, hear, and see.
>
> (2010: 5)

In contrast, the understanding of "belief" that material religion writers object to is disembodied and discursive. Meyer argues that in 'conventional understandings of religion . . . spirit is privileged above matter' (2011: 58). Personal doctrine and private spiritual encounter are perceived as the true heart of religion, while materiality is merely its contingent expression.

This dismissive attitude is frequently linked by scholars of material religion to the legacy of Protestantism (see Orsi 2005; Morgan 2010; Vasquez 2011; Engelke 2012; Houtman and Meyer 2012, among others). In many nineteenth- and early twentieth-century theories of religion, spiritual beings were considered to take material form only in less advanced traditions, while 'among civilized Protestant Christians, who stood at the apex of religious evolution, spirits would have no physical presence' (Engelke 2012: 211). Protestant prejudice encouraged scholars to emphasise the superiority of a Protestant style of internal, personal spirituality, and to therefore 'overlook – or, perhaps better, look *through* – religion's material forms' (Houtman and Meyer 2012: 11). Protestant scholars refought the religious wars of previous centuries through their studies of other world religions, too: according to Robert Orsi, for example, 'scholarship on "Hindu" ritual echoed with anti-Catholic contempt' (2005: 178). Writers in the field of material religion seek to use these arguments to demonstrate that non-material study of religion is inadequate as scholarship (because of its unconfessed theological bias) and deeply problematic (because of its origins in colonial racial politics).

There are reasons to be cautious about overstating this thesis of Protestant bias. First, as Engelke points out, the de-emphasising of materiality is not unique to studies of religion: this is 'a basic intellectual dynamic of modernity' (2012: 211), widely shared across the humanities subjects. Second, even within Christianity, tensions over the relationship between matter and spirit are much older than the Protestant Reformation. Third, while it may be true that 'the use of . . . material means in addressing God was a key bone of contention between Catholics and Protestants (especially Calvinists) after the Reformation' (Houtman and Meyer 2012: 7), materiality was also a source of internal conflict within both traditions. Hostility to matter is not universally shared among Protestant churches.

Nonetheless, these ongoing discussions about the origins and biases of modernity, science and the idea of "religion" are of great value. Sociologists of religion will recognise parallels here with debates in our own field, including not only the critical study of the concept of "religion" but also emerging attention to non-religion and the long-running debates over the origins and extent of secularisation. Hostility to the "anti-modern" materiality of religion does still persist today, and we should be careful to recognise any influence those attitudes may exert in public or academic discourse.

For sociologists, however, the contrast between "material" and "immaterial" understandings of religion is not limited to the distinction between things and doctrines. Material religion can also offer a fruitful challenge to sociology's focus on society, social structure, institutions, identities and roles. Materiality reminds us to focus on the particular, contextual and personal, appreciating the complex networks of human and non-human actors that combine to generate what appears to us as the social (Latour 2005). Classic sociological themes of class, gender, ethnicity or power can all be analysed in terms of access to and deployment of material resources, as the chapters in this volume will show.

The lifecycle of material culture: introducing the volume

This book explores the field of material religion through a range of disciplines, including sociology, anthropology, cultural studies and media studies. We have chosen not to structure our approach around a list of topics (like architecture, clothing and ritual) or themes (e.g. the role of material culture in tensions between religious and non-religious groups). Instead, our volume follows the lifecycle of an object, identifying three key phases that demand material analysis: **production**, **classification** and **circulation**.

This three-part structure has been developed by **David Morgan**, who explains his approach in Chapter 1. Morgan proposes that we should understand material analysis as

> a series of inquiries that move from consideration of the concrete features of an individual object to comparison with other objects like it to its circulation and use and finally to what the object does and how it may be understood to perform different kinds of cultural work.

To understand an object and its place in material culture, we must first consider its "production": what it is made of, how it has been designed and how it was made. If we apply this approach to the example of St Cuthbert's cross, the small ornament found in Cuthbert's grave by James Raine in 1827, we would begin by noting its expensive materials: gold and red garnets. It is small, just 6 cm across, but intricately designed. A large round gemstone in the centre is surrounded by four smaller ones, and each arm of the cross is paved with a mosaic of twelve stones. One arm has been broken, repaired and broken again. Its design strongly suggests an Anglo-Saxon origin, contemporary with St Cuthbert, so consideration of the object's manufacture would include discussion of the trade routes and goldsmith techniques available at the time.

In the second phase of analysis, Morgan encourages us to consider an object's "classification". What does the object do, what category of objects is it assigned to and how does it reproduce or adapt older styles and materials? Here, our consideration of Cuthbert's cross begins to become more speculative. The cross is designed to be worn around the neck, but it seems out of place on the body of a famously ascetic monk. Similar crosses have been found in the burials of high-status women (Willem 2013: 94), which might suggest that this cross was not originally intended for Cuthbert at all. In terms of remediation, the most obvious antecedent for this golden cross is the original cross of wood, but its design – outlined in raised dots, hammered into the gold – is also reminiscent of illuminated manuscripts, like the Lindisfarne Gospels. It has often been suggested that the abstract designs and patterns found on manuscripts, including the use of lines of dots, is a painted remediation of contemporary styles of jewellery, carving and metalwork.

In the final phase of analysis, Morgan calls for attention to the object's "circulation". We must consider not only the object itself, but also how people engage with it, including 'the registers of sensation that apprehend the object, the techniques of the body that object activates, and the value or salience that is generated by the use of the object in religious practice' (Morgan, this volume). Objects have 'a social career' in which they are transported, exchanged and put to work in unexpected new ways (Morgan, this volume).

The social career of St Cuthbert's cross is rather mysterious. Its unexpectedly rich materials and feminine design have already been mentioned, along with evidence of extensive use and repair. The cross was discovered for the first time in 1827, and was not mentioned during previous openings of the tomb – even when the grave was ransacked in 1539. The website of the Durham World Heritage Site suggests that 'the king's commissioners did not see it', because they failed to check the saint's robes (Durham World Heritage Site n.d.). That would have been a surprising oversight, but the only alternative is that the jewel was not in the coffin at all. Historian David Willem suggests that it might have been added to the grave secretly – and illegally – when Cuthbert was reburied in 1542 (Willem 2013: 4).

Today, St Cuthbert's cross is a highlight of Durham Cathedral's exhibition of treasures and a key part of the cathedral's brand. The cross features in the cathedral's logo in a modified, now unbroken form, without any indication of its actual size. Copies of the cross began to be produced soon after the original was discovered, and the British Museum holds an enamelled version dating from the mid-nineteenth century (British Museum n.d.). That early commercial product was designed to hold a lock of hair, but visitors to the Durham Cathedral shop can now take home their own cross on a postcard, placemat, glass plaque, scarf, T-shirt or piece of replica jewellery, among other options. The wider appeal of the cross was marked in 2013, when its image was added to the flag of County Durham as a symbol of regional heritage.

Through material analysis, as David Morgan's chapter explains, we can study 'the way in which an object participates in making and sustaining a life-world'. The cross of St Cuthbert, most likely produced in the seventh century, is now deployed in the overlapping worlds of spirituality, marketing, tourism, commerce, regional politics, personal adornment and home decoration. It functions as a key marker of identity and distinction, and as a disposable token of a pleasant visit. Objects have always occupied this complex, multilayered role, mediating between individuals, communities, traditions and wider societies, shaping lived religion as well as religious conflict. As the chapters in this volume show, scholars across many disciplines have much to learn from the study of religion's materiality.

Production, classification, circulation: introducing the chapters

David Morgan's opening chapter is followed by three parts, each containing four essays that respond to one of his three categories. The first part, **Production**, includes chapters that pay particular attention to the medium, design and manufacture of objects.

Marion Bowman considers a very familiar object utilised in many religious contexts: the candle. Drawing on fieldwork and participant observation undertaken over many years, Bowman takes a comparative approach highlighting the importance of attention to production. Contrasting the Glastonbury Candle, an object designed and produced with particular religious functions in mind, with the tea light, a ubiquitous household item put to work to perform such functions, Bowman explores 'the productive work that lies in people's actions and intentions' shaping the candles' use.

Martin Wood invites us into Jalarām's kitchen to explore the role of food in the lives of Jalarām Bāpā devotees in Greenford, London. Presenting data collected in ethnographic fieldwork, Wood examines the connections between sacred food practices and the ethical and ideological commitments of the group. Wood argues that for devotees the preparation and offering of food to others, regardless of their social rank or religious commitments, are simultaneously a reenactment of the central narrative of the group's history and an opportunity to outwork in the present ethical principles established in the past. Wood demonstrates that attention to the process of production illuminates understanding of this, as mundane and everyday food is understood to become extraordinary, a material means by which blessing is bestowed.

Carl Morris considers the production of music by contemporary Muslim musicians, examining the 'conceptual, cultural and economic' conditions in which music is generated. Presenting findings from ethnographic research in the 'Muslim music scene', Morris explores the factors at work that enable and constrain musical production. Morris argues that a considerable degree of self-consciousness is evident in Muslim musicians, revealing the significance of the shifting social context of contemporary Britain in shaping the creative process and output.

Leading us into another creative world, **Tim Hutchings** asks what insights we can glean regarding the role of digital media in shaping religious life-worlds. Taking two contrasting examples, online memorials and digital Bibles, Hutchings argues that digital media should be included within considerations of material religion, demonstrating similarities between digital and physical objects in their function in shaping religious practice. However, Hutchings argues, attention to digital media is also important because of its distinctive characteristics, offering religious users significantly different, and rapidly changing, means of engagement.

The second part of the volume shifts the focus to the realm of **Classification**, considering the function, purpose, adaptation, reproduction and remediation of objects. Essays in this part pay attention to 'what kind of thing' an object is (Morgan, this volume) and how it compares to other things.

Graham Harvey opens this section with an exploration of the function of art and buildings, arguing that such objects are understood – at least by some – not as things but as persons. Harvey traces modernity's taken-for-granted assumptions about things to the conflicts of early modern Europe, and offers some alternatives to 'the modernist marginalisation of matter'. Harvey uses four examples of indigenous engagements with things to suggest that a relational dynamic can be at work in the interaction between person and object. In other words, Harvey argues, 'things are members of societies as much as humans and other animals are.'

From an anthropological perspective, **Timothy Carroll** suggests that engagement with the field often entails encounters with objects which defy analytical categorisation. Drawing on ethnographic research in an Eastern Orthodox monastery on Mount Athos in Greece, Carroll demonstrates that attention to classification can illuminate how seemingly distinct things, relics, clothing and gestures, may share a common function and therefore be rightly understood as objects 'of the same class'.

Maria Nita considers the ways in which Christian climate activists draw upon religious tradition in their understanding of and engagement with place and argues that the rituals enacted 're-orient' space, encouraging a different perspective on the planet. Through consideration of the ways in which the 'sacred books or icons' traditionally adorning altars are replaced by 'acorns, leaves and feathers', Nita explores how objects may be remediated. This use of organic objects in a sacred context by participants demonstrates how new material mediums may be employed to convey a familiar motif, highlighting how remediation 'negotiates change while maintaining continuity' (Morgan, this volume).

This part closes with a contribution by **Janet Eccles and Rebecca Catto** considering a developing area in the sociology of religion, that of non-religion and atheism. Drawing on data from research projects with both young atheists and female atheists, they consider atheism from a material perspective, exploring whether 'denial of belief can be displayed through clothing, ritual, objects and, particularly, space'. Paying attention to the function and designation of place/space, they argue that the responses of atheists in their study suggest an understanding of space as 'secular sacred', demonstrating a commitment to keeping certain everyday places free from religion and feelings of 'profanation' when religion encroaches.

In the final part of the book the **Circulation** of objects, their deployment, repurpose and reception, takes centre stage.

Douglas Davies explores the interaction between thought, action, objects and identity in relation to the universal human experience of death. Burial, cremation, icons and relics are used to investigate the role of things in the relationship between "mental" and "material" culture. For example the practice of scattering the ashes of a deceased person now occurs in many very different locations in contemporary Britain, and this material act supports a 'circulation of memory' in which the dead symbolically 'wander' through places significant to them.

Elisabeth Arweck presents findings from a project exploring 'young people's attitudes to religious diversity' and examines their understandings of material expressions of religion. Arweck argues that the young people demonstrate considerable awareness of the cultural factors that are at work shaping the everyday deployment, circulation and reception of religious symbols, clothing and dietary observances.

Drawing on ethnographic work undertaken at the British Museum's 2012 exhibition on Hajj, **Steph Berns** explores 'the social career' (Morgan, this volume) of objects moved from their usual setting to that of the museum. Berns focuses on the sitara, the textile covering of the Ka`ba, 'the spiritual focus of Islam'. The sitara journeyed to London from Mecca for the exhibition, and Berns explores the impact of this new context, examining the ways in which this prompts different modes of engagement and reception.

In our final chapter, **Terhi Utriainen** explores 'angel practices', such as healings, angel card readings and angel visitations. She explores how, within the Lutheran context of Finland, such 'angel happenings' are moments in which the traditional figure of the angel is circulated in new forms and ways. Through participant observation among a group of women engaged in the practice of creating an 'angel talisman' and its subsequent translation, by some, into a 'prayer ornament', Utriainen identifies how the circulation and repurposing of the angel work to provide a focus to help navigate the problems of everyday life. Such angel practices are illustrative of the ways in which traditional, language-centred forms of religion may become entwined with alternative, material expressions.

The contributors introduced above include sociologists of religion, anthropologists, media scholars and experts in visual studies. The study of materiality can provide a point of intersection between these and other disciplines, bringing together our distinctive discourses and methodologies to analyse embodied human interactions with the stuff of religion. Our chapters range from the beginning of an object's life to its end, from the ephemerality of candles to the permanence of museums, and from the solidity of statues to the apparent intangibility of music or digital media. We hope that this collection will serve to demonstrate once again that the study of materiality, the production, classification and circulation of things, is of the greatest relevance for theoretical debates across the whole field of the study of religion.

Works cited

Arweck, Elisabeth and William Keenan. 2006. 'Introduction: Material Varieties of Religious Expression'. In *Materializing Religion*, eds. Elisabeth Arweck and William Keenan, 1–20. Farnham: Ashgate.

Bailey, Richard. 1989. 'St Cuthbert's Relics: Some Neglected Evidence.' In *St Cuthbert, His Cult and His Community to AD 1200*, eds. Gerald Bonner, David Rollason and Claire Stancliffe, 231–246. Woodbridge: The Boydell Press.

British Museum. n.d. 'Collection Online: Replica/Jewellery Case/Cross Pendant'. http://www.britishmuseum.org/research/collection_online/collection_object_details.aspx?objectId=82633&partId=1. Accessed 08/03/2016.

Durham World Heritage Site. n.d. 'The Keeper of the Shrine.' https://www.durhamworldheritagesite.com/architecture/cathedral/intro/cuthbert-shrine/keeper-of-the-shrine. Accessed 08/03/2016.

Engelke, Matthew. 2012. 'Material Religion.' In *The Cambridge Companion to Religious Studies*, ed. Robert Orsi, 209–229. Cambridge: Cambridge University Press.
Grieve, Gregory Price. 2015. 'Digital.' In *Key Terms in Material Religion*, ed. S. Brent Plate, 55–62. London: Bloomsbury.
Houtman, Dick and Birgit Meyer. 2012. 'Introduction: Material Religion – How Things Matter.' In *Things: Religion and the Question of Materiality*, eds. Dick Houtman and Birgit Meyer, 1–26. New York: Fordham University Press.
Meyer, Birgit. 2011. 'Medium.' *Material Religion* 7(1): 58–64.
Meyer, Birgit, David Morgan, Crispin Paine and S. Brent Plate. 2010. 'The Origin and Mission of Material Religion.' *Religion* 40: 207–211.
———. 2011. 'Introduction: Key Words in Material Religion.' *Material Religion* 7(1): 4–8.
Morgan, David. 2010. 'Introduction: The Matter of Belief.' In *Religion and Material Culture: The Matter of Belief*, ed. David Morgan, 1–18. Abingdon: Routledge.
Orsi, Robert. 2005. *Between Heaven and Earth: The Religious Worlds People Make and the Scholars Who Study Them*. Princeton, NJ: Princeton University Press.
Plate, S. Brent. 2015. 'Material Religion: An Introduction.' In *Key Terms in Material Religion*, ed. S. Brent Plate, 1–8. London: Bloomsbury.
Raine, James. 1828. *Saint Cuthbert: With an Account of the State in Which His Remains Were Found Upon the Opening of His Tomb in Durham Cathedral, in the Year MDCCCXXVII*. Durham, NC: Geoffrey Andrews.
Sadgrove, Michael. 2007. 'Benedict and Cuthbert: Two Saints for Durham.' Sermon preached in Durham Cathedral, 18 March. http://www.durhamcathedral.co.uk/ worshipandmusic/sermon-archive/benedict-and-cuthbert-two-saints-for-durham. Accessed 08/03/2016.
Stolow, Jeremy, S. Brent Plate, David Morgan and Amy Whitehead. 2015. 'On the Agency of Religious Objects: A Conversation', 29 October. http://materialreligions.blogspot.se/2015/10/on-agency-of-religious-objects.html. Accessed 08/03/2016.
Strhan, Anna. 2015. *Aliens and Strangers? The Struggle for Coherence in the Everyday Lives of Evangelicals*. Oxford: Oxford University Press.
Vásquez, Manuel. 2011. *More than Belief: A Materialist Theory of Religion*. Oxford: Oxford University Press.
Willem, David. 2013. *St Cuthbert's Corpse: A Life After Death*. Durham, NC: Sacristy Press.

1 Material analysis and the study of religion

David Morgan

Discussion of the materiality of religion has become more common in recent years, resulting in a host of instructive studies ranging from the production and reception of objects, images, spaces, clothing and food to the study of practices, the senses and the history of thought about them.[1] Less attention, however, has been devoted to consideration of the kinds of questions one poses in conducting the material analysis and interpretation that compose the empirical study of materiality. The paucity of procedural reflection among scholars of religion compromises the materialisation of the study of religion because it fails to provide scholars not trained in material analysis with the tools they need to undertake empirical studies. Scholars of religion tend to be well-prepared in the investigation of languages, texts and the history of ideas, but less so in the study of objects, spaces, bodies and the practices of using them that make up religions in one way or another.

I propose here a sustained reflection on the means of material analysis and critical definitions of material culture that enable the study of religions as embodied, physical and felt forms of social and historical phenomena. Making materiality *evidential* is the task. By this I mean foregrounding such material evidence as images, emotions, sensations, spaces, food, dress or the material practices of putting the body to work. The challenge is to resist using these phenomena as illustrations of what remains the truly immaterial basis for studying religions. It is, after all, far more traditional to approach the study of religion with a set of themes or problems that are set wholly within the medium of theories and texts, answerable by applying abstract reasoning to non-material evidences, such as literary sources or philosophical debates. Certainly this counts as the study of religion no less than does material analysis. The problem is that it has tended to dominate academic investigation to the point of excluding other kinds of evidence. The rise of material culture studies in religious studies over the past two decades has moved towards correcting this tendency, but a significant challenge persists in making material analysis a readily usable method. This book will contribute importantly to addressing that challenge.

We can frame the study of an object's materiality in a series of steps that follow it from production to use. Doing so should not be allowed to privilege intent or the genius of a maker if we balance production with reception and if we understand the origins of an object to precede the object in the history of its medium and the craft and manufacture that produce it no less than the tools and ability of the person making it. The object is an instance of a material culture that precedes it and is renewed and extended by it. By material culture I mean not only the object's physical characteristics but also the registers of sensation that apprehend the object, the techniques of the body that object activates, and the value or salience that is generated by the use of the object in religious practice. Material culture, in other words, is more than an object. It is the way in which an object participates in making and sustaining a life-world. To study religious material culture is to study how people build and maintain the cultural domains that are the shape of their social lives. This approach presumes that objects, spaces, food, clothing and the practices of using them are not secondary to a religion but primary aspects of it.

In practice, material analysis consists of a series of inquiries that move from consideration of the concrete features of an individual object to comparison with other objects like it to its circulation and use and finally to what the object does and how it may be understood to perform different kinds of cultural work. This procedure can be parsed in many ways, but I will map it out as a process that consists of at least nine aspects or moments, each of which captures a key aspect of an object's materiality and its relevance for those who put the object to religious use. These are the principal foci of analysis, the handles by which scholars take hold of objects in order to treat them as primary evidence. The nine aspects are: medium, design, manufacture, function, comparison, remediation, deployment, reception and ideology or cultural work. I will organise these nine into three successive groupings: production, classification and circulation. These nine form what amount procedurally to nine consecutive steps in analysis. Running throughout these steps are a number of key analytical themes that occupy scholars, which I will take up in tandem with discussion of each of the nine steps of analysis. In order to keep the reflection concrete, I will focus my remarks on a number of related objects (Figures 1.1–1.5), which will be helpfully compared with one another to put the analytical terms and categories I adduce to work.

A final note is important to make as a preface to what follows. My intention is not to transform the study of religion into the specialised study of objects, but rather to offer a way to make materiality an available datum for scholars of religion who discern a useful connection of objects to what they study. Objects are a mode of evidence whose characteristics yield value only when interrogated constructively. There is much that is important and relevant to learn from them. But if we are unable to hear their testimony, they remain mute in our accounts and religions tend to remain textual and intellectual – that is conformed to the evidence that most scholars are trained to analyse.

Production

Material analysis commences with scrutiny of an object's *medium*. What an object is made from enables and shapes our perception of it. A medium carries form or content, bearing it across space or time, between people. In many of the most important instances, a medium becomes indistinguishable from what it bears. In works of art, for example, the value of the object is in part its maker's performance in a particular medium. In the performance of a liturgy or listening to a speaker, the medium is also a connection in which a relationship takes place. More than the information that is otherwise conveyed, the medium of music, chant or elocution is how a community is experienced. Disparate parties come together or are mediated in a medium.

In the case of Figure 1.1, a woodcarving of Jesus, the Christian deity is represented. A feeling, idea, ideal or message is presented in the delicate shape of wood. When a devotee fondles the figure, prays to it, proudly displays it and gazes tenderly upon it each day, the object is clearly a medium that has merged with its content. To touch and behold the object is to convey to Jesus what the devotee feels about him.

The feel of Jesus in the case of Figure 1.1 is something we can apprehend ourselves, at least to a certain degree. The smoothed wood surface, the light weight of the object, the delicate details are all features of this particular species of wood. The close grain of the wood allows for the detailing as well as the smooth, uninterrupted surface. No knots or discolouration mars the even planes and contours. The eye and the hand move over the surface in uninhibited gradation. Light falls softly on the figure, casting diffuse shadows that serve to reveal the gradually undulating surface and a columnar volume. The treatment of the wood moves effortlessly from long folds of drapery to the tiny articulation of fingers, heart emblem, hair and facial details. Another medium would not allow this delivery of form. Imagine a knotty length of scrub pine or a figure modelled in cement.

Consider the different effects of other media commonly used to portray figures of Jesus bearing the Sacred Heart. Figure 1.2 is a solid cast of plaster, made from a two-piece rubber mould and painted with a spray gun and details by hand. This means that the hands must cling to the surface of the body since they are the result of a mould, not free-form carving, as in Figure 1.1. The same is clear in Figure 1.3, a hollow metal cast that has been covered with a coating of gold paint. In order to keep the process inexpensive, hands and robes avoid deep undercuts, which require more complex forms of casting, and therefore greater expense. The same can be said of the dashboard figure (Figure 1.4), a two-piece plastic moulding.[2]

A more elaborately treated version of the subject is Figure 1.5, a hollow cast with deep undercuts and a free-hanging hand. This figure was probably created using a multiple-piece agar mould, a gelatinous substance derived from algae and used in creating dental moulds as well as for figure casting before the development of latex moulds in the early twentieth century.[3] It was entirely

Figure 1.1 Albrecht Buchmiller, Sacred Heart of Jesus, ca. 1950, wood, 8 3/4 inches high.

Figure 1.2 Sacred Heart of Jesus, Columbia Statuary, no. 110, solid cast plaster, ca. 1930s, 12 1/2 inches high. Collection of the author.

Figure 1.3 Sacred Heart of Jesus, early twentieth century, pot metal, 6 inches high. Collection of the author.

Figure 1.4 Sacred Heart of Jesus, dashboard figure with suction cup, Hartland Plastics, mid-twentieth century, 5 1/2 inches high. Collection of the author.

Figure 1.5 Sacred Heart of Jesus, produced by in Olot, Catalonia, by Moderna Sagrada Familia P. Lluís, early twentieth century, hand-painted hollow cast plaster, 17 1/2 inches. Collection of the author.

hand-painted and bears considerable detailing work as well as subtle variations of tone. This strongly suggests that the piece was created in the early twentieth century when spray guns were not used to paint the figures, but assembly lines of artisans decorated the surfaces by hand. The delicacy of the figure and the degree and fine nature of ornamentation of Figure 1.5 suggest that its cost was higher and its clientele more demanding. A stamp on the backside of the figure indicates it was created in Olot, a town in eastern Catalonia that was home to several firms specialising in the production of saints' images beginning in 1880.[4]

The liability of a hollow cast is clear, however, in the broken fingers of the left hand. The figure's delicacy makes it a risk for easy damage. The same is true of the woodcarving, where several fingers are missing (see Figure 1.1). Yet the very delicacy means a more distinctive object, one that cuts a more engaging figure, displays finer workmanship, costs more and participates with a more lavish setting to create a special place for devotion. It is evident that each medium affords a different range of treatments, from detail work to finish. The medium allows different kinds of working, resulting in effects that suit certain circumstances more than others.

Size, setting and finish are features of each medium that hinge directly on the *design* of objects, like the figures discussed here. By design I mean the organisation or structure of an object, which is the arrangement of forms in the body of a medium. Formal organisation bears intention, which is why the word "design" means both the configuration of an object and the intention carried within it. We need to consider how the medium accommodates or affords the object's design by asking why the object was made this way and not another.

Clearly, medium and design work closely with one another. Design is the form a medium takes. Recognising an object's design means discerning the intention it bears. Design aligns medium to the process of manufacture as well as to the object's intended function. In all of the five figures reproduced here, it is evident that the design seeks to protect the integrity of the figure from breakage by securing the hands to the torso, by distributing the falling folds of the robes in such a way that the figure takes the shape of a column. A bowed head is linked with quietly displayed hands and an overall repose of the figure achieved in narrow shoulders to convey a feeling of serenity and silence. The figures are designed, in other words, to produce an effect that suits their purpose.

The overall shape of each figure tends to be something like a canoe: narrow at top and bottom, widest at the centre. Often, the slightest sway is introduced in the right hip and left knee (only Figure 1.1 reverses this). This suggests the presence of the body, but stops far short of accenting it, subordinating its sensual effect and power to a mass of drapery whose folds and patterns safely conceal flesh. But it may be more than that. Beneath the thick robes, the anatomy subtly registers a distribution of weight that puts the figure at standing rest. No movement vibrates through the folds of drapery. The objects focus our attention on and by means of their very motionlessness. The figures bring the eye to rest, collecting attention in the endeavour to calm the mind with a grace that emphasises sweetness and delicacy as the correspondence between body and soul.

The third aspect of production to be discussed is *manufacture*. In fact, we have already mentioned it in the discussion of medium by pointing out the techniques of casting used to create several of the figures of Jesus. Manufacture, the physical production of an object, has everything to do with medium and design since the means of production must suit the nature of a medium and the design or formation in which a medium is invested. Pushing a medium beyond its limits will result in a figure's easy demise. Manufacture involves expense and skill that are directly relevant to the marketing of the objects and more. Skill pertains to the culture of practice, status, knowledge and availability of resources that imbue objects with value. An object's expense affects its sale and display as well as its function, circulation and reception, not to mention the cultural work it performs. Moreover, manufacture pertains to the supporting technologies of production, which reveal much about the division of labour, scientific knowledge, the investment of wealth and the social location of producers. Therefore a careful description of an object's methods of manufacture reveals a great deal, serving as a kind of window on the social worlds of production.

For instance, a trade in plaster saint figures arose in the eighteenth and nineteenth centuries in Europe and migrated to the United States with Catholic immigrants. International firms established a presence in cities with migrant Catholics – Boston, New York, Chicago, Milwaukee and Philadelphia. Often, firms in the United States were established by immigrant craftsmen. Pietro and Antonio Allegrini founded the Pennsylvania Statuary Company in Philadelphia around 1919. Ermano Moroder created Moroder Studios in Milwaukee in the mid-1940s. Emanuele Fontanini registered copyrights in the early 1950s for Catholic objects produced by Boston Statuary Products Corporation. Angelo and Cesare Ghibesi produced Catholic imagery for Jersey Statuary Company in the 1950s. Columbia Statuary was a firm based in Chicago that imported work from Italy and produced its own statues, which were registered for copyright beginning in the mid-1930s. Its religious works date from the middle of the century.[5] Figure 1.2 is an example.

Most firms combined religious production with non-religious items and also articulated their production, ranging from prestige markets to very affordable figures like Figure 1.2, whose modest size (12 1/2 inches) made it ideal for private use in the home or monastery cell. The pricing structure for plaster figures varied from a few dollars to several hundred. Sales catalogues allow us to reconstruct a sense of the range and use for different products. They provide the options presented to consumers and reflect the uses consumers brought to their purchase. Moreover, seeing the variety of options allows us to gather a collective sense of the taste or aesthetic sensibility that the vendor imagined that customers would appreciate. Comparing catalogues over time allows us to determine what succeeded and what did not, what met with consumer interest and what dropped out as failing to satisfy demand.

In the case of Figure 1.1, by contrast, an entirely different mode of manufacture is at stake. This is a woodcarving produced by a German carver for sale at the 1950 Passion Play in Oberammergau, in southern Germany. The carver,

Albrecht Buchmiller, worked in a centuries-old tradition of German wood-carving, which produced religious figures and scenes for use in shrines and altars. But Buchmiller's figure, eight and a half inches high, was not designed for use in a church. He carved this and many figures like it for sale as souvenirs to those attending the Passion Play or visiting the site of Oberammergau as tourists. The object was not inexpensive: it sold for fifty-five German marks in 1950. In 1955, one US dollar equalled 4.21 German marks.[6] Nevertheless, larger, more elaborate carvings would not accommodate the market for such a souvenir. Visitors to Oberammergau wanted a small souvenir they could take home in a suitcase or handbag or post to a family member.

A key analytical theme to understand in the study of production is the concept of affordance.[7] I noted earlier that a medium affords a particular treatment. If one wants a shiny surface, cast metal or glazed porcelain is suitable. If large editions of inexpensive copies are the goal, plaster works very well. Wood is the medium of choice for figures to evoke a venerable tradition of craftsmanship as well as the hand-tooled look that affords minute detailing as well as a range of possible finishes – from the rough hewn to the matte finish, to a surface that receives paint or applications such as gold leaf. A medium affords or allows certain possibilities and produces certain kinds of effects. An object's design and manufacture need to be in harmony with its medium's affordances for the sake of successful production.

The affordances of medium, manufacture and display tell us a great deal about the effect and intention of an object, and may illuminate a great deal about its reception by suggesting how an object may appeal to users and the marketplace. A heavy object like that in Figure 1.3 would make for a very dangerous dashboard decoration, whereas the lightness of the object in Figure 1.4 suits the purpose very well, allowing the figure to adhere to a car dash with no more than a latex suction cup enclosed in its base. A delicately crafted wood object like the one in Figure 1.1 is light enough for the dashboard, but would suffer serious damage if it became unattached, and might attract a thief by sitting in plain sight inside the car. So the very cheapness and mass-produced quality of the statue in Figure 1.4 attune it to the site and purpose of the dashboard.

Classification

When we look at an object whose function we do not recognise, we are inclined to ask, "What is this thing?" Bill Brown (2001) pointed out in a widely read essay that we are not likely to ask that question until the thing fails to do what it normally is intended to do. When a window is so dirty that it is no longer transparent, no longer able to act like a window, we may well wonder what it is. An object's *function* is its identity because function speaks to purpose. This is the first analytical step in the category of classifying an object. To know what an object does or is meant to do tells us a great deal about what it is, where it belongs, for whom it was designed to operate in such a way, what they expected of it, what it did for them, the system of value in which the object operated, and the world view that assigned it a place within an overarching scheme of values.

Did the figures reproduced here instruct and remind devotees of their spiritual duties? Did the figures reassure, calm, inspire or uplift them? Did the figures establish contact for devotees with their heavenly referent? Was Jesus somehow present in the imagery? Did the objects serve as amulets or talismans for their owners? Did they mark powerful sites where prayer or pledge was made more efficacious? Learning the answers to these questions tells us more about function because they lead to inquiry about how to use them. How were they somatic technologies for accessing Jesus? Was their power keyed to display? To prescribed techniques of visual or tactile engagement?

I have titled the second cluster of determinations in material analysis "classification" because each of them – function, comparison and remediation – allows us to specify an object. By that I mean assigning an object a place within a taxonomy, determining what kind of thing it is. More than function per se, this means locating an object within a system of classification. Every individual object belongs to a species of such objects, according to what it does, what it resembles, where it fits, how it relates to other things like it, how it differs and what is generically unique and absolutely unique about it. I have already noted the importance of function, which tells us so much about what kind of a thing this or that object is. But we can hardly begin to specify a thing if we are unable to compare it to others like it.

For *comparison* to ensue, therefore, we need a group of comparable artefacts. I like to call this set the archive. The definitive value of material analysis depends heavily on the construction of an archive for purposes of comparison. An archive illuminates the genealogy of family resemblances, revealing important information about where a thing comes from and why it takes the shape it does. A key technique used by art historians in this procedure is iconography, which consists of tracing the descent of patterns or motifs in the history of a subject matter. Note, for example, the pattern of Jesus' hands in the five images reproduced here. Figures 1.4 and 1.5 share the motif of one arm outstretched and the other touching the Sacred Heart on Jesus' chest. Figures 1.1–1.3 gather both hands about the heart, though Figures 1.2 and 1.3 share the act of parting the tunic to display Jesus' heart. With each change of pattern, we may note new intentions or new purposes for the object. Such differences can help us date objects, locate them in different traditions and site innovations in interpretation and function of the object. Getting the archive right means conducting valid comparisons, comparing apples with apples and oranges with oranges.

An important feature that affects classification is *remediation*.[8] Remediation is a reissuing of a product in a new medium or format – from wood sculpture to plastic or cast metal, from a painting to a decal or a printed T-shirt. This is a highly common feature of (re)production that reassigns the object to a new register of use and availability. In doing so, remediation reinterprets an old theme. I place it within the category of classification because it consists of placing the artefact in a new interpretive context. A new medium means a new setting, different use or function, different audience and probably a different cost and means of acquisition. Remediation reclassifies the object. But clearly remediation does more than classify an artefact. As a form of reproduction, it touches on the category of production as well as circulation. Reproduction means new uses to which people will put the item as well as new forms of circulation.

The prevalence of remediation reminds us that human culture is inherently conservative, tending to reproduce itself over and over. And for good reason: preserving the past is a way to stabilise the present and the future. In a world where nothing lasts, where scarcity constantly threatens well-being, where competition for resources is ongoing, and in which the young and the converted must constantly be formed to participate productively in social life, reproducing social arrangements, ideals, symbols and practices is a premium. Reproducing social order means creating a playing field that operates under constant rules that can be mastered for improving one's situation and favouring one's group. As the practice of reproducing motifs from one medium to another, remediation allows something novel to be added to something familiar, thereby keeping the traditional motif up-to-date and available. The five images examined here are good examples.

Statues of the standing figure revealing the Sacred Heart do not precede the nineteenth century, and became firmly established devotional iconography in the construction of the Basilica of the Sacred Heart at Montmartre in the last two decades of the century. A large figure of Jesus, placed on the exterior of the building, draws aside his tunic to reveal the Sacred Heart with one hand and gestures to viewers with the other (similar to Figure 1.5). The figure was created for the basilica around 1900 by sculptor Gustave Michel (Morgan 2008: 48n77). A practice of erecting statues followed in Europe and elsewhere. Smaller statuary of the Sacred Heart cast in a stone composite medium that was suitable for use in churches and churchyards was available for sale in the 1881–82 *Catalogue of Church Ornaments, Vestments, Material for Vestments, and Regalia* issued by the international firm of Benziger Brothers, which had American offices in New York, Cincinnati and St Louis at this time.

Commercial reproduction of the Sacred Heart burgeoned in the twentieth century, ranging from small plaster statues like Figures 1.2 and 1.5 to woodcarving such as Figure 1.1 and metal and plastic items such as Figures 1.3 and 1.4. The motif migrated from one medium to the next as determined by use, commerce, clientele and available industrial technology. Hartland Plastics, Inc., based in Hartland, Wisconsin, in business from 1939 to 1978, produced plastic action figures, baseball players and television cowboy characters, such as Roy Rogers, Dale Evans and the Lone Ranger and Tonto.[9] The firm also produced religious objects, such as Jesus light switch fixtures, the Infant of Prague, First Communion figurines and car dash Sacred Heart figures, such as Figure 1.4.

The car dash was one place to practice a certain form of devotion that was different from the bedroom, sanctuary, pilgrimage shrine or workplace. Remediation means adapting a motif to a new medium whose affordances favour its use in a new setting. A figurine like Figure 1.3 is designed to emulate the precious objects used in high liturgical services and placed on altars, reliquaries and processional crosses. Composed of what is commonly known as "pot metal," a variously formulated alloy of tin, lead, copper and zinc, the figure offers the advantage of weight and patina. The surface suggests gold and the weight supports the idea. Such objects stand on domestic altars and oratories, gracing bedrooms and desks. The car dash Jesus (Figure 1.3) is lightweight and durable, impervious to damage when the suction cup loses its grip and the object falls from its perch. If it becomes soiled, it is easily washed. If it is stolen or lost, it is readily replaced at little expense. And with these advantages it is able to travel with the devotee, taking its blessing on the road, into the wide world of chance and accident. Remediation negotiates change while maintaining continuity.

Circulation

Remediation leads to changes in circulation. By adapting to new circumstances, the object in a new medium is able to go places and do things that its predecessors in other media were unable to undertake. As I said, culture is conservative in its tendency constantly to reproduce. From an economic perspective, constancy is a better bet because it means less outlay and risk than change requires. So there are economic pressures not to change just as there are rewards for successful innovation, but those rewards come with a greater chance of failure.

The incessant act of reproduction generates what I am calling *deployment*, which is the endless circulation of artefacts. Statues such as those pictured here circulate, and they are deployed in new media, or remediated. Deployment happens in many ways – in commerce, collecting, gifting, domestic and public ritual, in entertainment and in piety. Deployment means commerce of all kinds, remediation of all kinds and display. Objects are commonly repurposed.

The medium for this is exchange – trading, bartering, gifting or monetary commerce. Objects are collected by entrepreneurs, dealers and collectors who invest in their resale value and collectability, which are driven by the limited supply or scarcity of the figures. Most of the objects pictured here belong to an era of Catholic immigration that has passed.[10] The companies that produced these items are largely no longer active, meaning that the objects themselves are becoming finite. Some have been remediated in new media, such as resin, which is more durable and comparable in price. Plaster, pot metal, porcelain and hard plastic moulding are now less common media for the production of religious statuary. Collectors, auction houses, antique dealers and entrepreneurs now form a large commercial industry that acquires objects in estate sales and circulates them for resale. As a result, the objects have shifted in classification: from devotional images to collectible artefacts. Their resale value is often higher than their original price. Instead of the resin objects being purchased in church goods stores, the "vintage" objects are acquired in auctions and in antique stores. They are no longer displayed as objects for the pious use of prayer and intercession, but as works of art or as historical or ethnic artefacts, as antiques or museum pieces.

28 *David Morgan*

Reception is a focus for material analysis when we understand it in three different ways. First, remediation and deployment as forms of circulation can put objects to different uses, offering evidence of the appeal of an artefact that is often reproduced, made less expensive by remediation in a different medium or using a new industrial technique that makes production less expensive by boosting scale or reducing time or labour. We can speak of the material reception of a motif in the evidence of remediation. Another aspect of material reception is the registration of physical use in the wear of an object. Figure 1.3 bears clear wear marks on the head and back shoulders of the figure, where the gold patina is completely absent and the metal surface has worn way by repeated contact, suggesting perhaps that the small figure was held in the hand of a devotee or stroked fondly where it stood. We can also note the indication of repeated touching on the nose of Jesus in Figure 1.5. The wear mark suggests that people visiting the image stroke its nose in an act of affection that also registers their presence before him. Material reception is also evident in the darkened appearance of this figure, which is likely the result of candle smoke and incense. This image, nearly 18 inches high, carefully embellished with hand-painted details, mould lines completely removed and deep undercuts apparent in the execution of the robe, hands and hair, was used on the altar of a church or shrine. Reception tells us something important about mode of display, use and audience.

Third, reception refers to the uses to which objects are put by devotees that may vary from original or designed intent. In this sense, reception is the private or local appropriation of objects to needs that the makers may not have anticipated. Objects, it is important to realise, are not finished when they leave the studio or manufactory. The narratives and practices that devotees report regarding the power or appeal of images of Jesus, for example, may make church authorities uneasy, or even alarmed. Some arbiters of taste in the Catholic Church have even launched vigorous attacks on popular taste. One German Catholic academic writer, Richard Egenter (1967), denounced a prayer card of the Sacred Heart of Jesus as "a sentimentalized and debased version of a generalized type derived from Old Masters, completely lacking in any spiritual truth or reality." The artist, he charged, did not respond "to personal feeling but to commercial demand."[11] Egenter objected to the remediation of "old masters" and impugned the commercial process as introducing a motive that undermined piety. It is a classic critique of religious kitsch, which is understood to substitute sentiment and the marketplace for authentic feeling and expression.

It should be clear that circulation refers to the social career of objects. As they circulate, they gain new value.[12] Their deployment and reception place them in contexts of exchange value, rarity, repurposing and taxonomic shifts that change their identity, appeal, purpose and value. But there is a final aspect of circulation to consider, the *ideological* or *cultural work* they perform. I have indicated that culture reproduces its motifs and symbols, remediating and deploying artefacts over and over again to help organise the life-worlds in which people exist. Thinkers from Aristotle to Mauss and Bourdieu have used the idea of the habitus to explain the constructive power of sensation that operates in culture. By habitus is meant the set of habits, thoughts and feelings that form a kind of enduring regime whose purpose is to organise human action into coherent patterns that allow people to live communally. In her study of religion, anthropologist Birgit Meyer (2006: 20) has called this "sensational form," by which she intends the "condensation of practices, attitudes and ideas that structure experiences of the transcendental." This is not unlike Bourdieu's description of habitus as "a system of lasting, transposable dispositions which, integrating past experiences, functions at every moment as a matrix of perceptions, appreciations, and actions and makes possible the achievement of infinitely diversified tasks" (Bourdieu 1977: 82).

The habitus, in other words, generates possibilities of behaviour, producing both individual and collective practices. Marcel Mauss (1973: 73) had already used the term habitus to convey the acquired ability that varied among peoples. This is what he meant by "techniques of the body," those characteristic ways of doing things as mundane as sitting, walking, eating or throwing a ball. Michel Maffesoli (1996) likewise drew attention to the shared or social characteristic of human behaviour, conceiving of the aesthetic (again, influenced by Aristotle) or sensuous style of behaviour as cultivating tastes or faculties for shared ways of feeling.

> Certain studies of the cult of the body – bodybuilding, diets, the press and magazines, dress fashion, sporting activities – demonstrate the indubitable way in which one constructs, cares for, and embellishes the body, partly under the gaze of the other, and partly so that it will be seen by the other. So even what might appear as individualism turns out to be, once more, a manifestation of tribal hedonism.
>
> (Maffesoli 1996: 35)

A key aspect of the cultural work of embodiment as learned behaviour, meaning everything from wearing clothing and learning how to swim to techniques of prayer and looking at images, is to create social bonds with those who constitute the social body to which one belongs.

Pierre Bourdieu (1977) helps us understand further the ideological significance of habitus or sensational form in his description of bodily *hexis* (acquired ability, from Aristotle) as

> political mythology realized, *em-bodied*, turned into a permanent disposition, a durable manner of standing, speaking, and thereby of *feeling* and *thinking*. The oppositions which mythico-ritual logic makes between the male and the female and which organize the whole system of values reappear, for example, in the gestures and movements of the body, in the form of the oppositions between the straight and the bent, or between assurance and restraint.
>
> (1977: 93–94)

Why is this political? Because the system of values that informs standing, speaking, feeling and thinking naturalises their embodiment, normalising, for instance, what men do versus what women do. Such distinctions become the nature of things. The body takes the shape of the truth taught by practice, language and ideas. The techniques of the body that members of a society learn become second nature – that is they are consonant with reality. This is the ideological function of embodiment and the material culture to which it belongs. And this is why I have underscored the reproductive function of material culture. We secure the nature of things in the practices and objects that our mediations reiterate.

Of course, culture is not merely mimetic.[13] It constantly changes, occasionally in a revolutionary transformation. But much more commonly, cultural change occurs as small variations on an accepted paradigm. The texture of daily life consists of iterations of the structures that people inherit and wish to maintain as the reliable organisation of everyday existence.

The trajectory of material analysis runs from the physical properties of a medium and the production of artefacts to the classification of its function and reproduction determined by its relation to other things like it, to the dynamics of circulation whereby the object acquires value and helps to construct a people's sense of community and shared reality. What makes an artefact sacred? This is a topic that takes us to another and very large topic, so it must suffice to say here that any object or bodily practice that connects one to forces that protect, heal or nurture is at least on the verge of becoming religious, even if that force is the state, mother nature, human goodness or a purpose-driven cosmic principle like ecological harmony. Religion, in other words, is the engagement of powerful agencies to enhance life and charge it with purpose. The sacred is any object or practice that secures such agencies. In the study of material culture, a religion is best approached in terms of a networking of numerous agents – people, objects, rites, places, communities, gods, saints and ancestors. The material analysis I have described is able to assess the formation and coupling of objects within far-flung webs of relationships.[14]

By placing this brief definition at the end of my account, I hope to make clear that the lion's share of any religion is not the gods or demons or spirits who stand beyond this world but the human beings who invoke them in what they do. This is not to make a theological statement on their reality or lack of it, but to suggest that taking materiality seriously means focusing our attention on the things and conditions that embody the relations that organise a religious life-world. Religion, in the end, is a kind of work devoted to world-making that is inseparable from the bodies and objects that benefit or suffer from the social and cultural structures that religions help secure.

Notes

1 Even a brief selection of recent work from a very large literature indicates the density and range of studies in terms of subject matter, religious tradition, geography and historical period: Morgan (2015); Dwyer-McNulty (2014); Promey (2014); Fleming and Mann (2014); Paine (2013); Garnett and Rosser (2013); Noyes (2013); Katz (2010); King (2010).

2 On plastic moulding see http://www.plasticmoulding.ca/history.htm. Accessed 14 July 2014.
3 For historical accounts of the techniques of casting see Quinn (1940) and Clarke (1946).
4 http://www.museusants.cat/english/history/idx_historia_uk.php. Accessed 16 July 2014. The sculpture includes a stamp that indicates it was produced in Olot by Moderna Sagrada Familia P. Lluís Mas. This firm was not among the original group founded before 1900.
5 *Catalog* (1936: no. 1, 2, 225, no. 2, 136, 250, no. 3, 3, 123, and no. 4, 241) lists copyright entries for Columbia Statuary. These numbers appear on the rear side of the base of many religious figures along with the initials "C.S." These numbers were not inventory numbers but product identification indicators registered with the US Copyright Office in the Library of Congress in order to protect them from violation by competitors who might reproduce the design.
6 http://www.nationsencyclopedia.com/economies/Europe/Germany-MONEY.html. Accessed 14 July 2014. A gallon of gasoline cost 20 cents in 1950 in the United States. Adjusting for inflation, the buying power of one dollar in 1950 was equivalent to $9.87 in 2014. http://www.dollartimes.com/calculators/inflation.htm. Accessed 14 July 2014.
7 The concept of affordance was coined by Gibson (1986: 127), by which he meant "the complementarity of the animal and the environment" in which it existed. An environment affords, furnishes or offers certain characteristics to the organisms that live in it. Gibson stressed that affordance is a relationship between the two, animal and environment, because the value or meaning of a property is determined not absolutely but relative to the life enabled by the ecology in which the animal participates. Thus, the idea of affordance is very relevant to the study of material culture because it prompts us to think about things in their setting. The physical features of a medium composing a thing are what relate it to its ecology, which is an environment of interacting forces and properties.
8 The concept has been extensively discussed by Bolter and Grusin (1999).
9 On Hartland Plastics, Inc., see http://dollreference.com/hartland_action_figures.html, accessed 15 July 2014.
10 Most, perhaps, but not all. In 1992, the trademark of Columbia Statuary was acquired by a California-based firm, Willits Designs International, Inc., although the new ownership appears to cover only porcelain statuettes. See http://www.trademarkia.com/columbia-statuary-74338121.html.
11 Egenter (1967: caption to Figure 15, unpaginated inset, and p. 48). For further discussion of issues of Catholic taste and mass-produced commodities see McDannell (1995: 163–197).
12 This idea has been instructively examined by Kopytoff (1986).
13 For a thoughtful consideration of reproduction and change in Bourdieu, see McCloud (2012).
14 I have explored the analysis of religious images within the perspective of network studies in Morgan (2014).

Works cited

Bolter, Jay David and Richard Grusin. 1999. *Remediation: Understanding New Media*. Cambridge: MIT Press.
Bourdieu, Pierre. 1977. *Outline of a Theory of Practice*, tr. Richard Nice. Cambridge: Cambridge University Press.
Brown, Bill. 2001. 'Thing Theory.' *Critical Inquiry* 28(1): 1–22.
Clarke, Carl Dame. 1946. *Molding and Casting for Moulage Workers, Sculptors, Artists, Physicians, Dentists, Criminologists, Craftsmen, Pattern Makers and Architectural Modelers*. Baltimore, MD: Standards Arts Press.

Dwyer-McNulty, Sally. 2014. *Common Threads: A Cultural History of Clothing in American Catholicism*. Chapel Hill: University of North Carolina Press.

Egenter, Richard. 1967. *The Desecration of Christ*, tr. Edward Quinn, ed. Nicolete Gray. Chicago: Franciscan Herald Press.

Fleming, Benjamin J. and Richard D. Mann, eds. 2014. *Material Culture and Asian Religions: Text, Image, Object*. London: Routledge.

Garnett, Jane and Gervase Rosser. 2013. *Spectacular Miracles: Transforming Images in Italy from the Renaissance to the Present*. London: Reaktion.

Gibson, James. 1986. *The Ecological Approach to Visual Perception*. New York: Psychology Press.

Katz, Maya Balakirsky. 2010. *The Visual Culture of Chabad*. Cambridge: Cambridge University Press.

King, E. Frances. 2010. *Material Religion and Popular Culture*. London: Routledge.

Kopytoff, Igor. 1986. 'The Cultural Biography of Things: Commoditization as Process'. In *The Social Life of Things: Commodities in Cultural Perspective*, ed. Arjun Appadurai, 64–91. Cambridge: Cambridge University Press.

Library of Congress Copyright Office. 1936. *Catalog of Copyright Entries for the Year 1935*. Washington, DC: Government Printing Office.

Maffesoli, Michel. 1996. *The Contemplation of the World: Figures of Community Style*, tr. Susan Emanuel. Minneapolis: University of Minnesota Press.

Mauss, Marcel. 1973. 'Techniques of the Body.' *Economy and Society* 2: 70–88.

McCloud, Sean. 2012. 'The Possibilities of Change in a World of Constraint: Individual and Social Transformation in the Work of Pierre Bourdieu.' *Bulletin for the Study of Religion* 41(1): 1–8.

McDannell, Colleen. 1995. *Material Christianity: Religion and Popular Culture in America*. New Haven, CT: Yale University Press.

Meyer, Birgit. 2006. *Religious Sensations: Why Media, Aesthetics and Power Matter in the Study of Contemporary Religion*. Amsterdam: Vrije Universiteit.

Morgan, David. 2008. *The Sacred Heart of Jesus: The Visual Evolution of a Devotion*. Amsterdam: Amsterdam University Press.

———. 2014. 'The Ecology of Images: Seeing and the Study of Religion.' *Religion and Society: Advances in Research* 5: 83–105.

———. 2015. *The Forge of Vision: A Visual History of Modern Christianity*. Berkeley: University of California Press.

Paine, Crispin. 2013. *Religious Objects in Museums: Private Lives and Public Duties*. London: Bloomsbury.

Promey, Sally M., ed. 2014. *Sensational Religion: Sensory Cultures in Material Practice*. Berkeley: University of California Press.

Quinn, James H. 1940. *Rubber Molds and Plaster Casts in the Paleontological Laboratory*. Chicago: Field Museum of Natural History.

Part 1
Production

2 From production to performance

Candles, creativity and connectivity

Marion Bowman

Introduction

As folklorist Henry Glassie points out, 'we live in material culture, depend upon it, take it for granted, and realise through it our grandest aspirations' (Glassie 1999: 1).

One of the main tasks of the material religion scholar is, quite literally, to notice things – by which, of course, I mean to notice *things*. My research has been grounded for many years in vernacular religious theory, articulated by American folklorist Leonard Primiano as 'an interdisciplinary approach to the study of the religious lives of individuals with special attention to the process of religious belief, the verbal, behavioral, and material expressions of religious belief, and the ultimate object of religious belief' (1995: 44). Paying special attention to 'material expressions of belief' and to the materials employed in 'doing' religion of necessity involves an 'on the ground' approach to the study of religion. For me, 'making materiality *evidential*' (Morgan, this volume) has resulted in years of fieldwork, participant observation, photographing material culture, acquiring numerous examples of material culture related to vernacular religion, and discovering wherever possible what things are doing; what they express; what they are thought to do; why they are employed in myriad contexts, formal and informal, institutional and domestic, public and private. If we are truly to engage with 'religion as it is lived: as human beings encounter, understand, interpret, and practice it' (Primiano 1995: 44), material religiosity and religious materiality must take centre stage.

Recognising material culture as 'the way in which an object participates in making and sustaining a life-world' (Morgan, this volume), in this chapter I examine some of the creative, tangible ways in which contemporary beliefs, practices and worldviews are expressed, encapsulated and enacted in different ways by, through and with material culture in the form of candles. Although candles are employed in myriad religious contexts for 'spiritual' purposes, they are so ubiquitous that as scholars we risk overlooking, underestimating or simply misconstruing the breadth of tasks they perform, the complexity of their usage, the affordances of their medium, and shifts in their production, specification, circulation and remediation – in short, how they 'work' in terms of material religion. Candles highlight what Primiano describes as 'the very qualities so important to lived religion: ambiguity, power, and creativity' (2012: 39).

The candle's medium, wax with a wick, 'affords or allows certain possibilities and produces certain kinds of effects' (Morgan, this volume). The candle's most obvious and basic utilitarian purpose is to give light, although candles are also employed to measure and mark time and to provide heat. Candles have been used globally for millennia, formally and informally, as both institutional ritual accoutrements and individual devotional devices. While focusing on candles primarily in relation to production, it will be necessary to include under this heading not simply the material production of candles but also the productive work in people's actions and intent: 'what the object does and how it may be understood to perform different kinds of cultural work' (Morgan, this volume). Both within and beyond institutional settings candles have been and continue to be used to remember the dead, honour other-than-human beings, mark sacred sites and materialise thoughts, intentions, aspirations and feelings of love, devotion, thanksgiving, loss or concern. Candles are 'performative' objects, able – like relics – to '"do" things by virtue of their very nature, in the right ritual/ cultural/ emotional/ religious environment' (Strong 2004: 238). In relation to institutional religion, world-building, worldview maintenance and everyday life, candles can convey, express or produce a range of purposes, meanings and emotions.

The candle's medium and affordances are central to its utility and ubiquity in terms of material religion. Applying fire (via a match, a taper, a cigarette lighter, another candle) to a candle involves physical engagement with it, and the heat and light produced are physically experienced. The flame itself can be visually, aesthetically, emotionally and/or meditatively engaging; it produces different effects for, and on, different people. The candle is an inanimate object that becomes activated, expressive, indeed animate, through the lighting of the wick to produce a flame. The affordances of wick in wax mean that the candle continues to burn after the human interaction that brings about the flame, leaving a continued presence in the actor's absence. Significantly, candle lighting can be performed with or without precise articulation of the exact meaning attributed to what is being done by the candle-provider, lighter or observer.

Candles provide excellent vehicles for studying how people perceive, use and interact with objects, and how they create, shape and narrate object biography. The fieldwork material and case studies drawn upon for this chapter derive from years of close observation and photographic recording of material religion in a variety of contexts; from long-term ethnological study of the town of Glastonbury, which has consistently highlighted material culture there (e.g. Bowman 1993, 2004, 2005, 2008, 2011, 2013, 2015); and from initial research conducted in relation to the project 'Pilgrimage and England's Cathedrals, Past and Present', funded by the Arts and Humanities Research Council (AHRC).[1] As the chapter is framed around production, I will contrast the Glastonbury Candle, highly focused and articulated in both production and purpose, and the tea light, which might be characterised as 'neutral' in its production but multivalent in its performative use. The themes of materiality, relationality and connectivity recur throughout.

Case study 1: the Glastonbury Candle

Glastonbury, a small town in the south-west of England, is the focus of and home to a variety of religiously aligned groups and individuals (e.g. Christians, Baha'is), Goddess devotees, Pagans, Druids, non-aligned spiritual seekers, 'native' Glastonians and incomers who have felt 'drawn' to Glastonbury, between whom at times there has been distrust, misunderstanding and animosity.

The material informing this case study has been gathered through participant observation, formal and informal conversations, photography and acquisition of material culture at Glastonbury over two decades. Online sources have also been invaluable, as the employment of social media has been intrinsic to the circulation, promotion and performativity of the Glastonbury Candle.

Guy Redden argues that at Body Mind Spirit Fairs, 'products are presented side-by side and the activities of many otherwise independent actors are interwoven' (2005: 237). These are 'intermediary spaces', 'catalysing networked relationships between diverse actors (both providers and participants) through presentation of multiple options for belief and practice' (2005: 237). As I have argued elsewhere (Bowman 2013), the town of Glastonbury in the southwest of England itself functions as an 'intermediary space'. The goods and services on offer there are similar in kind to those found at Fairs (crystals, 'esoteric' books, 'New Age' and Pagan paraphernalia, healing goods and experiences, yoga and meditation requisites and so on), but in Glastonbury they are a permanent part of the fabric of everyday life. Because of this locational interweaving of 'otherwise independent actors', it is both an environment that can embrace, accommodate and affirm an immense spectrum of belief and praxis, but also one that has witnessed much contestation.

In 2007 the Glastonbury Pilgrim Reception Centre (commonly known as PRC) was established, operating with the definition of pilgrim simply as 'One who makes a journey to a sacred place'. The PRC's stated objectives were twofold: 'To actively help in building Glastonbury as a centre of pilgrimage for people of all faiths and beliefs' and 'To offer a range of services to pilgrims, visitors, residents and researchers including information, teaching and support'. The PRC website explained:

> Today in the twenty-first century, there has been a huge resurgence of interest in the town as a centre of pilgrimage. But now, instead of a centre of Christian pilgrimage, Glastonbury has fully emerged as a place that recognises and honours all faiths and beliefs and all those on a sacred journey.
>
> (Glastonbury Pilgrim Reception Centre n.d. [a])

The PRC attracted volunteers from a variety of spiritual backgrounds and provided the sort of specialist information, publications and artefacts not found in ordinary tourist information centres: information on the various religious and spiritual groups in Glastonbury and their activities, workshops and rituals; maps locating various earth energy lines in and around the town. Online, the

38 *Marion Bowman*

PRC has maintained a visually attractive website, providing both information and the opportunity to purchase items online to raise funds for the Centre.

The Glastonbury Candle (Figure 2.1) provides the most significant example of materiality, commodification and community building pioneered by the

Figure 2.1 The Glastonbury Candle at the Pilgrim Reception Centre, Glastonbury. Photograph Marion Bowman.

PRC. It was developed in 2010 in conjunction with Starchild, a long-standing Glastonbury business making and selling incenses, essences, candles and other paraphernalia for personal and ritual use. Measuring 5 cm in diameter and standing 35 cm high, the Glastonbury Candle was manufactured locally in blue. According to the PRC's website, 'In many cultures and beliefs, blue is seen as a very sacred colour and represents faith, devotion, peace, inner knowledge, love, tranquillity and harmony' (Glastonbury Pilgrim Reception Centre n.d. [b]). The Candle, according to its label, is infused with 'herbs, trees and flowers, including the Glastonbury Thorn' that have been 'collected in tune with the cycles of the Moon from various sites in and around Glastonbury'. It has been described as 'an excellent representation of the Whole that is Glastonbury and also goes some small way in helping to celebrate our ethos of honouring all paths' (Glastonbury Pilgrim Reception Centre n.d. [c]). The Glastonbury Candle is small-scale and artisanal in its production; the wax has been given a specific, significant colour and infused with carefully chosen ingredients, collected at meaningful times; the place of its manufacture is considered important. Though potentially multifunctional (it could, after all, be used simply to provide light or for decorative effect), it has been intentionally produced for specific spiritual and communal purposes and effects.

The Glastonbury Candle was a highly targeted and purposefully produced item which has been used tactically to promote and express community cohesion, particularly through the 'Glastonbury Candle Journey.' One specific Glastonbury Candle was 'activated' by being lit and blessed in a ceremony at the PRC in July 2010. Since that time a series of Glastonbury Candles, lit in succession from that original Candle and housed in a large glass lantern, have travelled around Glastonbury and beyond. From the start, the PRC website pointed out that the Candle's 'Pilgrimage' round Glastonbury could be followed on the Glastonbury Candle page of the online shop, or through the Candle's Facebook page. The meticulous documentation of the Candle's journey reveals that it has spent time at ever more diverse venues and occasions. These have included the United Reformed Church, the Goddess Conference, the Anglican-led Holy Thorn Ceremony, Glastonbury Natural Health Centre, Archangel Michael Healing Centre, and shops such as Yin Yang and Starchild. It has been lit ceremonially by Sufis, Buddhists, Anthroposophists, Pagans and Sai Baba devotees. Not only did the Glastonbury Candle become a fixture of PRC meetings and events, but also it gradually appeared at the monthly Town Council meeting in the Town Hall, at the weekly indoor market and in pubs and cafes.

In April 2012 the renamed Glastonbury Unity Candle was the focal point of a 'Celebration of Harmony and Healing' organised by Morgana West of the PRC and led by the mayor of Glastonbury to celebrate 'Unity through Diversity'.

> Starting at the Pilgrim Reception Centre, its journey throughout the town saw it calling in at thirty different places, including temples, churches and sacred sites, until reaching its final destination at Chalice Well Gardens,

where more than fifty different faith and belief representatives had gathered for a simple ceremony beneath the two ancient yew trees. Each representative was given a half-sized Glastonbury Unity Candle and had brought with them a small blue glass bottle containing water which had been gathered from many places in and around Glastonbury.

Each individual was invited to come into the circle and pour the water into a glass bowl, specially engraved with the words Glastonbury 2012, Harmony and Healing. Each one lit their own Glastonbury Unity Candle from the flame that had journeyed around the town and, following a declaration of their faith, their path or their beliefs, they offered their own blessings on Glastonbury, its people and on out into the wider world.
(Glastonbury Pilgrim Reception Centre n.d. [d])

This event deftly used the Candle to address a number of issues and motifs relating to division and diversity within Glastonbury. The Candle as focal point of a procession both referred to and deflected from the use made of processions in Glastonbury to carry particular images (whether the Virgin Mary during Roman Catholic pilgrimages or a form of the Goddess in the Goddess Conference processions) to stake claims to the town by and for particular groups (Bowman 2004). Representatives of different groups participated in the central ritual of candle lighting and were able to make distinctive but non-confrontational declarations of their worldviews, but the focus was on blessing Glastonbury *as a whole*. Many within and beyond Glastonbury see the Glastonbury Candle Journey and the activities of the PRC as significant enterprises in creating a new level of interaction between the town's varied factions, fostering an acknowledgement of difference in worldviews and lifestyles that need not rule out cooperation and respectful coexistence. As the 'Unity through Diversity' website now declares,

In its familiar lantern, the Unity Candle is taken out onto the land in ceremonies of all kinds, attends churches, temples and other sacred venues, weddings, anniversaries, baby-namings, christenings, funerals, talks, workshops, conferences, festivals and concerts.

Each host lights the Candle in a way that is appropriate to them so they are personally and energetically engaged in the physical process of igniting the light. Being pro-actively involved reminds us that our individual thoughts and deeds are a vital and integral part of the whole and that only by co-evolving with one another, and with nature, in a constructive and coherent relationship, can we contribute towards creating a better future for all of humanity.
(Glastonbury Pilgrim Reception Centre n.d. [b])

The theme of materiality, relationality and connectivity can be seen in the context of a community, with the Glastonbury Candle embodying, expressing and actualising the relativism that increasingly has become the town's *modus operandi*. Many in Glastonbury are content to acknowledge their religion or spiritual path as only one among several possibilities, or to understand that this perception, which tends to emphasise personal choice and supports eclecticism and tolerance, is widely held.[2] Through the PRC site and the Candle's Facebook page, its involvement in a variety of ritual contexts and sojourns at a great range of venues reified and reinforced visions of inclusivity and cohesion in a highly disparate setting. The Candle's multivalence materialised the aspiration of community building and cohesion in a spiritually diverse context. The biography of the Glastonbury Candle, recorded online, demonstrates, in a religiously non-traditional, non-institutional setting, 'the dynamics of circulation whereby the object acquires value and helps to construct a people's sense of community and shared reality' (Morgan, this volume). In a fascinating shift from object biography to agency, or 'a medium becom[ing] indistinguishable from what it bears' (Morgan, this volume), on November 28, 2015, I received a text message reading 'Dear Marion, The Glastonbury Unity Candle invites you to join A Vigil for the Earth'.

While the iconic Candle in its lantern is the focus of much attention, the majority of Glastonbury Candles are commodities, bought and used by individuals. However, this is a candle that comes with a lot of information, with clearly articulated instructions, suggestions and assumptions about how the candle might be used and what sort of work the candle might perform. The paper label on my candle, purchased in 2013, states that 'Lighting the candle and focussing on the flame will connect you to the energies of Glastonbury and remind you of your own inner flame and the Divine Spark that resides in us all.' There is the suggestion that 'If you have purchased your candle in this sacred place, consider taking it to the places that you feel drawn to, light it for a few moments and visualise the special energies and magic of Glastonbury flowing into the candle.' (In Glastonbury, talk of energy is common across a range of modes of spiritual seeking and practice.) Stapled into the leaflet accompanying Candles is a taper 'lit from the activated candle so that you might light it and use it to ignite your own Unity Candle and carry the energies onwards.' The leaflet text continues:

> By witnessing the flame spark into life, we are reminded of our own inner flame and of how, regardless of our differences, we are all connected in the same Light.
> Many of us have come to realise and accept that our thoughts have energy. If, when we light the Glastonbury Unity Candle and reflect on all that light brings into our lives, perhaps the dark places in the world around us grow a little brighter.

The purchase of a Glastonbury Candle involved the acquisition of an assemblage of materials (the candle, the label, the leaflet and the taper), invited a range of interactions with the candle through lighting and suggested a number of ways in which candle and taper (wick and wax in different formats) could be performative, bringing spiritual benefit and connectivity with Glastonbury. The label and the leaflet encapsulate and convey a number of significant assumptions about individual spirituality, the nature of 'energy' and the power of visualisation, the sacredness and specialness of Glastonbury and the properties of the candle as a material conduit to and for the immaterial and spiritual.

The production, manufacture and marketing of the Glastonbury Candle and its paraphernalia are highly intentional, specialised and context-specific. By way of contrast, the second case study focuses upon the mass-manufactured tea light.

Case study 2: tea lights, context and cathedral

The tea light, so called because of its original function in teapot warmers, is generally a solid circle of paraffin/vegetable wax with a wick, roughly 38 mm in diameter and 15 mm deep, most often housed in an aluminium or plastic 'cup'. Its casing makes the tea light both highly portable and 'self-sufficient'; it can be used without further equipment in virtually any location. Manufacturers tend to claim a burning time of around four hours. As they are cheap enough to be bulk bought and require no paraphernalia, tea lights can be massed to create installations, such as circles, crosses, spirals, labyrinths, numbers and words (see e.g. Sedakova 2015). Lit and spent tea lights in the public domain thus mark sites of all-night vigils, expressions of solidarity and protest, spontaneous mourning and other temporary incursions of religious materiality into notionally secular space. The tea light casing remaining after the wax has burned away creates debris, which can be problematic (see Figure 2.2), but which also provides testimony to these and other, more private acts.

Precisely because the tea light is so neutral and ubiquitous, the production of material religiosity/religious materiality in relation to a tea light is literally in people's own hands. In this respect tea lights can be compared with relics, which are likewise 'defined as much by where they are located and what people do with them as they are by what they physically are' (Schopen 1998: 260). For this reason, the second case study pairs the neutral, mass-produced tea light with the highly specific context of a Christian cathedral.

Candles have played a considerable material, devotional and ritual role in the Christian tradition, their medium and affordances providing immense scope for symbolic exposition. Historian Eamon Duffy notes that pre-Reformation sermons for Candlemas (a festival associated with the triumph of light over darkness) frequently articulated that 'the processional candles on the feast were carried to represent Jesus, and underlined the point with an elaborate exposition of the significance of wax, wick, and flame as representing Jesus' body, soul, and godhead' (Duffy 1992: 18). The AHRC-funded project 'Pilgrimage and England's Cathedrals, Past and Present' has provided opportunities to observe and interrogate cathedral life through participant observation, informal conversations, questionnaires, emails and interviews with cathedral visitors, volunteers, guides, clergy and staff. *Inter alia*, we have been able to observe praxis and performance, and converse with people about normally unarticulated beliefs,

Figure 2.2 Tea light debris at Virtuous Well, Trellech, Wales. Photograph Marion Bowman.

intentions and personal acts involving candles. For the purposes of this chapter, I shall concentrate upon tea lights in the context of Westminster Cathedral.

Westminster Cathedral, London (the Metropolitan Cathedral of the Most Precious Blood), is the mother church of the Roman Catholic Church in England and Wales. Candles are an obvious part of devotional life there: the scent of hot wax strikes one on entry and tea lights are consistently burning on racks before various saints and in assorted chapels (Figure 2.3). I was told by a volunteer of one laywoman who, as her own contribution to the life of the Cathedral, regularly goes round the different candle racks first thing in the morning and lights a single candle, to ensure that no racks are bare and giving later visitors encouragement and a means of lighting their candles. Donation for the tea lights is encouraged, but this is framed as an offering rather than a purchase.

The signs relating to candles observed in Westminster Cathedral in March 2015 were A4 laminated sheets, generally attached to the metal container for donations (see Figure 2.3); the red and gold Cathedral logo appeared top centre of the sheet, and then these words:

Jesus said: I have come into the world, so that whoever believes in me may not remain in darkness.

Lighting a candle is a prayer: When we have gone it stays alight, kindling in the hearts and minds of others the prayers we have already offered for the sad, the sick, the suffering, the peace of the world, and prayers of thankfulness too.

Lighting a candle is a parable: Giving light to others, it burns itself out. Christ gave himself for others – He calls us to give ourselves.

Lighting a candle is a symbol: of love and hope – of light and warmth – our world needs them all.

Figure 2.3 Racks of lit tea lights in red plastic containers at the Chapel of Holy Souls, Westminster Cathedral, London. Photograph Marion Bowman.

Explicitly Christian messages and meanings here are related to both the material and symbolic characteristics of candles. The cathedral's signs reinforce the range of emotions, beliefs and worldviews that might be expressed and encapsulated through the act of candle lighting, with relationality and connectivity implied, but not explicitly stated, in relation to saints and the dead.

People produce meaning in the choice of placement of a tea light, expressing preference and reflecting relationality. Racks are located at strategic points beside or within chapels with specific dedications (Lady Chapel, Chapel of St Patrick and the Saints of Ireland, Chapel of the Holy Souls, Chapel of the Blessed Sacrament), before a statue (e.g. St Anthony) or picture (e.g. Our Lady of Perpetual Help), and the numbers of candles burning in each rack can signal their varying degrees of popularity. Placement is also affected by the liturgical season; the number of tea lights burning at the Chapel of the Holy Souls, unsurprisingly, increases around All Souls' Day.

Within Westminster Cathedral there are 'devotional hotspots' where the massing of lit tea lights is obvious through sight, scent and even heat. From a week of participant observation stationed beside an entrance, it became obvious that the focal point of a visit to the cathedral for numerous people of varied ethnicities is the statue of St Anthony (Figure 2.4). St Anthony is traditionally associated with the poor (devotional activity related to him frequently involves leaving a donation for 'St Anthony's poor'), is considered good at finding lost things[3] and is popular throughout much of the Catholic world. An elderly man who visits the cathedral nearly every day told me that he usually lights a candle if someone is unwell; when I asked him where, he responded 'St Anthony, he's usually the one they love' (Fieldnotes, 4/3/2015). One volunteer commented that on busy days the overcrowding of the candles before St Anthony can be problematic; volunteers keep an eye on racks to remove spent tea lights to create space, but it is considered wrong and disrespectful to remove lit candles.

The statue is mounted on the wall, and people commonly reach up and hold St Anthony's foot while praying to/communicating with him. On the marble surface below are cards that can be used for requesting prayers for particular people and placed in a basket; the basket was piled high with cards by the end of the week, although I noticed that many people who paused or lit a candle there did not write on a prayer card. The wording on the cards available beside the statue of St Anthony very specifically articulate ideas about candles and their affordances, relationality and agency:

Lord,
May this candle be a light for you to enlighten me in my difficulties and decisions.
May it be a fire for you to burn out of me all pride, selfishness and impurity.
May it be a flame for you to bring warmth into my heart towards my family, my neighbours and all those who meet me.
Through the prayers of Mary Virgin and Mother I place in your care those I come to pray for (especially . . . [blank space where name can be written in])

46 *Marion Bowman*

    I cannot stay long with you in this church; in leaving this candle I wish to give to you something of myself.
    Help me to continue my prayer into everything I do this day.
    Amen

I observed one woman who had spent a long time in front of the statue take ten one pound coins from her bag, insert these in the donation box, choose ten tea lights, carefully place them in a line on the top row of the right candle rack (repositioning someone else's lit candle to do so) and light

Figure 2.4 Statue of St Anthony, Westminster Cathedral, London. Photograph Marion Bowman.

them. This was a devotional 'installation'; the quantity of candles and their proximity to the saint were clearly significant, reflecting and materialising her relationship and interaction with St Anthony. On another occasion, a woman who had spent some time before the statue of St Anthony was clearly very upset when a strong gust of wind blew open the swing door opposite the statue, extinguishing the candles. She involved a couple of bystanders in a rather frantic (and slightly dangerous) effort to bring lit tea lights from another rack to relight the candles before St Anthony. It seemed imperative to her and the others involved that the candles be relit and the devotional *status quo ante* be restored immediately. In these examples we can discern a trajectory running

> from the physical properties of a medium [wax] and the production of artefacts [the tea lights] to the classification of its function and reproduction determined by its relation to other things like it [assemblage on racks of devotional candles in a particular location], to the dynamics of circulation whereby the object acquires value and helps to construct a people's sense of community and shared reality.
>
> (Morgan, this volume)

People can buy tea lights (or larger candles) with plastic casing bearing the image of a saint or a particular aspect of Mary (e.g. Our Lady of Lourdes) at the cathedral shop. St Patrick candles tend to be placed at the candle rack for what is commonly called St Patrick's chapel, while Marian candles tend to appear in relation to the Lady Chapel, or before the image of Our Lady of Perpetual Help on a side aisle pillar. In these cases, while the wax and wick materiality remains constant, the casing of the tea lights has been modified to achieve specificity; they are purchased to identify or reinforce a devotional focus, to express a relational preference. Purposeful production is further reinforced by purposeful placement. However, one cannot tell from simple observation precisely what is going on. Conversation reveals, for example, that a candle bearing the image of a *relation's* favourite saint might be placed in the cathedral on her/his behalf, thereby bringing the relative into what is considered an especially sacred or significant space. It is also possible to buy in the cathedral shop cards with the message 'I lit a candle for you in Westminster Cathedral'. Layers of physical and spiritual relationality and connectivity are thus materialised through a candle's production and purchase, and through performances relating to the physically present and non-present, to the living and the dead, to human and other-than-human beings.

One Westminster Cathedral employee, who lights a plain tea light every day for her deceased father at St Patrick's chapel, generously expanded for me the role of the candles for her personal construction of worldview, community and shared reality:

> I light candles for people all the time. Some dead, some living.

When I light a candle to my [father] I am sending up love and feeling a link to him through that little light and usually a quick 'God Bless'.

I always like to light my candles at St Patrick's chapel because of my strong pride in my Irish roots and if I am feeling sad or want to share something with [my father] I will stand for a few moments and chat to him. Although I am sure he will be fully aware of things already it doesn't hurt to have a word!

A candle is a great way to focus the mind too and to be able to switch off and watch its light and be drawn in to prayer through it.

As another example, I lit a candle for my cousin . . . She underwent a mastectomy and I sent up a prayer and lots of love to her. Again this little light symbolised the link across the miles attached to a prayer that I almost 'see' being lifted and floated over to the person I am sending it to.

I know that probably sounds daft! So when it is to someone living it floats to them and I see them being surrounded in love and calmness and God's love and my thoughts of them.

When I send up a prayer to [my father] or my uncle . . . or for someone else who has passed away I imagine it floating upwards and onwards into the sky and that the person can see me sending this thought to them and is aware that I remember them in many different ways and one of them is through a prayer asking God to keep them close even in death.

(Personal email communication, 6/3/2015)

This example is redolent with materiality, connectivity and relationality, demonstrating 'the way in which an object participates in making and sustaining a life-world' (Morgan, this volume). As Gosden observes, 'emotions are materially constituted and material culture is emotionally constituted' (2004: 39).

The biography of the Glastonbury Candle and the performative uses of the tea light in Westminster cathedral demonstrate different ways in which an object 'participates in making and sustaining a life-world' (Morgan, this volume). The Glastonbury Candle is not portable and ubiquitous, unlike the tea light. It needs to be contained in some way (e.g. in a lantern – see Figure 2.1) and is envisaged as both containing and projecting Glastonbury in some sense, through its infusions of herbs and essences from Glastonbury and potential to be 'charged' with the energies of Glastonbury. The plain tea lights used in the Westminster Cathedral examples, by comparison, are materially neutral in their production but gain performative power and significance through their employment in specific contexts and configurations. Their use is directed at an institutional level through signs, the cards below the statue of St Anthony and the positioning of candle racks, but there is nevertheless considerable scope for 'ambiguity, power, and creativity' (Primiano 2012: 390) at the individual level. It is interesting to note the similarity between the aspiration that 'If, when we light the Glastonbury Unity Candle and reflect on all that light brings into our lives, perhaps the dark places in the world around us grow a little brighter' and the sign in Westminster Cathedral declaring that 'Lighting a candle is a symbol of love and hope – of light and warmth – our world needs them all.'

In both cases, in the end, people interact with and produce meaning through the candles in their own way, for ultimately that is the multivalent nature of candles, brought about by the affordances of wax and wick, conjoined with the embodied human activity of adding flame.

Conclusion

In this chapter I have concentrated on production in relation to candles, specifically the contrasting examples of tea lights and the Glastonbury Candle, materially both combinations of wax and wick. Tea lights, as mass-produced objects not purposefully or exclusively produced as religious objects *per se*, have focused attention on the productive work that lies in people's actions and intentions, the relationality and connectivity enacted and maintained through these material objects with other human beings (living and dead), with other-than-human beings, and with the past and place. The Glastonbury Candle, by contrast, is a complex, carefully crafted, intentional object. Although by its very nature transitory, it reflects the production values of more lasting items of religious materiality, underlining the importance of studying production in relation to the ephemeral as well as the more lasting and obvious products of lived religion.

I have demonstrated throughout this chapter that the theme of materiality, relationality and connectivity recurs in careful consideration of material religion. As various chapters in this book attest, a number of trends in the study of religion are contributing currently to a more nuanced understanding of material religion, and indeed religion *per se*. While the significance of materiality was never absent from folkloristic, ethnographic and anthropological engagement with religion (see e.g. Bowman and Valk 2012), '[w]ithin religious studies and the human sciences more broadly, there has been a growing interest in what the study of materiality offers for our understanding of the lived experience and practices of religion' (Engelke 2011: 209).

In addition to materiality, a recognition of the importance of relationality – and a relationality that is inclusive of 'other-than-human' beings and things – is increasingly informing approaches to studying religion and the material dimensions thereof (see e.g. Harvey 2005; Whitehead 2013). Mika Lassander has advocated combining elements from Primiano's vernacular religious approach (e.g. recognising the importance of individual creativity) and Latour's actor network theory (ANT; Latour 1987), suggesting that 'a major contribution of ANT to social research lies in paying attention to the active role non-humans play; how things ... make people do things' (Lassander 2012: 241–242). Connectivity likewise emerges as vital; Paul Tremlett argues that religions (old and new) should be regarded as 'nodes that link people, places and objects together in particular ways' (Tremlett 2013: 473).

Glassie claims that material culture often 'reports thoughts and actions that resist verbal formulation' (1999: 46). While this is undoubtedly true, religious materiality does far more: it produces, mediates, enables and enacts those thoughts and actions in the never-ending work of world-making and maintenance.

Notes

1 Working with Durham Cathedral, York Minster, Canterbury Cathedral and Westminster Cathedral, 'Pilgrimage and England's Cathedrals, Past and Present' is examining pilgrimage and engagement with sacred sites in England from the eleventh to the twenty-first centuries, and assessing the growing significance of England's cathedrals as sacred/heritage/tourist sites today. Team members: principal investigator Dee Dyas and researchers John Jenkins and Tiina Sepp, University of York; co-investigators Marion Bowman, The Open University, and Simon Coleman, University of Toronto. For more information, see http://www.pilgrimageandcathedrals.ac.uk.
2 While this does not work for people who feel strongly that their religion/spiritual path represents *the* truth, I was told by an Anglican vicar who formerly worked in Glastonbury that talking about 'my truth' rather than 'the truth' had opened up opportunities for significant interaction and working practically with a number of groups and individuals, and was therefore a legitimate and successful strategy.
3 I first heard the prayer 'Good St Anthony come around, something's lost that can't be found' while conducting fieldwork in Newfoundland in the late 1970s.

Works cited

Bowman, Marion. 1993. 'Drawn to Glastonbury'. In *Pilgrimage in Popular Culture*, eds. Ian Reader and Tony Walter, 29–62. Basingstoke and London: Macmillan.

———. 2004. 'Procession and Possession in Glastonbury: Continuity, Change and the Manipulation of Tradition'. *Folklore* 115(3): 1–13.

———. 2005. 'Ancient Avalon, New Jerusalem, Heart Chakra of Planet Earth: Localisation and Globalisation in Glastonbury'. *Numen* 52(2): 157–190.

———. 2008. 'Going with the Flow: Contemporary Pilgrimage in Glastonbury'. In *Shrines and Pilgrimage in the Modern World: New Itineraries into the Sacred*, ed. Peter Jan Margy, 241–280. Amsterdam: Amsterdam University Press.

———. 2011. 'Understanding Glastonbury as a Site of Consumption'. In *Religion, Media and Culture: A Reader*, eds. Gordon Lynch, Jolyon Mitchell and Anna Strhan, 11–22. London: Routledge.

———. 2013. 'Valuing Spirituality: Commodification, Consumption and Community in Glastonbury'. In *Religion in Consumer Society: Brands, Consumers and Markets*, eds. Francois Gauthier and Tuomas Martikainen, 207–224. Farnham and Burlington, VA: Ashgate.

———. 2015. '"Helping Glastonbury to Come into Its Own": Practical Spirituality, Materiality, and Community Cohesion in Glastonbury'. In *Practical Spiritualities in a Media Age*, eds. Curtis C. Coats and Monica M. Emerich, 51–65. London and New York: Bloomsbury Academic.

Bowman, Marion and Ülo Valk, eds. 2012. *Vernacular Religion in Everyday Life: Expressions of Belief*. Abingdon and New York: Routledge.

Duffy, Eamon. 1992. *The Stripping of the Altars: Traditional Religion in England 1400–1580*. New Haven, CT and London: Yale University Press.

Engelke, Mathew. 2011. 'Material Religion'. In *The Cambridge Companion to Religious Studies*, ed. Robert A. Orsi, 209–229. Cambridge: Cambridge University Press.

Glassie, Henry. 1999. *Material Culture*. Bloomington and Indianapolis: Indiana University Press.

Glastonbury Pilgrim Reception Centre. n.d. (a). 'About Us'. http://www.glastonbury-pilgrim.co.uk/#glastonbury-pilgrim-centre-about-us.php. Accessed 12/01/2012.

———. n.d. (b). 'The Glastonbury Unity Candle'. http://www.unitythroughdiversity.org/the-unity-candle.html. Accessed 09/03/2015.

———. n.d. (c). 'The Glastonbury Candle'. http://www.glastonbury-pilgrim.co.uk/#giftshop/the-glastonbury-candle.php. Accessed 12/01/2012.

———. n.d. (d). 'Glastonbury 2012: A Celebration of Harmony and Healing Inspiring Unity through Diversity.' http://www.unitythroughdiversity.org/glastonbury-2012-find-out-where-it-all-started.html. Accessed 08/03/2016.

Gosden, Chris. 2004. 'Aesthetics, Intelligence, and Emotions. Implications for Archaeology'. In *Rethinking Materiality: The Engagement of Mind with the Material World*, eds. E. Demarrais, C. Gosden and C. Renfrew, 33–43. Cambridge: McDonald Institute for Archaeological Research Volumes.

Harvey, Graham. 2005. *Animism: Respecting the Living World*. London: Hurst.

Lassander, Mika T. 2012. "Grappling with Liquid Modernity: Investigating Post-Secular Religion". In *Post-Secular Society*, eds. Peter Nynäs, Mika T Lassander and Terhi Utriainen, 239–267. Piscataway: Transaction.

Latour, Bruno. 1987. *Science in Action: How to Follow Scientists and Engineers through Society*. Milton Keynes: Open University Press.

Primiano, Leonard. 1995. 'Vernacular Religion and the Search for Method in Religious Folklife'. *Western Folklore* 54(1): 37–56.

———. 2012. 'Afterword – Manifestations of the Religious Vernacular: Ambiguity, Power, and Creativity'. In *Vernacular Religion in Everyday Life: Expressions of Belief*, eds. Marion Bowman and Ülo Valk, 382–394. Abingdon and New York: Routledge.

Redden, Guy. 2005. 'The New Age: Towards a Market Model'. *Journal of Contemporary Religion* 20(2): 231–246.

Schopen, Gregory. 1998. 'Relic'. In *Critical Terms for Religious Studies*, ed. M.-C. Taylor, 256–268. Chicago and London: University of Chicago Press.

Sedakova, Irina. 2015. 'Magico- Religious Symbolism of a Candle in the Slavic Calendar Rituals'. In *The Ritual Year 10: Magic in Rituals and Rituals in Magic*, eds. Tatiana Minniyakhmetova and Kamila Velkoborska, 141–151. Innsbruck, Tartu: ELM Scholarly Press.

Strong, J.S. 2004. *Relics of the Buddha*. Princeton, NJ: Princeton University Press.

Tremlett, Paul-François. 2013. 'The Problem with the Jargon of Inauthenticity: Toward a Materialist Repositioning of the Analysis of Postmodern Religion'. *Culture and Religion: An Interdisciplinary Journal* 14(4): 463–476.

Whitehead, Amy. 2013. *Religious Statues and Personhood: Testing the Role of Materiality*. London and New York: Bloomsbury.

3 Blessed food from Jalarām's kitchen

Narrative, continuity and service among Jalarām Bāpā devotees in London

Martin Wood

Introduction

In the last 100 years, the figure of Jalarām Bāpā (1799–1881) has been transformed from regional Gujarātī *Lohāna*[1] saint to transnational Hindu phenomenon. In the UK alone the Jalarām Bāpā tradition has established two substantial places of devotional worship (*mandira*) specifically dedicated to him: the Jalarām Prathana Mandir in Leicester and the Shree Jalarām Mandir Greenford, London.[2] While there are no official figures, trustees and devotees at both *mandira* speak of hundreds of thousands of *bhaktas* (devotees) attending regular devotional worship and major festivals on an annual basis. Furthermore, his image or *mūrti* can be found in numerous pan-Hindu, Sanātana Dharma[3] *mandira* and on domestic shrines in Gujarātī homes around the country. In this essay I will focus specifically on the UK diaspora context based on qualitative field research undertaken at the tradition's West London Greenford *Mandir*.[4] My research examines how devotees understand the relationship between the production and consumption of sacred food or *prasādam* and how this underpins certain aspects of the tradition's ethical ideology.

What interests us here is the tradition's central commitment to maintaining a strong social ethic based on charity for all, an ethic underpinned by the miraculous events or *parchās*[5] that characterise the tradition's hagiographies and narratives. This ethical approach is referred to as Jalarām *seva* or service to others irrespective of religion or social status, and it takes place through the preparation and serving of blessed food from the *mandir*'s charitable kitchen or *sadavrat*.[6] Jalarām *seva*, both *prabhu* and *jan*, divine and human, employs blessed food as the medium of both transformation and transmission and allows devotees to fully engage with and, to an extent, re-enact the tradition's core narrative. In short, the vehicle of *prasādam* allows devotees to put into action today the ethical principles that underpin the tradition and that were established in nineteenth-century Gujarāt. As Morgan suggests (in this volume), the medium, in this case *prasādam* from Jalarām's kitchen, 'carries form [and] content, bearing it across space [and] time, between people' – and, in this case, the divine. Here we see that the ethical and spiritual message of Jalarām has been absorbed by the *prasādam*, affecting the circumstances of those who consume it. What is also important here is the process of production, a process that transforms the initial mundane food object into something spiritually charged and beyond the ordinary – something that bears specific intention.

Field research and hagiography

The majority of Gujarātī Hindus arrived in the UK from East Africa between 1968 and 1972, escaping the political and social oppression of Idi Amin's Pan-African policies. It was not until the 1980s and 1990s, however, that academics in the field of the study of religions began to undertake sustained research concerning the beliefs and practices of Hindus in this country (e.g. Ballard 1994; Brear 1986; Burghart 1987; Jackson and Nesbit 1993; Knott 1986; Mattausch 1993, 1998; Nye 1995). Following Raymond Williams's first work on the Swāmīnārāyan tradition (1994, 2001) there has been a steady interest in the lives and events of Hindu saints associated with the Gujarāt region of Western India, much of which has provided a valuable focus on the US and UK diasporic context (Williams 2001; Kim 2008, 2013; Wood 2008, 2010a, 2010b).

Few, however, have made any specific mention of the Jalarām Bāpā tradition. Michaelson (1987) provides a fascinating insight into the domestic activities of Jalarām Bāpā devotees but elsewhere only brief mentions of the saint have been made (Jackson and Nesbitt 1993; Bowen 2006). Other than Wood (2010a, 2010b, 2015), there has been little work on the life of and the miraculous events surrounding this increasingly popular Gujarātī religious figure. In some respects this is not surprising as during his life few would have known about Jalarām Bāpā beyond Virpur, the village where he grew up and lived for most of his life, located in the Saurashtra region of Gujarāt.[7] While he made a considerable impact on those in the immediate area, he would have maintained only a modest following. It seems that it was only after his death and the subsequent migration of Gujarātī Hindus at the end of the nineteenth century that his place in the socio-religious fabric of the Gujarāt and beyond became secure.

The contemporary, transglobal significance of Jalarām Bāpā contrasts somewhat with the fact that no literature was produced on him, textual or scholarly, during his lifetime. According to devotees, Jalarām did not commit any of his teachings to paper or produce any autobiographical accounts of the events of his life and it would appear that the majority of the narratives, stories and indeed myths concerning Jalarām and his teachings have been either transmitted orally or come directly from the work of Saubhagyachand Rajdev (1947). Rajdev, a firm Jalarām devotee, travelled extensively in the Virpur region during the 1940s, speaking to devotees who had encountered Jalarām and collecting stories and testimonies concerning their experiences of his blessings. *Bhakta Shri Jalarām* ('Jalarām the Devotee') also contains the stories of devotees living in East Africa and is considered by most in the UK to be the best source for the saint's life. Due to the fact that Rajdev's work, while substantial, has been only partially translated into English (1966), this research also relies upon the more contemporary hagiographies that have drawn directly on Rajdev and that likewise re-present the life and teachings of Jalarām Bāpā in English: *Jalarām Bāpā* by Ramanlal Soni (1984) and *Shri Jalarām Vandana* by Rekhaben Shah (2000). Furthermore, I have complemented this with material from various temple guidebooks and the websites produced by Jalarām Bāpā *mandira* in the US and UK.[8]

These hagiographies are extremely important in interpreting and understanding the tradition's ethical commitment. I have, however, had to detach myself from the rigid concerns of historical accuracy as many of the events related in the hagiographies of Jalarām may not have taken place in the way that they have been presented. I therefore concur with Rinehart's view when he suggests that narratives can act as 'useful sources of information on the ... social and religious concerns of the communities that produced and (who continue to) read them' (1999: 8). These hagiographical accounts, as compiled by devotees, allow us to gain a deeper understanding of the wider socio-religious context within which the Greenford community locates itself.

This research is further underpinned and contextualised by an ethnographic approach in the field, specifically at the Greenford Jalarām Bāpā *mandir*. This has involved taking into consideration a number of factors, including language, gender, age and generation. For example many of the older female devotees with whom I have worked preferred to speak in their mother tongue, requiring the assistance of a translator, while second- and third-generation devotees are fluent in both written and spoken English. At times it has proved difficult to fully engage with ordinary, regularly visiting devotees, because their time is often limited and they are mostly attending the *mandir* for devotional purposes. However, many made a substantial contribution to this project. One also has to find a balance between the views of ordinary devotees and those of temple committee members, religious specialists and community leaders. Devotees occasionally appeared reticent to comment on certain issues of belief and practice and suggested that I speak to the temple *pandits*, because 'they know all the answers'.

Devotees of Jalarām Bāpā in Greenford are drawing on a long tradition of *seva* through the distribution of free food to those in need irrespective of religion or social status. According to the hagiographical accounts of his life, the foundations of this ethical and social ideology were laid when Jalarām Bāpā began to fulfil his *sadavrat* in the form of a charitable kitchen (Soni 1984: 7–10; Shah 2000: 14–20). The year was 1820 (1876 bright half of Margh, Vikram era)[9] and the saint had recently married after returning from a *tīrtha yatra* (pilgrimage) of India's most significant pilgrimage sites. Upon his return he visited a renowned *guru*, Bhoja Bhagat (Bhojalrām), who accepted the twenty-year-old as his disciple. Jalarām was then reunited with his wife, Virbai Mā, and after establishing their household in Virpur they laboured in the fields of a local farmer who paid them in bundles of food grains.

Over time Jalarām and Virbai accumulated a substantial surplus of grain and eventually he asked her what they should do with it. Virbai replied, 'I know why you are asking me this ... You may start giving alms to the needy in the name of Rama ... God cares for those who care for others' (Soni 1984: 10). Jalarām then approached Bhojalrām and sought his permission to start dispensing free food to those in need. Bhojalrām replied, 'Do charity . . . Follow your dharma by thought, action and speech. Attribute all your actions to God . . . give as much as you can' (Soni 1984: 10). From then on, the saint's reputation for *parchās*, many of which involved the miraculous multiplication of food, spread through the region as did the welcome news of the charitable kitchen. The saint never turned anyone away regardless of social status or religious conviction, and the *sadavrat* kitchen constantly fed those in need as famine and economic hardship plagued the region.

It was not, however, until Jalarām's death, on 23rd February 1881, that the *sadavrat* received the direct attention of the divine. Hariram, Jalarām and Virbai's grandson, had arranged for a great gathering of *sādhus* (religious renunciants) at their *ashram* (a monastery or abode of ascetics) to mark the passing of the saint. All of those present had been fed when suddenly a 'great sadhu from unknown places' (Kataria 2010: 33) bowed to the congregation and entered the kitchen's storeroom, reappearing with a *ladoo* sweet in his hand. He then crushed the sweet and spread the crumbs about the place exclaiming, 'This is the everful granary' (Soni 1984: 64). 'Let this store never get dry' (Rajdev 1966: 72; Kataria 2010: 33). Both Rajdev's and Kataria's narrative suggests that the *sādhu* was 'the lord himself (who) came in the guise of the sadhu to give his blessings to the *sadavrat*' (Rajdev 1966: 72; Kataria 2010: 33). Soni comments that 'even today the store of Jalarām's ashram is ever full' and that 'he is ever here with us. Bāpā is immortal' (Soni 1984: 64).

Today the original *sadavrat* kitchen in Virpur continues to feed thousands of devotees who arrive on a twice daily basis to partake of the free *prasādam* (see ahead) that is offered, and as in the narratives, it is believed that the food never runs out and the stores never run dry no matter how many people turn up. One hundred and ninety years after Jalarām Bāpā established his first charitable kitchen in Virpur, almost to the day, the Greenford *mandir* opened its own *sadavrat* kitchen. According to one of the trustees, writing in the Shree Jalarām Greenford Newsletter No. 8 (Mojaria 2013),

> In 2010, UK had started feeling the pinch of global recession. Many a family's, especially the new immigrants' household budgets were in the doldrums. The trustees were quick to respond and rise to the occasion. A word was spread for the newly started free daily kitchen (sadavarat), serving meals seven days a week to the attendees, irrespective of caste, colour and creed. It saw many . . . families through very difficult times.

The kitchen now feeds a large number of Hindu and non-Hindu devotees from a variety of migrant backgrounds seven days a week. Devotees speak of Thursday and Saturday *mandir* services attracting between 500 and 1,000 devotees for *pūjā* (worship, especially of an image, in this case of Jalarām and Rama) and up to 150 for *prasādam*. As with the hagiographical tradition of the 'everful granary', it is believed by devotees that the food never runs out, no matter how hard the economic times are or how many turn up for *prasādam*. It is precisely this relationship between narrative, *parchā* and the contemporary practice of *seva* that I intend to explore.

Blessed food – *prasādam*

By distributing free food, the Jalarām community is addressing not only the material requirements of the hungry and those in need: they are also addressing the spiritual desires of those who consume it. All of the food that is prepared, served and distributed by the charitable kitchen is Jalarām *prasādam*, food that has been directly blessed by Jalarām Bāpā himself. The *sadavrat* and the food it produces are the mediums through which the ethical message of the Jalarām *seva* is mediated. This is a reciprocal relationship. As we shall see, the food acts as a conduit through which the blessings of the saint are transmitted to the devotee, but it also acts as the medium through which the devotion of the individuals involved in its production is mediated to the saint.

The basis of this reciprocal process revolves around the idea that food can be transformed from a mundane material into spiritually charged *prasādam*. It is generally understood by devotees that when one prepares and offers food to the *mūrti* or representation of the God/Goddess, *guru* or saint with the requisite sense of love and devotion, it will be accepted and consumed in a non-physical manner. That which is left over is believed to be of special religious significance to those who eat it. In this sense food produced under certain ritual conditions, using specific ingredients, not only mediates the love and devotion of the devotee to the saint but also mediates the blessing and grace of the saint to the devotee when later consumed.

Before this, however, the food has to undergo several transformations that will render it entirely different from its original mundane state. Firstly, the initial food commodity has to be vegetarian and *sattvic*. By this we are referring to the food's inherent *guṇa* or material quality, which in this case is pure and light and often takes the form of green vegetables, pulses, dairy products and rice. The understanding is that when one is focusing on God one should not consume food that is inherently and physiologically heavy or conversely excites the senses (*tamas* and *rajas* respectively), so meat, onions, garlic and excessively spicy ingredients are prohibited or avoided.

In the domestic arena, for devotional food to become a medium of spiritual intention it has to be produced under certain conditions. The devotee must be mindful of the need for physical and spiritual purity, involving washing hands and sometimes bathing as well as purifying one's mental and spiritual approach through singing or listening to *bhajans* (devotional hymns) and focusing mentally on the object of devotion. Now in a ritually pure state, the devotee will begin preparing the food with a sense of love and devotion. The food is being prepared for the deity only, and it is the emotions of the devotee that transform the food into something that is worthy of offering.

The food will never be tasted prior to offering. Once prepared, it will be put into special dishes called *thāl*s and allowed to cool. The food will then be placed at the feet of the *mūrti* and left for twenty minutes as the recipient sees, smells and consumes the subtle portion. Thus, the next part of the transformative process is now complete with the food fully removed from the material realm and relocated in the spiritual. The food will then be placed back into the main portion of the meal, which will likewise become transformed from mundane to spiritual, from ordinary to extraordinary. The final part of the transformative process takes place when the devotee consumes the food and is filled with the blessings and love of the deity or saint. This will elevate the devotee and in certain circumstances heal him or her of spiritual or physical ailments. *Prasādam* acts as a conduit between the devotees and the deity; it is the devotional glue that cements their relationship and the material that provides spiritual sustenance.

A similar process takes place at the Greenford *mandir*, but on a greater scale. I was invited to witness this by one of the temple's *paṇḍits*, Balkash, as he prepared for the Thursday midday *thāl* service. Thursday is the main devotional day in the Jalarām weekly ritual calendar and is fully dedicated to the saint, so the spiritual efficacy of the *prasādam* on this day is greatly increased. A set of designated *thāls*, in this case copper bowls, was placed on a tray and Jalarām's favourite foods, *kichiri* (a pulse dish), *shak* (vegetables) and special *rotli* (flat bread), were put in the bowls and then taken from the *mandir* kitchen to the *paṇḍit* in the main shrine area. Having received the food, *paṇḍit* Balkash closed the shrine curtains and explained to me that all the other deities on the shrine would be fed through Jalarām's *mūrti*. It should be explained that the *mūrtis* to be found in the *mandir* are thought of as entirely different to those to be found in the domestic sphere. The mundane representation, made of solid marble in the case of the Jalarām *mūrti*, will have been transformed from a material statue or icon during the *Bhav Prathista* ceremony where the essence of the saint is drawn down into the image. Put simply, the image or statue becomes consecrated by Jalarām's presence and his *mūrti* is treated as though it were Jalarām himself.

The food was placed at the feet of the Jalarām *mūrti* and *paṇḍit* Balkash removed the flower that had been placed in Jalarām's right hand, 'because Jalarām eats with his right hand'. *Paṇḍit* Balkash then offered water to Jalarām three times, one to wash his hands, one to wash his mouth and one to take a sip. The idea that Jalarām is ever present in the *mandir* was highlighted by the fact that the *paṇḍit* made sure there was sufficient time for the food to be properly consumed by the saint. The food was left at Jalarām's feet as *Paṇḍit* Balkash chanted the *Ram Mantra* 108 times in front of Jalarām, taking about fifteen minutes. I was then politely asked to leave the shrine area so that Jalarām could eat in private. The *thāls* were then taken back to the *mandir* kitchen and the freshly blessed food was mixed with the rest of the food before it was served to the many devotees and guests who had congregated to consume the Thursday *prasādam*. Whether any food physically went missing from the *thāls* on this occasion or physically increased I did not see.

Service – *seva*

As we have seen, food is an important medium for spiritual transformation in the Jalarām Bāpā tradition, but if we are to understand how *prasādam* also acts as a vehicle for ethical and charitable activity we need to understand the concept of *seva* in its widest sense. Broadly speaking, in Hinduism *seva* means service. As Warrier points out, this service could be 'directed towards society, towards an individual, towards one's parents, towards God or towards one's guru . . . in specific social and historical contexts, the notion of *seva* assumes particular meanings and orientations' (Warrier 2003: 264).

A brief survey of relevant research in the field reveals that the form of *seva* undertaken by devotees from diverse Hindu traditions also varies. The Swāmīnārāyan *sampradāya* has long promoted and engaged in specific forms of *seva* and is an integral part of everyday life. According to Kim, Swāmīnārāyan *seva* takes many forms, often involving physical or financial and material sacrifice, and is 'explicitly connected to their desire to please Akshar Guru and Purushottam Bhagwan' (Kim 2013: 134). In other words, Swāmīnārāyan *seva* is directed towards 'the abode of the supreme person' (Williams 2001: 237) and 'the highest divine reality' (Williams 2001: 240) respectively. In her exploration of another prominent Gujarātī *sampradāya*, Saha suggests that Puṣṭi Mārga devotees follow the founder's example of religious practice with *seva* taking the form of lifelong service to Kṛṣṇa. This form of *seva* 'requires members to . . . adhere to a strict moral code that places emphasis on vegetarianism, a life of constant humility and virtuousness, and maintaining an unswerving faith in Kṛṣṇa' (Saha 2013: 140).

According to Beckerlegge (2000: 59–82), Swami Vivekananda developed his ideology of service to humanity drawing on the example of his contemporary Swami Akhandananda. Akhandananda supported Vivekananda's promotion of organised service to humanity, and it is interesting to see that both men spent part or all of 1892 in the Gujarāt region. Here they may have encountered the Swāmīnārāyan *sampradāya*, whose *samnyāsins* (renunciants) were already carrying out the wishes of its founder, Sahajanand Swāmīnārāyan, in their pursuit of 'practical delivery of service to the *satsanga*' (Beckerlegge 2000: 64). It is not beyond the realms of possibility to imagine that they may also have encountered devotees of the recently passed Jalarām Bāpā: after all, Akhandananda in particular spent time in Junagadh, an important place of pilgrimage some 60 km from Virpur.

Another modern-day form of *seva* is demonstrated by the Mata Amritanandayami Mission. According to Warrier, here *seva* is rendered selflessly in the interests of maintaining, promoting and expanding the services of the mission itself. In this respect devotees follow the example of the mission's founder Mata, who proclaimed that serving humanity is the 'ultimate expression of selfless service and compassion' (Warrier 2003: 266).

We should also take into account the considerable programme of *seva* that has been undertaken by the International Society of Krishna Consciousness (ISKCON). Rather like the Jalarām tradition, the main vehicle of ISKCON *seva* is the distribution of free *sattvic* food in the form of ISKCON *prasādam*. As King points out ISKCON has great influence among diasporic Hindus (2012: 452). On a more global level, ISKCON has developed the 'Food for

Life' project, which comprises a 'network of kitchens, cafes, vans and mobile services, all providing free food . . . (claiming) to be the largest vegan and vegetarian non-profit food relief organisation with projects in over 60 countries and serving more than 1,500,000 free meals daily' (2012: 460) all consisting of ISKCON *prasādam*. The success of the programme lies in its reliance on the volunteers' *seva* as well as its spiritual and humanitarian aims, but also, according to King, on its promotion of Hindu values within a Western framework based upon democracy and egalitarianism (2012: 460). The 'Food for Life' project also has other aims. What is interesting about the project is its open frankness about its intentions to proselytise the message of its founder, Prabhupada, through the distribution of ISKCON *prasādam*. As Valpey points out, food is 'a major vehicle for missionary activity in ISKCON (and this) good tasting Krishna *prasādam* (is) then distributed to the public . . . as a means of gaining new recruits or spreading the message of Krishna Consciousness' (Valpey 2004: 51).

Jalarām *seva* and the Greenford *mandir*

While operating on a much smaller scale to that of ISKCON when it comes to the distribution of free food to those in need, the ethic of *seva* in the Jalarām tradition takes two distinct forms, both of which are fully expressed at the Greenford *mandir*. The first is *prabhu seva*, which, as with the Puṣṭi Mārga and Swāmīnārāyan *sampradāyas*, entails devotional service to the divine either directly or through the service of devotees. It should be noted that *prabhu seva* does not mean service to Jalarām Bāpā himself, who is, at least on a doctrinal level, considered to be fully human and not divine in any way. In this respect Jalarām should be seen as the conduit through which *seva* is directed to the divine in the form of Rama, but also, by extension, to all the other deities found on the *mandir* shrine.

The second form of *seva* is referred to as *jan seva* or direct service to humanity. This is expressed in many ways and the *mandir* engages in a variety of local charitable and social activities. Many devotees have signed up for the NHS organ donation programme, and the *mandir* community has raised substantial funds for numerous charities in the UK, East Africa and India, including eye and dental camps. Food donations beyond the *sadavrat* kitchen also characterise the tradition's wider role in the London region and it distributes thousands of free meals to the homeless in inner London, sends *Diwali*[10] *prasādam* to the inmates of Bronzefield Women's prison and has recently started to send donations to the Harrow food bank (Mojaria 2013).

Prabhu seva and *jan seva* are, however, intertwined and this is perfectly illustrated by the example of the Greenford *sadavrat*. The *mandir*'s senior *pandit*, Piyush Mehta, explained:

> In many sampradayas the devotes believe the responsibility is meant to serve the God, but in Jalarām Bāpā's philosophy you have to first serve the poor people, if you are helping the people, feeding the people, you are

feeding the God because in every human being there is God. So if you are helping and serving the people it means you are serving God, Jalarām Bāpā's philosophy was like that. So his teaching is very simple, feeding the people.

In essence, the Greenford *sadavrat* kitchen is Jalarām's philosophy made manifest in the here and now, and it operates according to his principles of selfless service to all. The U.K. context is of course different from that which is spoken of in the hagiographies: in comparison to nineteenth-century Gujarāt there is relatively little or no obvious poverty, hunger or economic hardship. *Paṇḍit* Piyush explained, however, that many of those who come to the kitchen are elderly people who live alone. Others are physically impaired or have just come out of hospital after life-changing operations and are brought to the *mandir* by family members who have given up daytime jobs to care for them. For many in these circumstances the preparation of meals at home was an arduous and often expensive task. Furthermore, the actual ideology, practice and experience of *jan seva* in the Jalarām Bāpā tradition differ from those forms examined earlier in that they are entirely underpinned by the belief that Jalarām himself is ever present and that the *parchās* illustrated in the hagiographical narratives are being replicated in the contemporary context.

By way of illustrating this, *Paṇḍit* Piyush explained that during his life Jalarām would ensure that enough food could be had by all, even if there were many more devotees than anticipated expecting to be fed. For example in one instance Jalarām increased 25 *ladoos* to 500 by simply placing a *tulsi* (sacred basil) leaf into the bowl containing them and half-covering it with a cloth (Shah 2000: 66). On another occasion he fed 150 horsemen from baskets of *ladoos* which remained 'full, even after all were given *prasādam*. All were amazed' (Soni 1984: 58). When I enquired if this had happened at the Greenford *mandir* Paṇḍit Piyush explained that cooked food did occasionally run out but

> You can go into the store (room) at any time and it is always full up, we never lack for food, this is Jalarām Bāpā's miracle ... It happens here ... you know, they cook food for perhaps 1,000 people and 2,000 people come, but there is still food left, it happens naturally, you can eat as much as you like and food is still there. Nobody goes from [here] without food.
> (Interview, Leicester, 2004)

As we have already come to appreciate, this same principle of multiplication of food when blessed and the understanding that it never runs out under any circumstances, but more especially when it comes to feeding devotees and those in need, are absolutely central to the promotion of Jalarām *seva*.

Jalarām's miraculous blessings are not confined to the commodities in the *mandir* storeroom. In recent years the *mandir* committee expanded its programme of *jan seva* to join with the Shree Satya Sai Narayan Seva Sanstha to help clothe and feed London's homeless. Again, echoes of this project's work can be found in the hagiographies. For example Jalarām as a young man was said to have clothed 'thousands of persons continuously for four days and yet the stock was not exhausted.' On another occasion, while working for a Bania (merchant) relative, he gave away 'cloth . . . pulses, rice and flour' to about a dozen *sādhus* who came to his shop. Whenever Jalarām's uncle measured the cloth, he 'found it was not an inch less' (Soni 1984: 5).

The project also saw devotees collecting and donating various commodities prior to distribution, such as biscuits, cakes and savouries and the stock stored in a warehouse in Queensbury, some five to six miles from the *mandir*. When I was conducting a portion of this research it was the week before Christmas 2013 and as such the distribution of the food parcels had reached its seasonal height. One of the informants from the Shree Satya Sai Narayan Seva Sanstha related to me that he fully expected the storeroom to remain full no matter how many parcels went out. The informant went on to explain: 'Since the Jalarām Mandir started to join us the store is never empty. Even after they have filled the bags on a Monday it would still be half full and the next day when they open it, it was almost full to the brim.'

It is believed by a number of devotees involved in this project that Jalarām had on one occasion been visibly present when donations of food had arrived at the warehouse. Needless to say these items of food were seen to be particularly blessed and distributed with care. Accounts of Jalarām's physical appearance after his death are plentiful and play a significant role in the hagiographies, but what is more important today is the central belief that Jalarām Bāpā is always present, visible or otherwise, where *seva* is being carried out in his name. *Pandit* Piyush explained: 'We all are the medium for his work; if you are doing seva you are inspired by Jalarām Bāpā. Jalarām Bāpā inspired you to do seva; always he is everywhere.' The Greenford *mandir* and the Shree Satya Sai Narayan Seva Sanstha now work on separate charitable projects, but Jalarām devotees continue to collectively contribute food and clothing to make parcels that are distributed in the Holborn district of inner London.

During his life, Jalarām considered this ethic of tireless and selfless service to be essential. Devotees believe that the fact that he was able to perform *jan seva* through his *parchās* reflected his own continuous efforts to please God through *prabhu seva*. This is something referred to by informants as *tapas charya*. *Pandit* Piyush explained the concept of *tapas charya* in terms of Jalarām's staff, his *danda*, which was seen as a metaphor for this continual support for humanity through feeding and healing, in some cases both at the same time. The Greenford *sadavrat* could, therefore, be interpreted as a perpetuation of 'Jalarām's *tap*'; his effort to support those in need with no thought of reward, as the *pandit* pointed out:

> There is nothing to gain from the sadvarat, it is all to give, we don't expect anything from anyone, and that is a sadvarat, if we expect something then it is not sadvarat . . . if you want social status then . . . (some) might come here and say I am doing seva, but God knows what is the seva.

That Jalarām is ever present and generous in this respect was further expanded upon by a member of the board of trustees:

> Every single volunteer who does seva is always rewarded with something by God ... We have people who have been doing seva since the mandir opened and they all have stories to say that they have been blessed with something from Bāpā.

Consuming the charitable food for its nutritional value should not be seen as the only way people benefit from Jalarām's *seva*. In this respect the devotees that I spoke to over several *sadavrat* lunches suggested that, like ISKCON devotees, one of the main reasons for coming to the kitchen was to partake in the spiritual qualities of the food. This was highlighted as one of the most important ways in which Jalarām Bāpā himself continued to perform *seva* for his devotees, through the medium of food that he blesses, on an ongoing basis.

The Jalarām tradition distinguishes itself from other devotional *sampradāyas*, such as the Swāmīnārāyan and ISKCON traditions, in that it places great emphasis on egalitarianism from the start. Unlike other *sampradāyas*, the food for Jalarām is not prepared by a trained religious specialist in a specifically designated and often ritually purified area. Rather, the food offered to Jalarām is prepared by volunteers in the ordinary industrial catering kitchen appended to the *mandir*. Here they work under the guidance not of a ritual specialist but of the kitchen manager, who herself is an ordinary paid member of the community.

The Jalarām tradition also distinguishes itself from ISKCON in one other respect. It has no intention of proselytising the teachings of Jalarām through the distribution of free *prasādam* from the *sadavrat* kitchen or any desire to convert anyone to the tradition. This is important as many members of other Hindu and non-Hindu communities regularly take advantage of the *mandir*'s hospitality when it comes to eating Jalarām's *prasādam*. On one occasion I spoke to a practising Sunni Muslim who, while also occasionally doing maintenance work for the *mandir*, regularly ate there. The food, he explained, was very delicious and he enjoyed eating it as often as he could. Furthermore, members of the local Ismailī Muslim community have also eaten there and on one occasion I was present as members of the Namdhari Sikh community made offerings in the form of food to Jalarām.

When it comes to the wider charitable effort, the food that is distributed to the homeless and in other projects is always Jalarām *prasādam*. I asked one of the trustees if this had been made clear to those receiving it, and he explained that every box of food had been labelled accordingly and the name of Jalarām is always said when serving the food. When I asked whether they thought that those receiving the food were aware of the spiritual qualities of the *prasādam* and the potential effect that it might have as an agent for conversion or promoting a spiritual agenda, the same trustee answered,

> No, we don't see it that way, we are not preaching our religion, we are just doing what Bāpā always did, that if you come to our house or to our city

we will always feed you . . . we are not there to convert people to our religion, we are just following Bāpā's example.

I have suggested in this chapter that, in order to fully understand how the Jalarām tradition has developed a distinct religious identity based upon the tradition of *seva* and miraculous blessings, we have to consider the nature of its core narratives not as history but as social and ethical identifiers. We need to sound a cautionary note, however, as it would be easy to conclude that the popular appeal of Jalarām Bāpā and the performance of *seva* in the community were based solely on miracles and that the entire ethical approach is motivated by the expectation of such miraculous blessings. The relationship between Jalarām Bāpā and his devotees and the *seva* that they perform is based on a great deal more than this. When devotees are volunteering in the kitchen they believe that they are not only benefitting wider society but also serving Jalarām himself, perpetuating his example of *jan seva*, as illustrated in the hagiographies. Furthermore, the overarching ethical principle of *seva* through the kitchen is far from one-way and this is inextricably linked with the production and the medium of sacred food. The kitchen prepares the food for Jalarām to consume and the food is then transformed into *prasādam*. The *prasādam* is then returned to the devotees and they benefit from its spiritual potential. Thus the circle of *seva* is complete on both a human and transcendental level, with the relationship between Jalarām and devotee fully cemented.

Devotees also believe that Jalarām continues to direct his service to humanity as a whole, not just to his devotees, as instanced by the tradition's commitment to *seva* for wider society in London. When it comes to the issue of miraculous blessings, the presence of Jalarām Bāpā and the continual replication of the events narrated in the hagiographies, we need only consider the beliefs concerning the everlasting storeroom and eternal *sadvarat* in Greenford. There is, however, a further layer of understanding when it comes to the role of such blessings. Many informants have suggested that miraculous blessings should be seen only as a path to a deeper understanding of Jalarām's spiritual and ethical message. The temple *paṇḍits* are constantly at pains to contextualise the miracles within this framework of understanding.

We can see the inseparable link between hagiography, tradition, miracles, *prasādam* and service to humanity played out in the Greenford Jalarām *sadvarat* kitchen. This relationship is ultimately reliant on two things. The first is the continued replication of the events and examples highlighted in the tradition's narratives. These form the hagiographical basis which is indispensable not only for devotees when it comes to the continuity of the tradition in the U.K. but also for scholars when it comes to the wider value of vernacular traditions in the ethnographic study of religion. The second factor in this relationship is the belief that Jalarām Bāpā himself is fully present. Although he is no longer with the devotees in the mortal sense, the rationale and practicalities of the perpetuation of his ethical principles depend upon this belief: without his presence the spiritual potential of food could not be realised and the production of *prasādam*, the material medium of the blessings and that which to an extent underpins the tradition's ethical ideology, would not be possible.

Notes

1 *Lohāna* – Hindu caste most associated with merchant trading (Daftary 2001: 132; Khan 2004: 32).
2 The Leicester *mandir* was specifically constructed and opened in 1995. The Greenford *mandir* has been located in a converted synagogue since 2000 and plans are currently being submitted for the construction of a new purpose-built *mandir* and community centre on the sight.
3 A self-designation of Hinduism by Hindus (Klostermaier 1998: 163).
4 The Greenford *mandir* is where the majority of my recent ethnographic field research has taken place, but this essay will also draw on previous research carried out at the Leicester *mandir*.
5 Whilst the term *parchā* (*paracha*) is not mentioned once in either Soni (1984) or Shah (2000), it is used regularly in preference to the word 'miracle' by devotees and on websites where it is said to refer to blessings from or direct experiences of Jalarām himself.
6 According to devotees, *sadavrat* is a religious obligation or eternal vow and the term is used interchangeably with the term 'charitable kitchen'.
7 Virpur is now considered to lie at the heart of the Jalarām Bāpā sacred landscape. It is the location of his house and the original *sadavrat* kitchen. There are numerous artefacts connected with the saint kept there, and it is the main hub of Jalarām pilgrimage and devotional activity in India.
8 http://www.Jalarammandir.co.uk/; http://www.Jalarambapa.com/; http://www.shreeJalaramsevatrust.org/; http://www.shreeJalarammandir.org/. All accessed 10/03/2016.
9 This refers to the lunar calendar used in *Gujarāt*, 'the first year of which corresponds to 57–56 B.C.E. according to Mukundcharandas (1999: 74) and Klostermaier (1998: 203), but 58 B.C.E. according to Kulke and Rothermund (1990: 76) and Basham (1954: 493)' (Wood 2015: 115, n2). This chapter uses the former calendrical dating, which is employed in the hagiographical accounts mentioned.
10 *Diwali* – the Hindu new year celebration.

Works cited

Ballard, Roger, ed. 1994. *Desh Pardesh: The South Asian Presence in Britain*. London: Hurst.
Basham, A.L. 1954. *The Wonder That Was India*. London: Sidgwick & Jackson.
Beckerlegge, Gwilym. 2000. 'Swami Akhandananda's Sevavrata (Vow of Service) and the Earliest Expressions of Service to Humanity in the Ramakrishna Math and Mission.' In *Gurus and Their Followers: New Religious Reform Movements in India*, ed. Anthony Copley, 59–79. Oxford: Oxford University Press.
Bowen, David. 2006. 'Hinduism: A Teacher's Approach'. *British Journal of Religious Education* 6(3): 128.
Brear, Douglas. 1986. 'A Unique Hindu Festival in England and India, 1985: A Phenomenological Analysis'. *Temenos* 2: 21–39.
Burghart, Richard. 1987. *Hinduism in Great Britain: Religion in an Alien Cultural Milieu*. London: Tavistock.
Daftary, Farhad. 2011. *A Modern History of the Ismailīs: Continuity and Change in a Muslim Community*. New York: Taurus.

Jackson, Robert and Eleanor Nesbitt. 1993. *Hindu Children in Britain*. Stoke on Trent: Trentham.
Kataria, Dhiraj. 2010. 'Shree Jalarāmbāpā: A Life Sketch.' www.jalarammandir.co.uk/upload/life_sketch.pdf. Accessed 07/11/2014.
Khan, Dominique-Sila. 2004. *Crossing the Threshold: Understanding Religious Identities in South Asia*. New York: Taurus.
Kim, Hannah. 2008. 'Managing Deterritorialisation, Sustaining Belief: The Bochasanwasi Shree Akshar Purrushottam Swāmīnārāyan Sanstha as Case Study and Ethnographic Foil'. In *New Religions & Globalisation: Empirical, Theoretical and Methodological Perspectives*, eds. Armin Geertz and Margit Warburg, 225–243. Aarhus: Arhus University Press.
———. 2013. 'Devotional Expressions in the *Swāmīnārāyan* Community'. In *Contemporary Hinduism*, ed. Pratap Kumar, 126–137. Durham, NC: Acumen.
King, Anna. 2012. 'Krishna's Prasādam: "Eating Our Way to Godhead".' *Material Religion* 8(4): 441–465.
Klostermaier, Klaus. 1998. *A Concise Encyclopedia of Hinduism*. Oxford: Oneworld.
Knott, Kim. 1986. *Hinduism in Leeds: A Study of Religious Practice in Indian Hindu Community and Related Groups*. Leeds: University of Leeds.
Kulke, Herman and Dietmar Rothermund. 1990. *A History of India*. London: Routledge.
Mattausch, John. 1993. *The Gujaratis and the British: A Social and Historical Survey, with Special Reference to the Gujarati Tradition of 'Arranging' Marriages*. Centre for Ethnic and Minority Studies, Royal Holloway College, Occasional Papers no. 1.
———. 1998. 'From Subjects to Citizens: British East African Asians.' *Journal of Ethnic and Migration Studies* 24: 121–141.
Michaelson, Maureen. 1987. 'Domestic Hinduism in a Gujarati Trading Caste.' In *Hinduism in Great Britain: Religion in an Alien Cultural Milieu*, ed. Richard Burghart, 32–49. London: Tavistock.
Mojaria, J. 2013. *Shree Jalaram Greenford Newsletter*, no. 8. Greenford: Shree Jalaram Mandir.
Mukundcharandas, Sadhu. 1999. *Handbook to the Vachanamrutam*. Amdavad: Swaminarayan Aksharpith.
Nye, Malory. 1995. *A Place for Our Gods*. Richmond: Curzon Press.
Rajdev, Saubhagyachand. 1947. *Bhakta Shri Jalarām*. Rajkot: Kankari.
———. 1966. *Bhakta Shri Jalarām*. Rajkot: Jai Hind Printing Press.
Rinehart, Robin. 1999. *One Lifetime, Many Lives: The Experience of Modern Hindu Hagiography*. Atlanta: American Academy of Religion.
Saha, Shandip. 2013. 'Krsna Devotion in Western India.' In *Contemporary Hinduism*, ed. Pratap Kumar, 138–147. Durham, NC: Acumen.
Shah, Rekhaben. 2000. *Shri* Jalarām *Vandana*. Surat: Sahitya Sankool.
Soni, Ramanlal. 1984. Jalarām *Bāpā*. Ahmedabad: Enka Prakashan Kendra.
Valpey, Kenneth. 2004. 'Krishna in Mleccha Desh: ISKON Temple Worship in Historical Perspective.' In *The Hare Krishna Movement: The Post-Charismatic Fate of a Religious Transplant*, eds. Edwin Bryant and Maria Ekstrand, 45–60. New York: Columbia University Press.
Warrier, Maya. 2003. 'The Seva Ethic and the Spirit of Institution Building in the Mata Amritanandamayi Mission.' In *Hinduism in Public and Private: Reform, Hindutva, Gender and Sampraday*, ed. Anthony Copley, 254–286. Oxford: Oxford University Press.
Williams, Raymond. 2001. *An Introduction to Swāmīnārāyan Hinduism*. Cambridge: Cambridge University Press.
Wood, Martin. 2008. 'Divine Appetites: Food Miracles, Authority and Religious Identities in the Gujarātī Hindu Diaspora.' *Journal of Contemporary Religion* 23(3): 337–353.

———. 2010a. 'Consuming Envy: Food, Authority and the Continuity of Vernacular Traditions in the Gujarātī Hindu Diaspora.' *Fieldwork in Religion* 5(1): 97–118.

———. 2010b. 'Jalarām Bāpā: The Public Expression of Regional, Vernacular Traditions among Gujarātī Hindus in the UK.' *The Journal of Hindu Studies* 3(2): 238–257.

———. 2015. 'Jalarām Bāpā: Miracles and Meaning in Nineteenth-Century Gujarāt.' In *Religious Transformation in Modern Asia*, ed. D. Kim, 115–138. Leiden: Brill.

4 Music and materialism
The emergence of alternative Muslim lifestyle cultures in Britain

Carl Morris

Introduction

In recent years there has been growing public and scholarly interest in British Muslim cultural production. While for the most part inadequately researched, the picture is one of an emergent middle-class generation of British Muslims who are shaping political, social and religious discourse through music, comedy, film, fashion, visual art and other forms of popular culture. While evidently composed of many different artistic forms, networks and subcultures (see Morris, 2016), this milieu just about hangs together as a cultural movement and helps to inform alternative Muslim lifestyle cultures for a younger generation of devout British Muslims.

Music has often played a leading role in these developments, particularly with the rise to public prominence of Muslim musicians in Britain during the mid-2000s. This music is characterised by a variety of styles – including nasheed (*a capella* religious songs) and hip hop – and remains a largely subcultural phenomenon. However, there are examples of Muslim musicians in Britain who have achieved mainstream and international success. The British-Azeri musician Sami Yusuf, for example, released his polished, professional and multimillion-selling album *My Ummah* in 2005. That album and Yusuf's subsequent career have led him to be regularly listed among the world's most influential Muslims by the website 'The Muslim 500' (http://themuslim500.com).

In this chapter I consider the production of music by Muslim musicians in Britain, analysing the conceptual, cultural and economic assumptions that underpin the process of producing music. As David Morgan outlines in the opening chapter of this collection, materiality can be analysed through the dimensions of production, specification and circulation. This is a helpful distinction – teasing out various aspects of materiality – but it is a process that equally requires a consideration of the interrelation *between* these stages of materiality. The genitive act of production itself, for example, is informed by a comprehension in the maker of need, usage, reception and wider cultural ideology. I therefore proceed in this chapter to offer a multifocal analysis of the materiality running through Muslim musical production in Britain. This involves considering the cultural and economic landscape that both limits and enables the production of music by Muslim musicians.

68 *Carl Morris*

The findings presented here are based on ethnographic research carried out across the UK in 2010–12. This included semi-structured interviews with twenty-two Muslim musicians, participant observation at musical and cultural events and an online survey completed by eighty-four Muslim music fans. The chapter is organised into three parts, covering musical genre, consumer culture and frameworks of production/distribution. By analysing in turn these conceptual, cultural and economic realities, I aim to demonstrate that Muslim musicians are acutely conscious of their position within a wider Muslim lifestyle culture – one that both shapes and is shaped by a process of musical production.

Muslim music: defining a genre

The act of producing music often brings with it a comprehension of placement within a wider cultural landscape. This involves the implicit or explicit categorisation of music through genre, and a resulting feedback loop that informs the process of production. In producing music, then, British Muslim musicians often debate whether there is a particular genre of music that might be labelled 'Muslim' or 'Islamic'. Even those who reject the term recognise that it has some practical and conceptual purchase. In handling the terms 'Muslim' or 'Islamic' music there tends to be a recognition of three features of such music: (1) music made by Muslim musicians; (2) music containing self-conscious Islamic or Muslim subjectivities; and (3) music that has a primary orientation towards a Muslim audience and consumer market. These loose criteria do, however, conceal various other complexities. I therefore propose a twofold typology that roughly divides Muslim musicians into one of two cultural streams: 'Islamic music' and 'Islamically conscious music'.

Islamic music is created by musicians who are more exclusively targeting communal and religious spheres of activity. These musicians produce paraliturgical music – music as a form of worship beyond core religious practice – that strengthens Muslim identity and focuses on local and communal belonging. Such music is produced as a means of connecting directly to Muslim cultural and religious networks, becoming an important cultural product in emergent Muslim markets and public spheres in the UK. The second stream of music – Islamically conscious music – incorporates a range of musicians who are more ambivalent in terms of their engagement with Muslim networks. It seems to me that while such music might directly reference Islam – and is certainly inspired by a Muslim worldview – it nonetheless attempts to deploy universal concepts in an effort to reach a wider audience. This music maintains a strong association with Muslim cultural and economic contexts, but it cannot be defined solely by these connections.

The first stream of Muslim music, Islamic music, is overtly immersed within Islamic discourse and attempts to reinforce the moral coherence of a distinct Muslim community. It is partly defined by sounds and lyrical content that reference the traditions, beliefs and religious figures distinguishing Islam as a unique religion. Yet it also includes music that deals with broader concepts of Islamic morality and spirituality – ranging from love and respect for one's

Music and materialism 69

mother to gratitude for the beauty of creation. In all instances there tends to be a clear rootedness in specific Islamic practices or beliefs. I suggest that such music can therefore be conceived as a form of paraliturgical practice. Indeed, it is perceived to exist within a spectrum of Islamic sound that is arguably reminiscent of Lois and Isma'il al Faruqi's typology of *handasah al sawt* (al Faruqi and al Faruqi 1986). According to this analysis, there is a hierarchy of performative sound directly shaped by a vocal tradition rooted in Quranic cantillation. This tradition holds Quranic cantillation as the exemplar sound, followed in order by: religious chants/poetry (zikr, na'at, etc.), vocal/instrumental improvisations, songs with serious themes and, finally, entertainment music (al Faruqi and al Faruqi 1986: 457–459). I believe that Islamic music falls into the second category of this typology – religious chants/poetry – and it is telling that musicians often discuss such music by utilising the concept of 'remembrance'. As with chanting, *zikr* and poetry, Islamic music is produced intentionally as a form of religious practice, celebration and reaffirmation.

In the UK, Islamic music usually manifests itself in the form of contemporary nasheeds – that is *a capella* pop songs containing traces of an Islamic poetic tradition. Yet it is important to remember that Islamic music is not confined to any one particular style – it is the words and intent that determine whether music might or might not be considered Islamic. As Amran, from Aashiq al-Rasul, explained, Islamic music covers multiple genres:

> Who can say it is to do with a particular genre, or that a certain genre only constitutes Islamic music? You can't say that, because you have today Islamic music composed and performed in many genres or styles, like Country and Western, Hip Hop, Rap, R&B.
>
> (Amran, 34, October 2010, Birmingham)

Referencing Kareem Salama, an American Muslim 'country and western' musician from rural Oklahoma, Amran is suggesting that it is the intention of the musician that marks music out as Islamic, not the actual style or genre of music itself. Indeed, according to Amran and many other musicians, of central importance is the intention to remember God and the Prophet Muhammad, as well as the desire to celebrate Islam and express a Muslim worldview:

> Intention is central in a Muslim's life, in whatever we do, if your intention is sincere, your prayer is accepted . . . [So] if I were to give a definition of Islamic music, it would be focussing on the words and meanings of the lyrics . . . Vocally, there are certain words which you could say are through and through Islamic. They remind or educate the listener about God or Prophet Muhammad, Peace Be Upon Him.
>
> (Amran, 34, October 2010, Birmingham)

Amran is arguing that the intention of the musician connects directly to the experience of the listener. Musicians and nasheed artists are therefore mediators of faith, transmitting religious experience and spiritual emotion through their performance and music. This requires a pureness of intent as well as a pureness of form. It emphasises communal gathering and the sharing of religious experience through the mediated form of music.

An examination of the music produced within this genre clearly demonstrates that four central themes repeatedly emerge to almost the exclusion of anything else:

- Praise to Allah and/or the Prophet Muhammad.
- Celebration of Muslim practice – most commonly Ramadan, Eid, the act of marriage and other practices relating to fasting, charity, prayer and pilgrimage.
- Reaffirmation of Islamic values – often relating to modesty, gender roles and respect for one's parents.
- Reference to Muslim history – whether specific historical events or highly respected individuals.

The predominant purpose of Islamic music, then, is to strengthen the bonds of communal solidarity and identity through shared beliefs, practices, values and history. In Britain, Islamic music – with an emphasis on tradition and meaning – is overwhelmingly produced in the stripped-down, modern nasheed style.

While the celebratory and communal role of Islamic music is perhaps most significant, it is also perceived to act as a form of religious pedagogy. Through Islamic music – in whatever form or style – Muslims are able to learn about their religion in an accessible way. This particularly applies to younger, British-born Muslims, who might struggle to grasp traditional forms of textual learning (which are often based on rigorous commentaries of the Qur'an and Hadith). Muslim musicians therefore often claim that Islamic music enables young Muslims to learn about their faith within a British cultural and social context. This view is shared by many practitioners of Islamic music, all of whom are seemingly happy to accept this broader definition. Yet here a conceptual dilemma is reached – for at what stage does Islamic music broaden its substantive content and simply become 'music'? I argue that it is possible to identify forms of music that, while textured by an Islamic ethos, cannot be narrowly categorised as 'Islamic music'. For analytical purposes, I refer to this genre as Islamically conscious music.

Islamically conscious music is marked by a desire to universalise the values and beliefs of Islam – to take an Islamic/Muslim worldview and produce music that will resonate with both Muslims and non-Muslims. Such music will therefore often focus on social and political issues that are especially relevant for Muslims, as well as spirituality and religion in a broader and less specifically 'Islamic' sense. The musicians who produce this music are often connected to Muslim cultural networks, but also to other subcultures and genre-specific contexts. This is particularly true of Muslim hip hop musicians, who have specifically discussed their sense of belonging to an 'underground UK hip hop scene'. In a sense, these musicians – including Poetic Pilgrimage, Mohammed Yahya, The Planets and Quest Rah – are often able to lay claim to both the cultural and religious capital associated with the field of Muslim cultural production (Bourdieu 1993), while simultaneously drawing on subcultural capital (Thornton 1995) in the cultural contexts of the UK, European and American hip hop scenes.

While hip hop is the musical style that might most commonly be described as Islamically conscious music, there are other notable instances, such as the folk rock of Silk Road, Yusuf Islam's recent venture back into pop music, and Sami Yusuf's attempt to create his own genre of music – so-called Spiritique. As Sami Yusuf has explained, Spiritique draws from Muslim musical traditions and expresses Islamic spirituality, but essentially tones down the specific and exclusionary references to Islam itself (references that are characteristic of nasheeds and Sami Yusuf's own early music): 'It incorporates and utilises Middle Eastern and Western harmonics, underpinned by spirituality. It's all-encompassing, all-inclusive . . . It will utilise music as a facilitator for spiritual appreciation, regardless of race and religion' (Sami Yusuf, quoted in Tusing, 2010). Sami Yusuf is reacting to the traditional characterisation of his music as 'Arab' or 'Islamic'. He has accordingly altered his lyrical content, shying away from overt Islamic discourse, as well as moving towards an exploration of universal themes around human rights, the nature of worldly existence and individual spiritual experience. These musicians will also often engage with political issues, particularly relating to geopolitics and a broadly anti-neoliberal agenda. Such themes are typical of music that would be included in this genre, right across the gamut of musical styles from hip hop through to pop music.

Despite variant musical styles, all of these musicians are largely comparable in their attempt to produce music that is inclusive beyond the traditional borders of religious belonging. They tend to reject any form of labelling that would place them squarely and exclusively into an Islamic or Muslim genre, as the hip hop musician Ayman explained:

> We're just making music and we happen to be Muslim as well, we don't put ourselves in that bracket where we're Islamic rappers or Muslim artists and rappers. Others may want to do otherwise, but we've never approached it that way, we've never really approached it that way. So, if I'm speaking to, you know, if there's an interview with a Muslim radio station or Muslim magazine and they mention it, then I'll talk about it, you know, but we don't use it as a selling point.
>
> (Ayman, 33, October 2011, London)

While Ayman joins numerous other musicians in rejecting a religiously defined label, he nonetheless stresses that his Islamic worldview naturally and visibly emerges through his music. This echoes comments made by other musicians who maintain a similarly cautious approach towards overtly expressing their Muslim identity through music. This includes the guitarist and folk rock musician Faraz, from Silk Road, who argues that his sense of being is central to his music: 'Islam just enthuses the way that we are and we live. We don't need to spell it out all the time, because it just oozes out in how you do stuff and how you see things' (Faraz, 34, October 2011, Birmingham). Faraz and Ayman – while practising very different styles of music – are both adamant that their Muslim background provides a rich array of personal and ethical experiences that artistically transcend any need for simplistic definition.

This stress on individuality and a unique Muslim perspective is advanced further by facets of intra-Muslim difference. Musicians regularly argue that they inherently bring their own unique backgrounds, identities and ideas to bear on their music. In doing so it is hoped that they can articulate something of their own individuality, while simultaneously providing a cultural point of contact for those with common experiences. Muslim musicians correspondingly raise a number of personal attributes – ranging from race and ethnicity through to gender and class – that they believe have value and should be asserted in the public sphere. The hip hop musician Muneera, from Poetic Pilgrimage, argues that this is especially true for Muslim women, who are often excluded or misrepresented in other contexts:

> It's essential for the voice of women to exist, you know, and we may not always reflect Islamic themes, but us being Muslim, it is a Muslim perspective, we're talking about love. When I'm talking about what I'm looking for in a husband, we're still reflecting that from a Muslim perspective, you know.
>
> (Muneera, 29, February 2011, Cardiff)

Islamically conscious music, then, is not overtly marked by Islamic concepts or by issues typically framed as 'Muslim'. Such music might cover a range of themes; yet all of these musicians would argue that Islam is the central filter through which their experiences and ideas are channelled.

At root, I am arguing that the defining concepts distinguishing Islamic music and Islamically conscious music are *community* and *individuality*. Islamic music is inseparably linked to a specific religious tradition; it attempts to reinforce Muslim practice, values and belonging through direct engagement with central Islamic discourses. In contrast, Islamically conscious music is about self-expression and individuality; it places an emphasis on reaching out, rather than laying down the tracks of community. Both genres of music are relevant and valuable, demonstrating the ways through which music can serve different needs. Yet this musical bifurcation furthermore points towards the complex attitude that Muslims in Britain have adopted towards wider society. There is a simultaneous and not necessarily paradoxical desire to reinforce Muslim communal identity, but also to bring Islamic beliefs to play within wider social and cultural conversations.

These artistic decisions are of course not detached from wider cultural and economic factors – musicians are inevitably forced to assess how their music can be 'placed' within a viable market. The label they attach to their music can determine exactly who will be willing to listen to (and buy) their music. The hip hop musician Quest Rah – a young and articulate Londoner, with filial roots in Egypt – has taken advantage of the security of a Muslim fanbase but also more recently tried to build a reputation within the wider hip hop scene in London:

> It's about what experiences you're coming from and what inspires you. If people want to label it, then that's up to them. There was more of a 'Muslim hip hop' scene at the time than there is now, so we were more comfortable with the label. But for the last couple of years, and how I feel now, it's more of a universal thing. I've always had a more balanced and universal approach to music. And I feel there's enough common principles within Islam that won't isolate people too.
>
> (Quest Rah, 25, October 2011, London)

Quest Rah originally developed his public profile within a Muslim cultural context, billing himself as a Muslim rapper in a Muslim hip hop scene. There were opportunities provided to him here that might not have been available if he had lacked that particular mark of identity. Nonetheless, his desire now is to reach out to a wider audience – a decision that presents both challenges and possibilities. This correspondingly raises the issue of Islamic branding and the role played by an 'Islamic' or 'Muslim' label in shaping the production of music.

Consumer culture and music

Islamic branding is usually understood through the concept of the global halal market – valued at US$150 billion (Fischer 2009) – and plays an increasingly important role in providing 'Islamic' products and services for Muslim consumers worldwide. Music is bound up with this developing consumer culture, but what specifically makes it 'Islamic'? What makes *any* type of consumer or cultural product Islamic? Certain styles of fashion might be considered 'Islamic' – with style and religious observance integrated through specific sartorial arrangements (Tarlo 2010) – as might hajj travel packages (McLoughlin 2009), Muslim smartphone apps (Bunt 2010) or the 'Islamic Barbie' (Yaqin 2007). Yet there are consumer products and forms of culture that have few, if any, implications for Muslim practice. Mecca Cola is often perceived as an anti-neoliberal Muslim consumer product, subverting the traditional dominance of Coca-Cola (Aggarwal et al. 2011). Does Mecca Cola therefore possess any unique qualities that mark it out as 'Islamic' – or does it become Islamic because it targets a specifically Muslim consumer market through clever branding? In the hard-edged world of global marketing, the answer might simply be that the identity of a cultural product is reflected back by the very market that breathes life into it.

Of central importance to the argument I advance here, then, is the suggestion that the production of Muslim music – both Islamic and Islamically conscious – is influenced by this comprehension of a Muslim consumer market. Growing beyond the simple provision of Islamic religious artefacts, halal food and other functional services, this consumer market is also increasingly about lifestyle and the reworking of mainstream Western products and practices. Little research has yet been done to examine this Islamic consumer culture, but it is worth quoting at length an insightful summary by Nabil Echchaibi:

> The stunning growth of the global halal industry ... has been accelerated by a wave of religious fervour among a social class of young, educated, and affluent Muslims who, according to the organizers of the World Halal Forum, wish to embrace an 'Islamic contemporary and global lifestyle'. It is still unclear what this Islamic lifestyle is, but a new market of consumer products, advertising, and commercial media programming is increasingly labeled 'Islamic' and slowly contributes to the rise of an alternative culture industry. Like all forms of consumption, such an elaborate Islamic consumer culture has deep implications for identity construction and constitutes a prime stage for the production and reproduction of what it means to be a modern Muslim in the twenty-first century.
>
> (Echchaibi 2012: 31–32)

Taking us beyond the specific characterisation of the halal market as a source of religiously permitted products, Echchaibi importantly brings the concept of identity to the forefront of Islamic consumerism. There are therefore two possible strands to the conceptualisation of a halal industry – that is practical and symbolic forms of consumerism.

Practical consumption relates to specific services and products that are required by Muslims for religious observance. This includes, for instance, halal food, prayer mats, beads and books, but also financial services, Muslim marriage websites, non-alcohol-based perfume and hajj travel packages. Such consumption is essentially about religious practice in some form – from direct religious activity and worship through to the necessary observance of religious strictures. These services and products are largely distributed through Muslim business networks that have developed in order to meet the specific religious needs of Muslims. Such networks include Islamic bookshops, health stores, supermarkets, butchers and clothes shops, but also a growing online presence where all-purpose purveyors of Islamic products can be found.

Islamic music, then, can more often be theorised as a form of *practical* consumption. As I argued earlier, Islamic music is aimed specifically at Muslims as a religious group and should be considered a form of paraliturgical worship. This is reflected in the distribution of such music. Islamic music is regularly sold through business networks that largely reject Islamically conscious music. This is partly due to the tendency for Islamic music to restrict the use of instrumentation – a controversial issue in the Muslim mainstream – but it also represents the fact that Islamic music sits comfortably alongside recordings of Quranic cantillation and audio lectures. Islamic music essentially serves a similar purpose for many: to facilitate and enhance Muslim religious practice. Walking into most Islamic bookshops around Britain, for example, one might find a selection of nasheeds and other forms of Islamic music arrayed between recordings of Quranic cantillation and books on Muslim lifestyle and Islamic philosophy.

Access to these networks of distribution can be essential for musicians to reach an audience that might otherwise be unreachable. The nasheed artist Amran remarked that producing an album without any instrumentation at all – just the human voice – immediately opened up a whole distribution network that was originally closed to his group, Aashiq al-Rasul: 'There are many Muslim shops or outlets that would not stock our songs, particularly those with musical accompaniment' (Amran, 34, October 2010, Birmingham). This particular mode of distribution – through specific sellers of general 'Islamic' products and services – serves to reinforce the status and specificity of Islamic music as a form of practical Muslim consumption. These business/religious networks exercise great power in determining to stock and therefore distribute only select and 'appropriate' products – everything else is subtly excluded from the Muslim mainstream and correct Islamic practice.

Symbolic consumption differs from practical consumption in the sense that symbolic products and services do not provide a specific religious function, but they are nonetheless still branded as 'Muslim' or 'Islamic'. Symbolic consumption is about lifestyle and identity – not necessarily about functionality. A prime example of this might be 'Eid party plates'. There is no practical reason – based on culture or religion – why ordinary plates cannot be used for Eid celebrations. The use of such plates instead signifies a declaration of Muslim identity and belonging through material and consumer culture. This is a benign and everyday example, but symbolic consumption is capable of additionally incorporating the socially charged subversion of mainstream branding and consumer culture. This is often done to critique the failings of wider society, but also as a means to inject Islamic ethics and ideologies into alternative cultural forms. Thus, 'Islamic Barbie' (Yaqin 2007) becomes the symbolic subversion of popularised sexuality, while Mecca Cola (Aggarwal et al. 2011) becomes the rejection of neoliberal hyper-capitalism. Through such products there is the gradual development of an alternative Islamic consumer lifestyle: a movement that advances substantive ethical and religious ideologies through symbolic and material culture. It is a cultural trend that claims to stand in contrast to the failings of mainstream consumer culture – it is in effect a form of ethical consumer culture.

While Muslim music is never purely symbolic – it always contains substantive lyrical content – it is nonetheless part of this alternative Islamic consumer lifestyle. Islamically conscious music is a means through which Muslims utilise music to challenge the perceived failings of popular culture. Thus, hip hop becomes the ideal vehicle to critique overconsumption, aggressive sexuality and social malaise. It can do this with particular effect through hip hop, specifically *because* mainstream hip hop so very often represents these specific failings – consider the hip hop stereotypes concerning sex, drugs and gun culture. As the

British-Mozambican rapper Mohammed Yahya explained, hip hop moved from being a vehicle for moral and intellectual debate to becoming a commodity for corporate profit:

> When hip hop started, there wasn't much money involved in it. It was a reflection of the daily experiences of the people – that's why they called it the CNN of the ghetto, or the black ghetto . . . they didn't really have a voice or someone that could speak out for them and represent them. So hip hop became that. But the music industry started changing, more money was pumped into it, and record label requests started growing too. So yeah, it became a business and with every business there are requirements. So unfortunately TV stations like MTV always promote, or give more exposure, to commercial hip hop artists whose labels have large budgets to pay to get on TV and unfortunately whose message is critically watered down.
>
> (Mohammed, 29, February 2011, London)

Mohammed and other Muslim hip hop artists believe passionately in their contribution to the 'underground' scene in Britain – that is a subcultural hip hop network, promoting 'conscious' lyrics and challenging the injustices of the world. This is a return to the perceived authenticity of the original and 'uncorrupted' hip hop culture of the 1980s and 1990s, but it is also a symbolic inversion of the contemporary commercialisation of hip hop. Muslim musicians – across a range of styles and genres – are scathing in their condemnation of 'sell-out' musicians at the pinnacle of the mainstream music industry. By practising music on a foundation of spirituality and ethical integrity, Muslim musicians argue that they can play a part in gradually altering attitudes towards the excessive lifestyles that are so glorified in contemporary culture. Music therefore becomes an integral part of this alternative consumer lifestyle.

The salience of Muslim music within a broader Islamic consumer culture can be highlighted though a consideration of the burgeoning Muslim clothes industry. Islamic fashion in the UK has been well documented by Emma Tarlo (2010), but nothing has been done to analyse the sartorial arrangements of Muslim musicians in Britain. Muslim musicians adopt a range of fashions: from the smart suits or casual jeans/T-shirts of contemporary nasheed artists, through to the Afro-inspired clothing of some African Caribbean musicians, to the street wear of Muslim hip hop musicians. The deployment of fashionable but culturally varied clothing allows the reimagining of such attire to become an embedded feature within the *habitus* of the 'global Muslim'.

The hip hop musician Ayman Raze takes this Islamic lifestyle approach further by designing his own range of clothing under the brand name Tawheed Is Unity – an organisation dedicated to Muslim development and expression through the arts. The name Tawheed Is Unity has been derived to evoke the solidarity of Muslims through the belief in one God – although the founder, Ayman, argues that this concept of unity can and should embrace non-Muslims as well. The motivations behind this clothing range are outlined on the Tawheed Is Unity website:

> Tawheed Is Unity began in 2006 as the brain child of **Ayman Raze** as an alternative clothing line for Muslims living in the West. Being involved with Hip Hop since the mid-90s, Ayman recognised the fact that young Muslims are steadily developing their own culture distinct from that of their parents and traditions. Being aware of the fact that whether you listen to Hip Hop or not, this is the Hip Hop generation and fashion is a key emphasis of the sub-culture, Ayman set about developing designs that would both represent Islam and the society and culture we are in.
>
> (Tawheed Is Unity n.d.)

The clothing range consists of a selection of 'sweatshop-free' T-shirts emblazoned with particular designs, several of which have the Arabic slogan '*Al Maarifah Quwah*' ('Knowledge Is Power') across the front. A recent addition to the clothing range involves an inversion of the famous 'Just Do It' slogan by the American company Nike – a company notorious for its use of cheap factory labour. This T-shirt (see Figure 4.1) displays the words 'Just Dua It', utilising the Islamic concept of supplication as a means to critique a notorious symbol of excessive Western capitalism.

Musicians, then, are part of a wider cultural movement that is attempting to provide more than just functional Muslim products, services and cultural forms – it is an attempt to create a consumer culture that is characterised by

Figure 4.1 A T-shirt design from the Tawheed Is Unity clothing range.
Source: Tawheed Is Unity.

a visible ethic. As Echchaibi points out, this cultural movement critically uses the 'toolbox of modernity' to subvert and reconstruct 'a "true" modern identity' (Echchaibi 2012: 38). Yet this desire to break with the perceived failings of mainstream consumerism raises the question of how exactly these musicians operate within the wider economy. As I shall demonstrate, a financially sustainable model for producing music – including ticket sales, promotional strategies and business structures – remains an important and inseparable characteristic of the 'Muslim music scene'.

Production frameworks and distribution

Professional and semi-professional Muslim musicians rarely operate outside of some kind of organised business framework. The decision that most Muslim musicians must make at some stage is whether to channel their professional career through an emerging Muslim cultural economy or to utilise the independent, subcultural business networks that are already in place. It appears that most Muslim musicians choose the former option. While mainstream and smaller independent record companies are of course theoretically available as one route for Muslim musicians, they often choose instead to release their music through companies that operate in an 'Islamically appropriate' manner. Either that, or they simply produce and release their music themselves, selling their CDs at events and through the Internet. With a sample of sixteen different musicians and/or groups, it is possible to examine the production company that they used to record and produce their album – in every instance Muslim musicians in this sample either signed themselves to an Islamic production company or released their music independently (see Table 4.1).

The six production companies listed were all established to facilitate the production and distribution of Muslim music. Four of these companies can broadly be described as supporting 'nasheed artists', while the other two – Crescent Moon Media and Tawheed Is Unity – have been established by musicians specifically to help provide a platform for 'Muslim hip hop' musicians in the UK. These companies all have an Islamic ethos of some kind and they regulate their activities accordingly. This might include a restriction concerning the use of

Table 4.1 Muslim musicians/groups organised by production company.

Production company	Musicians/Groups
Awakening Records	4
Meem Music	3
Mountain of Light Productions	1
Safar Media	1
Crescent Moon Media	1
Tawheed Is Unity	1
None	5

instrumentation or the management of lyrical content to align with perceived Islamic norms. Several of these production companies furthermore release audio lectures by Muslim *ulama* and other figures of religious note. Regardless of whether intentional, this can sometimes result in Muslim music becoming contained within an arc of religious pedagogy, rather than billed as a more straightforward form of 'halal entertainment'.

Islamic production companies vary in the support that they are able to offer to musicians. Awakening Records is the most successful Islamic production company, both in Britain and worldwide. Indeed, Awakening Records has taken Muslim music to an entirely new corporate level. Boasting an unconfirmed 500 million customers, Awakening Records supports some of the most successful and lucrative Muslim musicians – including Maher Zain, Hamza Robertson and Mesut Kurtis. Sami Yusuf himself began his career with Awakening Records, releasing his first two albums with the company before an undocumented dispute drove him elsewhere. Awakening Records engages in active media promotion, the organisation of events worldwide and the production of both music recordings and associated videos. The individual level of support provided to the musicians beneath the corporate shield of Awakening is unclear, though it apparently includes regular financial support for selected musicians. There is no doubt that these musicians must have extensive international appeal for such an arrangement to be financially viable – the UK Muslim market is seemingly insufficient by itself to generate the necessary returns. Perhaps for this reason Awakening Records is almost entirely focused on the contemporary pop/nasheed style of music that has so successfully penetrated Muslim markets across the world.

As well as a growth in Muslim production companies, it is also possible to note the tentative emergence of Muslim recording studios. Muslim musicians have in the past used any recording studio that can provide the technical support needed. Yet it is increasingly possible to find recording studios that overtly pitch for an 'Islamic market' (see Figure 4.2).

It is not entirely clear how an Islamic recording studio might offer a different service to a 'non-Islamic' recording studio. Yet the very emergence of these studios does serve to demonstrate two important points. First, there is clearly a growing technical and professional pool of expertise among Muslims in Britain, along with the business and financial resources that are required to sustain them on a commercial footing. Second, the demand for these services perhaps does something to indicate the interest in utilising audio recordings as a form of *da'wah* (religious invitation) by Muslims in Britain. Through its mission statement, the production company Crescent Moon Media vividly illustrates the desire that some Muslims have to use sound as a form of *da'wah*:

Crescent Moon Music is a company that was set up to show the beautiful side of Islam. All of the artists are talented musicians but are also Muslims. They enjoy talking about the deen and believe that the arts is probably the

80 Carl Morris

Figure 4.2 An advertisement for a recording studio in Birmingham.
Source: Audio Dawah.

most powerful way to talk to the youth. The main aim of the company is to bring good music to the listener. The company also wants to give dawah to non-Muslims and to show them that not all Muslims are terrorists.

(Crescent Moon Media, n.d.)

This combination of growing expertise and interest in utilising sound recordings for *da'wah* hints at the possibilities of a British Muslim music/audio market. While it is perhaps unlikely that the cassette culture of Egypt and other Muslim majority countries will be replicated in Britain (Hirschkind 2006), one might speculate that Muslims in Britain could potentially be at the forefront of an developing English-language online Islamic audio culture – from nasheeds and hip hop through to audio lectures, Islamic adverts and audio books.

Ironically, it is partly through the difficulties posed by the Internet that Muslim musicians have found themselves confronted by a challenging market environment. One of the concerns raised by Muslim musicians is the difficulty that they have in supporting themselves as professional musicians – this is in spite of the potential offered by a niche Muslim consumer market. While there are exceptions, most Muslim musicians view themselves as 'struggling artists'. Yusuf Islam and Sami Yusuf might have little difficulty in selling their music on a large scale, but for the most part Muslim musicians cannot rely on generating income as a professional musician. Internet downloading is often blamed for this difficulty. It is because of this financial context that almost every Muslim musician in Britain is engaged in employment unconnected to their role as a musician. This includes musicians who work as teachers, youth and community workers, charity fundraisers, bankers and managers. These Muslim musicians are essentially a cohort of successful professionals who use the remainder of their time and energy to write, record and perform their music. While an amateur/semi-professional model is often characteristic for subcultural musical genres, it is nonetheless important to understand the financial constraints that shape the production of Islamic and Islamically conscious music.

In asking why this might be the case it is necessary to consider exactly how Muslims in Britain access such music. The extent to which Muslim music fans are willing to pay for a recording, or for entry to a concert, determines the overall professional character and viability of Muslim music as a self-supporting cultural and economic venture. The online survey that I conducted with Muslim music fans provides an insight into this issue. It is of course necessary to account for the inbuilt biases of the survey itself: it is an Internet survey and it specifically targets self-identified Muslim music fans. Nonetheless, it helps us in beginning to construct a picture of Muslim music consumption.

The survey was distributed to approximately 1,500 British Muslims – that is those who have used social media to self-identify their interest in Muslim musicians. There were eighty-three returns – a response rate of 5.6% – representing a fairly normal return for an Internet survey (Sue and Ritter 2007). The survey consisted of thirty-nine questions, four of which asked specifically about music consumption. Q. 15 (Table 4.2) asked respondents to rank on a scale of 0–5 how important a particular method of listening to music is for them:

Table 4.2 Online survey.

Ranking	A	B	C	D	E
0	7	14	21	20	22
1	3	4	9	13	5
2	4	7	10	11	5
3	6	15	12	15	15
4	11	18	8	5	9
5	40	14	8	6	14

Key

A – Through the Internet
B – Another media source (radio, television etc.)
C – Through recordings bought in a shop
D – Borrowing or copying recordings
E – Live music or singing
Q. 15: 'If you listen to music, please indicate how important the following methods of listening are for you.'

The most striking figure relates to the Internet. Of the seventy-one people who responded to that particular category, forty marked the Internet as being of the highest importance as a method of listening to music. In contrast, far fewer respondents placed any great importance on recordings purchased in a shop, with twenty-one ranking shop-bought recordings as of the lowest importance. Alternative sources of media and live performances are a little more evenly distributed in their importance for respondents, although none equal the seeming significance of the Internet.

While music can, of course, be purchased for a fee through the Internet, these findings do suggest a weighting towards a method of consumption that increasingly holds little financial cost to the individual (e.g. illegal downloads and free streaming). This is certainly comparable with the situation facing the wider UK music industry, where there has been a notorious turn away from music retail outlets to online shopping, illegal downloading and freely distributed music on the Internet. As David Kusek and Gerd Leonhard (2005) presciently argued, music has gone from largely being a purchasable physical product – such as vinyl, tapes and CDs – to cultural information that is accessed through new media technology (often at no cost). In this new and evolving environment, it has been suggested that musicians and the associated music industry must turn away from music sales as traditionally conceived, to instead focus on live performance, merchandise and sponsorship/advertisement (Kusek and Leonhard 2005).

The survey is only one strand of data and should be viewed with caution, but it does support additional ethnographic findings that reach similar conclusions. Indeed, the Internet almost certainly undermines the actual sale of music. Amran – a long-standing nasheed performer with experiences of the music market that reach back into the 1990s – has argued that it is increasingly difficult to sell music because of illegal downloading:

> We headlined an event at Trafalgar Square, where there were twenty-five to thirty thousand people in the audience and everyone is singing our songs. We sang five or six songs and they're familiar with all of them. They must have listened to them from somewhere ... but this doesn't reflect in sales, so most probably it's illegal downloading or sharing.
> (Amran, 34, October 2010, Birmingham)

Amran is echoing a concern that many Muslim musicians have in relation to selling their music. They recognise that the Internet has unavoidably taken CD sales away from them and fundamentally undermined their ability to make a full-time living out of being a musician. Yet musicians acknowledge that the Internet is important as a tool to raise their profile, connect with fans and sustain the kind of musical and cultural scene that is required to generate an interest in their music. Several musicians have remarked – particularly in relation to hip hop and other niche genres of music – that their particular music scene *only* exists on the Internet. In a sense, then, while it is possible to identify the emergence of a fragile market base that can support Muslim musicians, the countervailing nature of the Internet nonetheless encourages the emergence of a powerful amateur cultural movement.

The future of a distinct Muslim music market therefore looks mixed. Particular forms of music with global appeal to an Islamic market will no doubt continue to thrive, but there will often be clear boundaries concerning style and lyrical content. Islamic pop and nasheeds, for example, must necessarily be inclusive enough to appeal across different Muslim markets, ranging from Britain and the United States through to Egypt and Indonesia. Conversely, alternative forms of music produced by Muslim musicians – including hip hop, folk rock and various syncretic styles – will most likely continue either as a semi-amateur movement in a Muslim subcultural context or as part of a genre-specific sub-culture (e.g. an underground hip hop scene). Despite these differences in trajectory and content, a common feature for British Muslim musicians will continue to be a high degree of self-consciousness. The societal context for Muslims in Britain – and indeed more widely – is evolving rapidly through generational, institutional and cultural change. Musicians not only are therefore grappling with these changes but also as producers of a material product remain mindful of where their music fits within a mixed cultural landscape and global economic market.

Acknowledgements

This research was carried out at the Centre for the Study of Islam in the UK, Cardiff University, with generous funding provided through the Jameel

Scholarship Programme. Special thanks are due to Professor Sophie Gilliat-Ray and Dr John Morgan O'Connell for their invaluable contribution.

Works cited

Aggarwal, Praveen, Kjell Knudsen and Ahmed Maamoun. 2011. 'Branding as Ideological Symbols: The Cola Wars'. *Journal of Business Case Studies* 5(2): 27–34.

al Faruqi, Lois Ibsen and Isma'il Raji al Faruqi. 1986. *The Cultural Atlas of Islam*. New York: MacMillan.

Bourdieu, Pierre. 1993. *The Field of Cultural Production*. Cambridge: Polity Press.

Bunt, Gary. 2010. 'Surfing the App Souq: Islamic Applications for Mobile Devices'. *CyberOrient: Online Journal of the Virtual Middle East* 4(1).

Crescent Moon Media, n.d. 'Mission Statement'. http://www.myspace.com/crescentmoonmusic [Accessed 21.11.12].

Echchaibi, Nabil. 2012. 'Mecca Cola and Burqinis: Muslim Consumption and Religious Identities'. In *Religion, Media and Culture: A Reader*, eds. Gordon Lynch, Jolyon Mitchell and Anna Strhan, 31–39. London: Routledge.

Fischer, Johan. 2009. 'Halal, Haram, or What? Creating Muslim Space in London'. In *Muslim Societies in the Age of Mass Consumption*, ed. Johanna Pink, 3–15. Newcastle upon Tyne: Cambridge Scholars.

Hirschkind, Charles. 2006. *The Ethical Soundscape: Cassette Sermons and Islamic Counterpublics*. New York: Columbia University Press.

Kusek, David and Gerd Leonhard. 2005. *The Future of Music: Manifesto for the Digital Music Revolution*. London: Omnibus Press.

McLoughlin, Seán. 2009. 'Holy Places, Contested Spaces: British Pakistani Accounts of Pilgrimage to Makkah and Madinah'. In *Muslims in Britain*, eds. Peter Hopkins and Richard Gale, 132–149. Edinburgh: Edinburgh University Press.

Morris, Carl. 2016. 'Finding a Voice: Young Muslims, Music and Religious Change in Britain'. In *Young British Muslims: Between Rhetoric and Realities*, ed. Sadek Hamid. Abingdon: Routledge.

Sue, Valerie M. and Lois A. Ritter. 2007. *Conducting Online Surveys*. London: SAGE.

Tarlo, Emma. 2010. *Visibly Muslim: Fashion, Politics, Faith*. Oxford: Berg.

Tawheed is Unity. n.d. 'About'. http://tawheedisunity.com/about/. Accessed 22.08.12.

Thornton, Sarah. 1995. *Club Cultures: Music, Media and Subcultural Capital*. Cambridge: Polity Press.

Tusing, David. 2010. 'Sami Yusuf Talks about Spiritique, His New Sound'. *Gulfnews.com*, 11 August. http://gulfnews.com/arts-entertainment/music/sami-yusuf-talks-about-spiritique-his-new-sound-1.666404. Accessed 09.02.12.

Yaqin, Amina. 2007. 'Islamic Barbie: The Politics of Gender and Performativity'. *Fashion Theory* 11(2–3): 173–188.

5 Augmented graves and virtual Bibles

Digital media and material religion

Tim Hutchings

Introduction

In the opening chapter of this volume, David Morgan speaks of material culture in terms of 'objects, spaces, bodies and the practices of using them ... images, emotions, sensations, spaces, food, dress or the material practices of putting the body to work.' 'To study religious material culture', he explains, 'is to study how people build and maintain the cultural domains that are the shape of their social lives', treating objects as primary aspects of what religion is and how it is lived.

This chapter seeks to explore and question this understanding of the material object by applying it to the realm of mediation. First, what would it mean to think of websites, mobile phone apps or QR codes as objects, to be studied as part of material cultures? Second, how can we apply Morgan's approach to "production" – in terms of medium, design and manufacture – to generate insights into the place of digital media in contemporary religion?

I will begin by tracing the Internet's shift over time from the alternative reality of "cyberspace" to its contemporary status as the mundane, often invisible infrastructure of everyday life. Understanding this change in our relationship with computer-mediated communication provides an important foundation for material analysis. I will then discuss digital technology and online content as kinds of "materiality", drawing on recent discussions in material religion and digital media studies.

To apply a material approach to the study of digital production, I will introduce examples taken from two rather different fields: digital Bibles and online memorials. As we shall see, the materiality of digital media is not limited to the level of technologies and devices. Digital software and content also function just like material objects: they are produced, classified and circulated, and they guide, structure, constrain and make concrete our actions and relations. By paying attention to the different dimensions of the materiality of media, we can gain a more nuanced understanding of the ways in which religion today is structured and provoked by material objects and their creators.

From cyberspace to infrastructure

In early visions of computer-mediated communication, the digital was positioned as the antithesis of embodiment and materiality. Computer networks offered us access to "cyberspace", a separate realm in which identity could be fluid, knowledge was open for access and all boundaries could be overcome by the masters of new technology. William Gibson famously defined "cyberspace" in his science fiction novel *Neuromancer* as 'a consensual hallucination experienced daily by billions' (1984: 67); for Case, his protagonist, cyberspace is 'a bodiless exultation', an experience of speed and power compared to which the human body is a prison of 'meat' (1984: 12).

Neuromancer became one of the foundational influences for the cyberpunk genre of science fiction. This style of writing attracted a fascinated audience in the early years of the Internet, for whom cyberpunk's discussions of fluid identities, the freedom of anonymity, corporate control and the subversive power of the hacker seemed to mirror what was already happening through computer networks. Even in these fictional accounts of cyberspace, however, materiality was crucial. The protagonists of early cyberpunk may have longed to escape from the flesh into disembodied experience, but their narratives were driven by material frustrations: bodily pain, broken technologies, the struggle to access the right connection at the right moment.

Over time, academic study and popular imagination have moved away from these early interests. As Internet use began to become more widespread in the late 1990s, digital cultures became increasingly tied to offline identities and social networks. Researchers are still studying the cultures of online communities, but ethnographer Christine Hine describes the contemporary Internet as 'embedded, embodied, and everyday' (Hine 2015). It is embedded, because the Internet is 'entwined in use with multiple forms of context and frames of meaning-making' (2015: 33); it 'means quite different things to different people' (2015: 38). The Internet is experienced as one option for action or communication, one alternative among others. It is embodied, because virtual identities are rarely separate from physical bodies: 'rather than being a transcendent cyberspatial site of experience, the Internet has often become a part of us' (2015: 41). Online social network sites like Facebook are used as 'a place to express an embodied self rather than a place to leave the body behind' (2015: 44). The Internet is everyday, acting as 'a mundane, invisible infrastructure' for society (2015: 46). As an infrastructure, the Internet structures choices and priorities, does work and makes decisions for us, but we become aware of it only when it is 'topicalised' in moments of crisis, ranging from national panic about jihadi radicalisation to the personal disaster of losing access to Wi-Fi. When infrastructure betrays us or fails us, we have a chance to relearn its significance.

Nonetheless, the early dream of the immaterial Internet remains powerful in much public discourse. To pick just one example, a recent issue of the Swedish popular philosophy magazine *Modern Filosofi* chose the Internet as its cover story (Modern Filosofi 2015), under the headline 'Do I Exist on the Internet? A Digital Humanity without a Body' ('*Finns jag på nätet? En digital människa utan kropp*'). Philosophers, we are told, do not agree. *Modern Filosofi* interviews two academic scholars (media theorist Amanda Lagerkvist and philosopher Fredrik Svenaeus) and frames their conversation as a classic cyberspatial debate, opposing digital immateriality against physical embodiment and the 'internet self' against 'my self in real life' (2015: 33). Our lived experience of the Internet may often be 'embedded, embodied, and everyday' (Hine 2015), but old hopes and fears remain.

Digital media as material religion

In one of the first issues of the journal *Material Religion*, Chris Arthur tentatively suggested that the Internet might be of interest to scholars of religious materiality. Digital content is a weak substitute for the real thing, he claims:

> the gravity of the tangible, the authentic, attends objects in a way that is impossible for the Web's spectral presences. However ingeniously they may construct their simulacra, there is always the whisper of the replica about them rather than the roar of the real.
>
> (Arthur 2005: 289)

Nonetheless, Arthur proposes, the Internet is full of images, sites and practices that could be considered a 'novel (virtual) materiality' (2005: 291), from museum exhibitions to meditation rooms and virtual pilgrimages. Scholars need to take these 'virtual artefacts' seriously.

Arthur was writing when the study of digital religion was in its infancy. Scholars initially found it difficult to take Internet religion seriously, and struggled to give much credence to practitioners' reports about the spiritual, personal and emotional significance of websites and online conversations. Researchers today are less likely to question the efficacy of online religious practices, and more likely to explore their integration into the everyday lives of users – reflecting the trend in Internet use and scholarship encountered earlier.

A decade later, digital media have become an accepted part of the study of religious materiality. A new volume of keywords in the study of material religion (edited by S. Brent Plate) includes a chapter on "Digital", in which Gregory Price Grieve argues that 'digital media have transformed the conditions of religious practice and people's relationships to each other and to the divine' (2015: 56). For example anyone can now open an "iRosary" app on their iPhone and digitally recreate the experience of thumbing through a string of beads. The app even causes the device to vibrate, to give a physical sensation to the hand as the user moves from one bead to the next. The app tries to faithfully represent the traditional Catholic practice of praying the rosary while using the multimedia storage power of digital media to give the user access to a library of prayers and imagery. Unlike Arthur, Grieve does not find this surprising; the use of digital media by religious communities and practitioners is now taken for granted.

Birgit Meyer has written extensively and influentially about the relationship between mediation and material religion, including an article titled 'Medium' for a keywords issue of *Material Religion* in 2011. Meyer argues that 'a focus on media is central to "rematerializing" our understanding of religion' (Meyer 2011: 60). Mediation 'produces belief' (2011: 61) by making the transcendent accessible, present and sense-able – and that process 'leads right to the question of religion and materiality' (2011: 60). Different traditions accept or reject different media forms, but their preferences are not static: 'the negotiation and adoption of new (or newly available) media . . . [are] central to the transformation, and hence continuation, of religion' (2011: 60). We can see one example of this development process in the contrast between Arthur's suspicion of inauthentic websites and Grieve's comfortable acceptance of mobile apps.

In the three articles we have just considered, Arthur, Grieve and Meyer insist that material culture scholars should pay attention to digital media. Surprisingly, however, they do not define what aspects of digital media they have in mind or what makes those aspects "material." All material religion might be a kind of mediation, as Meyer argues, but it doesn't necessarily follow that all media are material objects. This lack of clarity in defining the "material" is not just an oversight but a major feature of the field: discussions of material religion tend to be much clearer about what they oppose than about what they affirm, as Joanne McKenzie and I pointed out in our introduction to this volume.

Substantive definitions of the "materiality" of religion are not easy to find, and most surveys of the field prefer to identify a set of common themes and interests. S. Brent Plate's recent definition of the field is helpful (Plate 2015: 3) but creates a potential obstacle for our attention to the digital by describing the study of material religion as 'an investigation of the interactions between human bodies and physical objects'. "Physical" seems to rule out electronic media, but Plate then goes on to include "the Internet" as an example of a human-made object on the next page (2015: 4). An "object", it seems, is simply that which is not an idea, and even ideas 'begin in material reality' (2015: 4).

This leaves us with a problem. It is commonplace to include studies of digital media within the field of "material religion", and to use the concept of "mediation" to think about how material objects work religiously, but what does it actually mean to talk about the digital as part of material culture?

First, we must decide what aspects of the digital should be included in discussion of materiality, and what has to be left out. Arthur and Grieve both focus their attention on digital reproductions of the physical objects and images of conventional religion; should that physical-digital contrast be the limit of our concern? Digital religion today is much more diverse than this kind of remediation; volumes on material religion have addressed topics like online gaming, for example, which appear to go beyond such a limited approach (Aupers 2012).

Second, we should remember that re-materialising the digital is a political move, embedding media practice in everyday life in opposition to a particular vision of freedom and the future. Some early forms of online religious practice were explicitly hostile to the body, sharing the cyberpunk vision of computer-mediated escape from the limitations of materiality. These examples were uncommon, but Christian critics of online religion continue to accuse practitioners of longing for immateriality. Popular imagination of the digital has since moved away from "cyberspace" into a more embedded, infrastructural understanding of digital technologies, but we still need to remember that the materiality of the digital is not self-evident or politically neutral. Scholars of digital religion need to think more clearly about what exactly we are calling "material", and who benefits from that materialisation.

Materialising the digital

Fortunately for this discussion, the idea of "materiality" has been debated in great detail by digital media researchers, particularly in the digital humanities, human-computer interaction and the newer field of digital anthropology. Paul Leonardi (2010) identifies the key problem clearly: writers interested in "materiality" have tended to oppose the physical that can be touched against the conceptual that cannot, but digital software is neither physical nor conceptual. Material objects have affordances and properties that constrain people's interaction with them, while the conceptual realm – which for Leonardi includes norms, discourses, routines, institutions and rituals – offers greater freedom for improvisation. Software does not fit into either category; it structures what we can do, and yet it does not seem to be made of physical stuff.

In discussions of religion and material culture, we can identify two different ways of thinking about materiality: "essentialist" (in which material means physical) and "binary" (in which the material is defined through its opposition to some alternative, usually "belief"). For theorists of digital media, both options are problematic. Instead, digital theorists tend to take what we could term a "functionalist" approach, in which the "material" includes anything that acts like a physical object. Material things constrain our freedom of action and engage us in relationships; to the extent that digital media function in the same way, they are material.

Digital humanists have been particularly interested in what happens to a text when it is digitised, because the instantiation of a text in a medium strongly influences how we interact with it. To address this, some have proposed separating the structuring role of material objects from their physicality, a good example of the "functionalist" approach. According to Marlene Manoff, a librarian, 'electronic objects are material objects' (2006: 312), with their own distinctive range of material properties:

> When studying the history of the book, attention to materiality means analyzing such things as typography, binding, illustrations, and paper to understand their role in the creation of meaning. In a world of digital artifacts, textual scholars may consider a whole new range of physical objects and processes, including platforms, interfaces, standards, and coding ... and a new concern with the graphical elements of textuality.
>
> (2006: 312)

The imagined opponent here is not the scholar of beliefs but the careless archivist, who believes we can copy a text from one medium to another – by digitising a manuscript, or printing out an e-book – without a loss of meaning. For Manoff, 'the properties of electronic objects alter our ways of creating and consuming information' (2006: 311). Knowledge is always 'shaped by the technologies used to produce and distribute it'.

Designers of digital technologies have also been fascinated by materiality. Erica Robles and Mikael Wiberg have written a number of articles about the materiality of digital media, drawing on their collaborative work in interaction design. Robles and Wiberg point out that digital design has tended either to treat materiality as a metaphor – for example in user interfaces that whimsically reference files, folders, paperwork and desktops – or to hide computation invisibly within everyday physical objects – for example in the field of ubiquitous computing. They argue that 'information technology seems to exist in-between the material and the immaterial, with properties so flexible it almost can take on any form imaginable' (Robles and Wiberg 2010: 138), and they call for designers to explore this through a new focus on the aesthetic integration of digital and physical. Robles and Wiberg propose the concept of 'texture', which draws attention to the way underlying structure relates to surface appearances and 'advocates investigating the range of properties exhibited by digital and physical materials and crafting compositions from their relation' (2010: 142).

More recently, Heather Horst and Daniel Miller have argued that a commitment to materiality must be one of the key principles of digital anthropology, because digital worlds 'are neither more nor less material than the worlds that preceded them' (Horst and Miller 2012: 4). We must not reduce the world to social relations in our analysis – a particular temptation for sociologists – because 'social order itself is premised on a material order . . . it is impossible to become human other than through socializing within a material world of cultural artefacts' (Horst and Miller 2012: 24). This emphasis on human interactions with objects is commonplace in introductions to material religion, but Horst and Miller point out that we must also attend to 'the order, agency and relationships between things themselves and not just their relationship to persons' (2012: 24). In the digital environment, software can talk to software, data can be collected and analysed and Internet-connected objects can communicate with other objects, all without the involvement of human bodies.

So what, specifically, is material about digital worlds? Horst and Miller propose three answers: the materialities of 'digital infrastructure and technology', of 'content' and of 'context' (2012: 25). The materiality of 'infrastructure' reminds us that the digital is 'a material and mechanical process'. The digital is ultimately made up of binary zeros and ones, stored electronically; saving, accessing and deleting data can be difficult technical processes. Digital devices have a particular shape and feel, as Grieve observed in his study of the iRosary. Computers must be made and disposed of, and networks must be connected with wires and cables, all with considerable environmental consequences.

The materiality of 'content' includes information, webpages and virtual environments, the stuff produced, copied, accessed and circulated by digital technologies. Visual culture studies can show us that websites 'are systematically designed to seduce and entrap' their target audience, while repelling those whose attention is unwanted; online images, in other words, function just like any other kind of artwork. The final kind of digital materiality, 'context', reminds us that digital technologies can be used to help people and objects communicate and connect, producing 'a new kind of place' online with new boundaries, proximities and demands for attention (Horst and Miller 2012: 27).

As Horst and Miller demonstrate, study of digital media must pay close attention to its physicality, as well as to how our action is shaped and constrained by digital content and our relationality is structured by digital contexts. Robles and Wiberg offer an intriguing design approach to physicality through their concept of 'texture', while Manoff reminds us of the distinctiveness of the content and context of digital texts.

In the remainder of this chapter, I will explore these different kinds of materiality using examples drawn from recent research in the areas of Bible-reading and bereavement. In both cases, material objects have historically played a crucial role in mediating relationships between the living, the dead and the divine, engaging the body and the senses in ways that can at times be overwhelmingly intense. These objects have also been highly contested, acting as focal points for tension between and within religious traditions. As we shall see, Bibles and memorials are supposed to educate and form the religious user, through their materiality as well as their content.

First case study: digital media and the Bible

I have written extensively about digital Bibles elsewhere (e.g. Hutchings 2015), focusing particularly on the apps produced by an American company called YouVersion. YouVersion's Bible App has been installed more than 200 million times and offers free access to thousands of translations and audio versions in hundreds of different languages. Users can select from a wide range of reading plans, track their progress, program their app to issue regular reminders and share their favourite passages through social media.

YouVersion's Bible App is a material object, in all of the ways outlined earlier. It is accessed through a mobile phone or tablet with specific kinds of affordances and capabilities, making it possible for users to have the Bible with them at all times without needing to carry a physical book. The app is designed as a "persuasive technology", inviting the user to read and share the Bible more frequently, in line with traditional evangelical Christian understandings of how the Bible should be used. The Bible App's traditional approach to the work of reading is mirrored in some of its visual design, which follows the metaphorical approach critiqued by Robles and Wiberg (2010): the app's icon, for example, is a brown leather-bound book with a ribbon as a placeholder. The app also records data, which YouVersion can use to analyse user activity. The Bible App creates spaces and contexts for interaction between users, through shared use of devices, circulation of messages to followers through social media and mutual awareness among connected friends through the app's own newsfeed. All three aspects of Horst and Miller's framework for digital materiality are at work here: technology, content and context.

In this chapter, I will focus on a very different kind of digital Bible. 'Uncover' is a physical, printed book, a pocket-sized copy of Luke's Gospel, produced by the UK's Universities and Colleges Christian Fellowship (UCCF) in 2013. According to the UCCF website, the Uncover books 'have been hailed [by Christian leaders] as one of the best evangelistic resources ever to have been produced by UCCF', and more than 150,000 copies were distributed in 2013 (UCCF n.d.). While the Bible App tries to remediate the familiar image of a leather-bound Bible, Uncover resembles an ordinary student notebook accompanied by a series of online videos. Uncover combines physical and digital resources, and we can use this example to explore the materiality and immateriality of digital religion.

I discussed Uncover in an interview with UCCF's head of communications, Pod Bhogal, in 2013. UCCF does use digital media, including Facebook, Twitter and YouTube, but Bhogal argued that the most effective context for evangelism is local, relational and informal. In a personal conversation, Christian students can address the questions that most interest the individual they are seeking to persuade – an advantage over the more structured conversations required by courses like Alpha. Finding the right tone for Uncover was crucial to enabling this kind of engagement. 'We didn't want to tell people what to believe,' Bhogal explained, but to encourage conversation and to make the book 'as accessible and interactive as possible'. Every other page is blank for personal notes, and the inside covers of the book are decorated with images of pencils, rulers and other study equipment, framing the object as a tool for the student reader to mark and write on.

The digital element of the project appears in the form of QR codes, printed on many of the book's pages. If readers use their smartphone to scan one of these codes, they find an online video in one of two different series. The first, written and presented in six instalments by recent university graduates, leads the reader on a twenty-minute 'journey through the gospel'. Each video examines a section of the text and links to the next. According to Bhogal, this stream introduces the whole gospel 'in a way that is accessible and plausible, because the amount they have to read is reduced and they are using a medium they are familiar with'. If readers then return to the start of Uncover to read the whole gospel in linear order, they will encounter further QR codes linking to videos in which non-student "experts" answer questions about key aspects of Christian teaching.

UCCF thought carefully about how to combine digital and print. 'Different kinds of media have different kinds of appeals,' Bhogal explained: for example blank pages added opportunities that digital media would have struggled to provide. Despite the ease with which words can be typed and edited on a screen, the 'immediacy' of scribbling on paper still has 'relevancy and power'. On the other hand, including digital resources helps UCCF connect with its target audience: 'there's something about a hardback book that will never go out of fashion,' but digital media offers greater accessibility and convenience, and videos appeal to some readers more than text.

The physicality of Uncover's printed book is also intended to speak to cultural understandings of giving and reciprocity. 'The idea behind the hardback gospel is that we want it to be a gift,' Bhogal explained, to be presented by the Christian student to a non-Christian friend. As a gift, the physical book becomes a bond between giver and recipient and presents a material invitation to share an act of reading. Sending a link to a website, UCCF felt, would not have carried the same personal significance.

To work as a gift, Uncover had to pay careful attention to design. This was a product that had to be 'not cringey', so Uncover was modelled after the fashionable, expensive Moleskine line of notebooks, with an attractive hardcover design, additional paper sleeve and elastic strap – all visible, material suggestions of quality and value. There are clear parallels to be drawn here with the recent popularity of "niche Bibles", marketed with attractive, high-quality covers and demographic-specific commentary as gifts for children, or with the older tradition of high-quality Bibles designed as gifts and prizes. In each case, the physical object is designed to enact a relationship between giver and receiver, to convey a message about the quality of its textual contents, and to position the receiver under an obligation to read it.

A material approach to digital religion must consider the differences between digital and physical objects, as well as what they have in common. I have interviewed and surveyed users of digital Bible apps like YouVersion, and many of them expressed reservations about material consequences of shifting from print to screen (Hutchings 2015). Some argued that a digital Bible made it harder to remember where a particular passage lay in the overall structure of the canon, and reported that they were more likely to skim-read and jump between texts. For others, the loss was more emotional. One respondent reported that 'I feel more distanced from it' on screen, 'frustrated at not having the personal contact of the paper and print'. Their paper Bibles had built up memories and associations, as an object that they had received as a gift and carried with them through life. The physical form of Uncover has been designed by UCCF to encourage these kinds of material relationships with and through the book, dimensions that the organisation feared a digital-only Bible might struggle to generate.

Second case study: digital memorials

This brief discussion of memory leads us to our second area of study. Paper Bibles can act as memory objects, preserving constructions of relationships. As José van Dijck has argued, 'concrete objects stand for relational acts of memory', and we use them to inscribe and communicate our identity and 'to situate ourselves in contemporary and past cultures' as well as to trigger recall of particular memories (2007: 24). As our identities develop and evolve, we reformulate and edit our memory objects, which may involve discarding them, moving them to new places or altering their contents. A Bible may move from a prominent shelf to a less prominent storage box or back to a bedside table; it may be proudly displayed at a funeral; it may acquire a new cover, additional annotations or new additions to a family tree page. It may remain unchanged, embodying old memories and connections and awaiting their rediscovery by a future generation.

Memory objects play a particularly rich role in death, bereavement and commemoration. Memorialisation is of particular interest to scholars of religion – as demonstrated in a number of chapters in this book – because it can be used to explore the shifting boundaries between religion and non-religion. All social groups must find ways to re-establish the security of their social bonds after the loss of members, and some but not all of the resources required for this process are drawn from religious traditions.

In times of mourning, memory is materialised across the spectrum of public and private spaces: the living construct public memorials to the dead, erect gravestones in separate cemeteries, preserve family photographs in their homes and store personal items that may be seen by only one individual. Dorthe Refslund Christensen and Kjetil Sandvik have borrowed the language of digital media to refer to graves as "interfaces", surfaces through which the living can interact with and perform their connection to the dead (2014: 251). Digital technologies are now also very important in the memorial practices of many families and social groups, perpetuating some customs and transforming others.

In some cases, digital media have been used to augment physical memorials, just as Uncover added QR codes to a paper Bible. Some stonemasons have experimented with adding QR codes to graves, cutting a pattern onto the tombstone that can be scanned by a visitor's smartphone. The grave then becomes a physical link to a digital memorial, in which the dead can be commemorated through photographs, videos, messages and other media. As Stine Gotved has observed, this can generate problematic interruptions between public and private space (2015: 275). A very large QR code can be scanned from a discreet distance, but visually marks the grave; a very small code is discreetly hidden, but forces the visitor to invade the gravespace in order to access it. The grave itself may be considered a space of private emotion, but it lies within the more public cemetery, perhaps under the eye of other visitors. Digital resources may be more private in tone, but they can be accessed from anywhere in the world. A mobile phone is a personal communication device, but some would still consider the use of a phone unacceptable within the sacred, silent space of a cemetery. And, of course, there is no guarantee that QR codes will still be in use in the future.

A QR code connects a grave to a digital resource, allowing a person at the gravesite access to multi-modal memories of the deceased. Digital media are thus embedded into the context of cemetery visiting. A different kind of connection between digital and physical is enacted by websites like Billion Graves (billiongraves.com), which aims to serve local historians and family genealogists.

Using the Billion Graves app, visitors to graveyards can take photographs of each headstone, upload them to the website tagged with a GPS location, and then transcribe as much information as they can still read. This information is then stored in a searchable database, making it easier to find specific graves around the world. In this case, digital technology archives data about physical objects in order to help coordinate embodied visits to those objects.

A digital technology or resource can also become a memory object in its own right. The dead now leave behind a legacy of devices, accounts and online content, including their mobile phones, computers, folders of digital photographs, blogs, computer game characters and email accounts. The bereaved must choose to access, archive, discard or delete the continuing digital presence of those who have died, and this process is not always straightforward – accessing online accounts may require finding passwords, for example.

Designers have also experimented with memorials that combine physical and digital resources, experimenting with 'textured' materialities (to borrow Robles and Wiberg's terminology). These projects often remediate archives of photographs or other legacies, incorporating media traces of the deceased into multi-modal memorials. Daisuke Uriu and Naohito Okude's 'ThanatoFenestra' is of particular interest to scholars of religion, because it is based on a traditional Japanese Buddhist family altar. The user lights a real candle, positioned in front of a small round screen. The device registers each flickering movement of the flame – which could be caused by a puff of air blown by the user – and this triggers the display to cycle through a series of digital photographs of the deceased. A bowl of aromatic oil above the candle sends smoke rising past the image and 'cleanses their spirits . . . as if burning incense sticks' (Uriu and Okude 2010: 423).

Wendy Moncur, Elise van den Hoven, Miriam Julius and David Kirk have collaborated on a design project called 'Story Shell', working with a bereaved parent, Mayra, to create a 'bespoke, tangible, digital memorial' for her home (2015: 470). The object they produced is a smooth white sphere, comfortable to hold, manufactured with a 3D printer. Through a hole in the top, the user can see a spiral decoration, laser cut from paper. Beneath this lie a speaker, LED lights and a sensor. Technology is made invisible, a design tendency identified by Robles and Wiberg. Moncur and her colleagues do not explain this decision, but it is possible that they felt that visible electronics would be inappropriate for a memorial, falling outside the boundaries of the 'sensational form' (Meyer 2011) of contemporary grief.

When the user picks up the object, the sensor triggers replay of recorded stories in which Mayra talks about her son, Andrew, and the speaker is powerful enough to gently vibrate the sphere while the stories play. Unexpectedly, Mayra chose to address Andrew directly in her storytelling, and for the researchers 'this implied that our central design goal of presence had been realised, as Andrew was vividly present for Mayra during this experience' (Moncur et al. 2015: 476).

The use of LEDs echoes Uriu and Okudo's candle (2010), but Moncur and her colleagues make no mention of a religious or spiritual context for their use of light (or any other aspect of their design). As Marion Bowman demonstrates in her chapter in this book, candles and lights 'convey, express or produce a range of purposes, meanings and emotions', and they can do so 'with or without precise articulation of the exact meaning attributed to what is being done' (Bowman, this volume).

Memory objects can also be constructed or maintained entirely online. A YouTube video, for example, can be created to commemorate a life, place or event. When a Facebook user dies, his or her existing profile remains online, still connected to the living. This kind of "continuing bond" with the dead can prove traumatic for some, and Facebook now allows next-of-kin to delete or "memorialise" pages to limit and control the networks of the dead (Facebook n.d.).

Mourners are also creating memory objects and ritual practices in virtual worlds, as Anna Haverinen has shown in her work on memorialisation in the virtual world of Second Life (2014). Funeral events are now frequently held in game settings, and visitors to Second Life can find memorial chapels, graveyards, statues and crypts. Haverinen interviewed a group of friends at a cave in Second Life that had belonged to a role-player called Yuki. When Yuki died, her Second Life friends redecorated her cave as a memorial place, displaying a slideshow of photographs of both the game character and the player herself. They also added a burial mound, 'in order for it to resemble an actual memorial familiar from the offline world' (2014: 167) – partly as a substitute grave for those who would never be able to visit Yuki's home country offline. Yuki's story ends with a fascinating twist, as her friends begin wondering if her tragic death – which showed a number of curious inconsistencies – might have been a hoax, a dramatic way to move on from the community without breaking character. Such events are not unusual online, but in this case Haverinen's interviewees claim not to mind too much. After all, they say, they did enjoy the role-play.

These case studies of memorialisation can all be understood as material objects, using the definitions introduced earlier. At the most straightforward of Horst and Miller's three levels, "digital infrastructure of technology", physical objects are involved in their production, maintenance and access: QR codes in ink or stone, mobile phones with touch screens, high-powered computers capable of rendering the graphics of virtual worlds, 3D-printed plastic spheres hiding physical lights and speakers, and so on. At the "digital content" level, photographs, videos and audio recordings are preserved and circulated through these memorials, inserted into virtual worlds and social media profiles and connected to physical objects. Email accounts and other online repositories of content become troublesome legacies for the bereaved, who must find out how to access them and decide what they are willing to save or delete. Digital Bibles are often designed to train the user to read and think in new ways, and the common practice of communicating with the dead through Facebook is arguably encouraged by the design of that social networking site (Walter 2015). This brings us to the third level of materiality, "digital context": the architecture of Facebook positions us within a network of contacts that includes both the living and the dead, provides us with a range of options for more or less public communication, and uses algorithms to calculate which of our communications should be seen by which of our connections. Our social environment is structured by the media we use, even if we are unaware of the boundaries placed around us.

Conclusion: the production of digital objects

In his contribution to this volume, David Morgan suggests analysing the "production" of a material object in three stages: medium, design and manufacture. To conclude this chapter we will discuss each of these in turn, bringing together observations from the foregoing examples.

As we have seen, designers pay careful attention to the strengths and weaknesses of different media. In the case of Uncover, a range of media are combined into one product, reflecting particular understandings of how students think. As a paper book, Uncover can be framed as a gift to read with a friend; as a series of videos, it can offer direct, relatable instruction. YouVersion chose to develop a mobile app instead, using digital media to provide easy access to the text and encouraging collaborative and performative reading through social media. Memorials can be physical (the deceased's mobile phone), augmented (graves with QR codes), virtual (memory caves in Second Life) or networked (Facebook profile pages), or they can combine physical and digital in more nuanced ways, like Story Shell's use of plastic, paper, lights and audio recordings (Moncur et al. 2015). All of these examples try to exploit the affordances and minimise the limitations of particular media.

We have also seen examples of careful design. The creators of these books and memorials are trying to produce something that will resonate with and shape their target audiences. Adding QR codes to graves requires careful consideration, because users need to feel comfortable accessing them without breaking norms of graveyard conduct or disturbing other visitors. Yuki's cave included visual elements designed to help visitors recognise the site as a grave, and Story Shell's shape, feel and function were all designed to encourage Mayra to use the object, find it comforting and experience Andrew's presence. Uncover and YouVersion's Bible App are explicitly designed to change how users think: recipients are meant to be attracted into conversation by Uncover's look and content, while reading activity is tracked, analysed and prompted by the Bible App. Design does not determine reception, of course, and a thorough study of these objects would need to include attention to how users appropriate, resist or reject them – themes considered in the later stages of "classification" and "circulation" in Morgan's model of material analysis.

Analysis of manufacture includes the techniques, technologies and networks of an object's production and trade. QR codes can be added to graves only by experienced stonecarvers, so in this case digital technology is used to reinforce the dominance of an established industry. In contrast, Yuki's cave was created within Second Life by volunteer users of that virtual world, without any need to involve traditional memorial industries. Story Shell was produced through 3D printing, which also gives designers direct access to the processes and resources of manufacturing. YouVersion is a more complicated example: it is a digital product created by programmers, rather than printers, which liberates the company from dependence on the infrastructure of the publishing industry; however, this has enabled greater centralisation of control within the religious production economy. YouVersion is owned by the megachurch Life.Church, so its digital Bibles are being produced inside a Christian institution. In the digital marketplace, traditionally independent publishers like the United Bible Societies have been reduced to content producers for church-owned apps.

The study of material religion argues that religious practices, identities and relationships – including relationships between texts and readers, or between the living and the dead – are shaped by and enacted through material objects. Electronic and digital media have often been incorporated within considerations of the materiality of religion, and this essay has tried to demonstrate that this inclusiveness can be justified. Digital Bibles and memorials are material objects, both physically and functionally. They are created through physical processes, and made out of physical materials, but they can also – more interestingly – be shown to constrain and structure our action and relationships, just as material objects do. They can also be profitably studied through application of the methods of material analysis, as shown here using the first stage of David Morgan's nine-step model. At the same time, there are significant and meaningful differences for users between Bible apps and paper Bibles, or virtual world memorials and QR-code gravestones. Designers and users reflect at length on the opportunities, affordances and limitations of different digital and physical media, and our analysis of digital materiality cannot overlook those debates.

The material approach also helps to remind us of the embeddedness of religious content, ideas and practices in wider contexts. Bibles and memorials are produced in a specific medium by designers and manufacturers, and to understand them as material objects we have to consider a wide range of issues that are not exclusive to religion: media affordances, access to production systems, the structure of the marketplace, cultural understandings of gifts and obligations, and many other issues. Memorials can play a role in religious ritual, symbolically express religious ideas and connect the bereaved with an afterlife, but the need for memory objects is shared across religious and non-religious groups. As this chapter has tried to demonstrate, materiality can be the point of contact between the sociology of religion and research in anthropology, media studies, the digital humanities, design studies, memory studies and more. This is, perhaps, the most important advantage that the material turn can offer to the study of religion.

Works cited

Arthur, Chris. 2005. 'Material Religion in Cyberspace'. *Material Religion* 1(2): 289–293.

Aupers, Stef. 2012. 'Enchantment, Inc.: Online Gaming Between Spiritual Experience and Commodity Fetishism'. In *Things: Religion and the Question of Materiality*, eds. Dick Houtman and Birgit Meyer, 339–355. New York: Fordham University Press.

Christensen, Dorthe Refslund and Kjetil Sandvik. 2014. 'Death Ends a Life, Not a Relationship: Objects as Media on Children's Graves'. In *Mediating and Remediating Death*, eds. Dorthe Refslund Christensen and Kjetil Sandvik, 251–272. Farnham: Ashgate.

Facebook. n.d. 'What Will Happen to My Account If I Pass Away?' https://www.facebook.com/help/103897939701143. Accessed 01/03/2016.

Gibson, William. 1984. *Neuromancer*. New York: Ace Books.

Gotved, Stine. 2015. 'Privacy with Public Access: Digital Memorials on Quick Response Codes'. *Information, Communication & Society* 18(3): 269–280.

Grieve, Gregory Price. 2015. 'Digital'. In *Key Terms in Material Religion*, ed. S. Brent Plate, 55–62. London: Bloomsbury.

Haverinen, Anna. 2014. 'In-Game and Out-of-Game Mourning: On the Complexity of Grief in Virtual Worlds'. In *Mediating and Remediating Death*, eds. Dorthe Refslund Christensen and Kjetil Sandvik, 155–176. Farnham: Ashgate.

Hine, Christine. 2015. *Ethnography for the Internet: Embedded, Embodied and Everyday*. London: Bloomsbury.

Horst, Heather and Daniel Miller. 2012. 'The Digital and the Human: A Prospectus for Digital Anthropology'. In *Digital Anthropology*, eds. Heather Horst and Daniel Miller, 3–38. London: Berg.

Hutchings, Tim. 2015. 'E-Reading and the Christian Bible'. *Studies in Religion/Sciences Religieuses* 44(4): 423–440.

Leonardi, Paul. 2010. 'Digital Materiality: How Artifacts without Matter, Matter'. *First Monday* 15(6–7).

Manoff, Marlene. 2006. 'The Materiality of Digital Collections: Theoretical and Historical Perspectives.' *Libraries and the Academy* 6(3): 311–325.

Meyer, Birgit. 2011. 'Medium'. *Material Religion* 7(1): 58–64.

Modern Filosofi. 2015. 'Finns Jag på Nätet?' *Modern Filosofi* 2015(4): 33–34.

Moncur, Wendy, Elise van den Hoven, Miriam Julius and David Kirk. 2015. 'Story Shell: The Participatory Design of a Bespoke Digital Memorial'. *Proceedings of the 4th Participatory Innovation Conference 2015*: 470–477. The Hague: Hague University of Applied Science.

Plate, S. Brent. 2015. 'Introduction'. In *Key Terms in Material Religion*, ed. S. Brent Plate, 1–8. London: Bloomsbury.

Robles, Erica and Mikael Wiberg. 2010. 'Texturing the "Material" Turn in Interaction Design.' *Proceedings of the 4th International Conference on Tangible, Embedded, and Embodied Interaction*: 137–144. New York: ACM.

UCCF. n.d. 'UCCF to Make 50 000 Uncover Gospels Available to Churches'. https://www.uccf.org.uk/news/uccf-to-make-50000-uncover-gospels-available-to-churches.htm. Accessed 01/03/16.

Uriu, Daisuke and Naohito Okude. 2010. 'ThanatoFenestra: Photographic Family Altar Supporting a Ritual to Pray for the Deceased'. *Proceedings of the Conference on Designing Interactive Systems*, 422–425. New York: ACM.

van Dijck, José. 2007. *Mediated Memories in the Digital Age*. Stanford, CA: Stanford University Press.

Walter, Tony. 2015. 'New Media: Old Mourners: Online Memorial Culture as a Chapter in the History of Mourning.' *New Review of Hypermedia and Multimedia* 21(1–2): 10–24.

Part 2
Classification

6 Art works

A relational rather than representational understanding of art and buildings[1]

Graham Harvey

Are art and buildings "things" we interpret, representations of ideas, or participants in relationships? Questions like this lie behind my efforts to understand the many and varied ways in which people engage with material culture or "things." "Things" here includes putatively individual artefacts and found ("natural") objects as well as constellations or communities constituted by interactions and relations between different species (of artefact, object, humans and others). This is to play with the term "things" as a profligate or at least pregnant term, embracing both "artefact" and "assembly" or "council" in its possible meanings (see Latour and Weibel 2005). Thus, assemblies of artefacts might be experienced as "places" – that is meshworks of porously bounded locations within which and as which persons and things interact.

The following section outlines one root of the problem faced when we try to think about the lives of things. It is concerned with the continuing impact of an historical European crisis on what have become taken-for-granted modern assumptions about things and behaviours towards things. In order to see the potential for rethinking things (objects and places), I then offer four case studies about different ways of thinking about and through things. These will contrast what we might call representational knowledges with relational ones and aim to increase understanding of "animistic" engagements with things which/who might wish to speak to us in different voices.

What does "is" mean?

Early modern European conflicts proved to be definitive for the modern construction of religion as "believing" and particularly as "believing in transcendence." These violent upheavals, polemically misidentified as "Wars of Religion" rather than as the "Wars of Nation State Making" that they were, required the privatisation and interiorisation of religion (Cavanaugh 1995; King 2007). Reconstituting Christians primarily as "believers" (Ruel 1997) was a significant part of re-forming them as citizens of modern states rather than as members of transnational communities. These processes resonated with the Cartesian modernist trajectory towards further individualism and rationalism.

Much as these moves may have benefitted the constitution of modernist ways of being, behaving and thinking, they make the task of understanding the lived realities of religions more difficult. If religion really were a matter of private beliefs that do not have any contact or concern with the secular world of nation states, it would be an irrelevant and fatuous pastime. This does not do justice to the continuing social, political, ecological and other activities of religious people. Neither does it leave researchers with much to do beyond quibbling about what causes the "licensed insanities" of religious believing (Bowker 1987; Orsi 2012).

These conflicts (early modern and contemporary) over the meaning of "religion" and the place of religion (as a lived reality) in private and public arenas shape the context in which I seek to understand religious material cultures. This is because specific conflicts nested with early modernity's state-making wars also established modernity's relations with "art." That is, controversies concerned with the meaning and implications of a priest saying "this is my body" while holding a piece of bread or something bread-like are fundamental to the distancing notion of representation or symbolism.

It is not so much the meaning of "this" or "my body" as the meaning of "is" that concerns me. The more-than-rhetorical violence generated by emerging differences of opinion over what the words of the Christian Eucharist meant certainly had significant effects on the evolution of varieties of Protestant and Catholic Christianity. Importantly, however, the legacy of the re-formation of Christian liturgies and catechisms has had wider impact on what it has become possible or straightforward to think and say about art, material culture and, in one way or another, all "things." The equivalence between bread and body in a crucial ritual interaction with dynamic and powerful materiality (Chidester 2000; Bynum 2011) was so severely disrupted that it now seems self-evident that "is" means "represents" or "symbolises."

More verbosely, when we hear or read "is" in many contexts (not only that of Christian liturgy) we automatically translate it as "actually is not but will stand in for an idea or meaning I wish to convey." So, if I say "this photo is my wife" or "this photo is me visiting a temple," I cannot easily be taken to mean that I am married to a photograph or have a two-dimensional double which is currently elsewhere. However, when Maori hosts speak about a building as an ancestor, or when Zuni (Native Americans) insist that a museum inappropriately displays an object who is a relative, it may be that inserting representational terms or ideas misinterprets, misinforms and misdirects attention. This is not to suggest that Maori or Zuni forget that houses and masks are made. That the contrary is the case is what makes these relational knowledges such a powerful challenge to Western idealistic, matter-fearing dualism. Peter Pels, for instance, identifies a pervasive cultural "fear of matter" (evident in Descartes and Luther) that "prepared the way for the marginalization of material culture studies in early twentieth-century anthropology" by overemphasising the representative and symbolic functions attributed to things (Pels 2008: 266). Nonetheless, Tim Ingold challenges Pels and other scholars of the "material culture turn" for remaining "trapped in a discourse that opposes the mental and the material, and that cannot therefore countenance the properties of materials save as aspects of the inherent materiality of objects" (2007: 12; also see Vásquez 2011; Whitehead 2013). In short, it is hard not to dematerialise matter so that, as "materiality" and "material culture," it can serve as a stand-in for or solidification of the creativity, agency or intentionality of humans.

In the following sections I introduce four examples of alternatives to the modernist marginalisation of matter that impedes understanding of indigenous and popular relationships with "things." Firstly, reconsideration of "fetishes" contests the overemphasis on the artefactuality or made-ness of things. Then, negotiation over requests for the repatriation of Zuni masks challenges the normative stress placed on authenticity and uniqueness. Learning to engage with a Maori meeting house in Britain suggests alternatives to solely functional analyses. Finally, the animacy of stones in Anishinaabe grammar encourages a rethinking of the themes of projection and anthropomorphism in interpretations of indigenous knowledges.

Considered together (but not forgetting cultural specificity and diversity), these four cases might point towards a place from which to propel further the presentation, analysis and theorisation of religion and religions as vernacular (Primiano 2012), lived (McGuire 2008) and embodied, emplaced and performative (Vásquez 2011). My intention is to do something quite different from suggesting that "there are other ways to think or act" or even that "other cultures are interesting or, in their own terms, rational." Rather, I seek to strengthen the trajectory of the relational turn in multi- and interdisciplinary studies that recognises interactions with matter as relations or interactions.

My approach is intimately committed to dialogue "somewhere" other than the "all-knowing, omniscient 'nowhere'" usually privileged in scholarly practice (Coburn et al. 2013: 335). In part, I seek to understand how some people consider it quite ordinary to treat buildings and other things as persons (a term that carries a considerable weight in this and related discussions; e.g. Harvey 2013b). On our return from these case studies that seem "elsewhere" (Harvey 2013a), we ought to see how curious it is that things "here" are so often, unreflectively, removed from life (Ingold 2011: 28–29). To that end, each case study highlights some aspect of human-thing interaction, and together they ought to contribute to an understanding that things are members of societies as much as humans and other animals are.

Personable fetishes

When presented with an object labelled "fetish" one might draw the conclusion that its defining characteristic is artefactuality. The term "fetish" originated when Portuguese colonial traders entered West African markets and failed to recognise the similarity between local relations with material cultures and their own relations with more familiar objects. In particular, they failed to appreciate the ways in which things were valued both by themselves and by "fetishists"

(Whitehead 2013: 153–187, drawing on Mauss 2006 [1923]; Graeber 2005 and others). Emphasising the made-ness of other people's things and exempting European matters from devaluation, while further elevating "faith," "believing" and "transcendence," have subsequently skewed both religious and scholarly knowledges and approaches to matter. It is worth noting that Charles de Brosses, who coined "*fetichisme*" in 1760, somehow associated it not with construction but with "fate" and "the fey" (de Brosses 1970; see also Latour 2010: 3). That is there is something peculiar about these things and those who own them.

Tord Olsson cites one of his Bambara hosts, Sungo Traoré, as having introduced himself by saying, "We are not Muslims, we are fetishists" (2013: 230). A friend of Olsson's in Bamako, Mali's capital, Sumankuru Kanté, has "*féticheur*" listed on his ID card as his profession. Although these Malians are entirely at home in the modernist world of consumerism and global communication systems, as Olsson demonstrates, they have not yet discovered that "fetishism" has, until recently, been deemed obsolete in scholarly discourse. However, just as the term "animism" is the subject of ongoing multidisciplinary revisitation (e.g. Bird-David 1999; Harvey 2013b), "fetishism" too is gaining increased value as academic currency (e.g. Pietz 1985, 1987, 1988; Hornborg 1992, 2006, 2013; Pels 1998; Masuzawa 2000; Latour 2000; Johnson 2000; Ingold 2006; Olsson 2013). So, even if Olsson's hosts remain rare in self-identifying as "fetishists," it is (as J. Z. Smith [1998] says of "religion") "our" scholarly critical term to be employed and debated rather than applied or imposed. It can work well to speak of vibrant ways in which some people engage with matter (made or found). As scholars seeking ways to speak insightfully and critically we may make careful use of terms like religion, animism and fetishism. The corollary must be that when we do so we must explain and justify our usage and not merely assert that "when *I* use a word ... it means just what I choose it to mean – neither more nor less" (Carroll 1962 [1872]: 274–275).

Olsson's (2013) eloquent discussion of contemporary Malian "fetishism" illuminates the possibilities opened up by "our" uses in dialogue with insiderly and indigenous self-identification. The following extract introduces fetishes:

> The type of artifact the Bambara themselves call "*fétiche*" when they speak French is in the Bambara language called *boli*, in the plural *boliw* ... To give a simplistic picture we might say that a certain *boli*-object is the body of a particular *boli*-person, or a portable altar that represents a particular other-than-human person ... Certain fetishes, however, are so big and heavy that they are as good as stationary. In the Bambara language the word *boli* is used as a generic term that refers both to this type of object and to the type of other-than-human person associated with such an object. Each such object has a proper name that is also the name of the other-than-human person that the object represents. A particular *boli*-object thus represents one other-than-human person only, rather than many. On the other hand, each *boli*-person is represented by a number of *boli*-objects, which have about

the same shape (similar external form and contain similar things) and are owned by different people.

(Olsson 2013: 232)

Olsson notes that his instructors take for granted that they live their lives together with both *boli*-persons and other "other than now physically living persons." They encourage appropriate decorum or etiquette in meeting such persons, largely in rituals in which "the parties announce their presence, and the relation between them is regulated" (2013: 228). In ritual discourse (as distinct from everyday language), Olsson says that he and his hosts deem it appropriate to "call these beings and objects persons"

> since they are sentient. They have the ability of perception, thinking and knowledge; they have the powers of volition, communication and agency. This is most evident in ritual situations. Moreover, when ritual participants reflect on the course of action in a ritual and upon the nature of the other-than-human agents of a ritual event, then one can speak about these agents as *mɔgɔw*, in the sense of "persons". The use of language in such a meta-ritual discourse is thus different from everyday language. For instance, in such a discourse, an object such as a fetish or a ritual mask can be characterized as a person. Bambara themselves then use the word *mɔgɔ*, person, as an analytical term.
>
> (Olsson 2013: 228)

That which might appear to be an artefact or thing (*fɛnw*) can be treated and apprehended as a person (*mɔgɔ*), particularly but not only in ritual interactions and discourse. Olsson's discussion suggests that *boli*-objects do not so much represent as present or make-present *boli*-persons. They are held to do the actions expected, desired or feared from other-than-living-human-persons. That is they receive sacrifices to encourage them to promote crops, they take possession of men and women in night-time séances, they respond to veneration by hunters in the bush and they dance in revels with secret societies. The carrying of one or more fetishes in leather bags as one travels is so prevalent that the term *tontigiya* (a metonymic compound indicating this "bag ownership") is both synonymous with *bamananya* (Bambara-hood) and definitive of Bambara traditional religion (Olsson 2013: 213).

For those of us tempted to wonder how people can mistake made objects for "persons," Bruno Latour offers a powerful reprimand and an invitation to think again. His *On the Modern Cult of the Factish Gods* (2010) places anti-fetishist, iconoclastic polemicists in the position of defending a nature-culture dualism that seems increasingly untenable. Asking "is it real or is it made?" misdirects our attention in a variety of ways, including seducing us into believing in inert matter. It is precisely the manufacture of technology that encourages scientists to trust the instruments that mediate "reality" to them (especially those bits of reality that are not visible without such mediation). Both scientific instruments and fetishes are manufactured by humans and, at the same time, are trusted to provide otherwise inaccessible information about how to relate to the world. The assumption that fetishists "believe" – an aspect of the "belief in believing" underlying definitive distinctions between religion and science – prevents rather than provokes understanding of the trustworthiness of carefully constructed artefacts for making further connections and enhancing relationships. To think differently about fetishes is to place them within the "parliament of things" (Latour and Weibel 2005) and the continuously socialising network of actors (Latour 2005).

As Tim Ingold indicates, the question we need to ask about fetishes is not "How is life in them?" but "How are they in life?" (2011: 28–29). Indeed, this question is one Ingold invites us to ask in relation not only to other interacting materials or things but also to all beings or persons, including ourselves. How are we in life? How do we move among and through the community of existences? Do we really experience objects as inert or do they work with us in making our shared world? In asking Ingold's question, we might place material culture studies in a far more interesting relationship with studies of society, culture and performance. With Peter Pels (1998, 2008) we might do something more vital than subsuming fetishes, things and matter within transcendent (human) cultures and/or emphasising their meanings and their representative or symbolic functions. We might reanimate understandings of the world as thoroughly interactive and communities as more inclusive and diverse.

Divine masks

Among the Zuni (from the south-west of what is now the United States), a *koko* (*kachina*) mask is sacred, powerful and personal. If someone (whether Zuni or anyone else) makes such a mask for a museum to display, Western ontology leads to the identification of such artefacts as "replicas." However, in Zuni theory, it is simply not possible to make copies or replicas of these masks or models of dancers wearing them. There can be no simulacra (Baudrillard 1988) of a kachina. This is not because of any technical difficulty in the making of masks, costumes or figurines. Technically speaking, almost anyone could make a *koko* mask, but absolutely no one can make a copy of them. If this seems enigmatic, the point is that anything that seems to be a copy of a *koko* mask is itself a *koko* mask. It is not a copy but the real thing again. Its production (however mechanical) cannot make it a reproduction (despite Benjamin 1936).

As Pia Altieri (2000) demonstrates, the only way to make a *koko* mask is to rely on Zuni sacred knowledge, and that knowledge knows no "replicas" but only masks *who* (as personal beings and therefore requiring personal pronouns) act in particular ways within the world. To concentrate on the making of things, in this case at least, is to attend to the wrong facts. While masks are made, so are all other kinds of persons (human as much as other-than-human, including "object persons"). In this case, the important facts for the Zuni – and for those who wish to understand and speak about these masks — are those facts concerned with the acts and performances of masks in various contexts.

These and other indigenous and relational facts about *koko* masks have come into conflict with the knowledges and practices of museum display cultures. Altieri (2000) contrasts the treatment of these masks with that of Zuni *Ahayu:da* ("Twin War Gods"). She demonstrates that the concept of individuated artefacts available for display contrasts with Zuni emphases on relationships and interactions. In negotiations over possible repatriation of Zuni "sacred" or "religious" artefacts, under the rubric of the Native American Graves Protection and Repatriation Act (NAGPRA), this difference of understanding became more apparent and, perhaps, more solidified and entrenched.

In the case of the *Ahayu:da*, a lengthy repatriation negotiation between Zuni Pueblo and the Smithsonian Institution resulted in a decision that "museums and collectors can stipulate that all *authentic* and *decontextualized Ahayu:da* are Zuni: *Ahayu:da* are cultural patrimony that cannot be bought, sold, removed or otherwise alienated from Zuni shrines" (Altieri 2000: 130). That is when Zuni can establish legal title to individual objects with a clear provenance from makers, owners and/or users, their *Ahayu:da* can be de-accessioned from Smithsonian and (following this precedent) other US museums and returned to their owners.

However, in the same negotiations, Zuni failed to persuade their interlocutors that all *koko* masks deserved similar protections and repatriation. This, as Altieri demonstrates, is because Zuni negotiators set out a case that all such masks were necessarily members of a class or community. Whether made by Zuni or others, whether made for Zuni or for others, and whether made for ceremony or display or any other purpose, *koko* masks are *koko* masks and, necessarily, Zuni intellectual, cultural and communal property. Neither maker nor "owner" of such masks has the right to give or sell them. It is simply but profoundly not possible for a *koko* mask to be alienated from the Zuni relational community. The same is true of putative "copies" of *Ahayu:da*: for Zuni they too are inalienable and authentic *Ahayu:da* while for Smithsonian and other museum curators they are replicas for display.

In short, some things are authentic even if they appear (to some observers) to be replicas. They are inherently relational and belong to and in the community for whom they make sense of and in traditional knowledge systems. The negotiators representing the US museums presume that masks become significant because of their representational significance, as created by makers and owners. The Zuni, in contrast, understand *koko* masks to be significant by virtue of being *koko* masks.

The individuation of particular things (e.g. by having a specific origin, maker, accession record or construction) does not equate to their personhood. Rather, things are lively within those relations with other things, persons, acts and events which Tim Ingold calls "meshworks" to emphasise their active and interactive nature (2007: 80; 2011: 84–86). That is in distinction with the way in which "network" has been misunderstood as a reference to mere connections or the joining of discrete dots, "meshwork" engages us with movements among, along, between and through possibilities for "becoming" within these processes and acts of relating.

Hinemihi: ancestor house

Since the 1950s, Maori living in Britain for short or long periods have met together to practise traditional performing arts as one means of learning, maintaining and displaying Maori culture and community. Ngati Ranana (translated on a T-shirt as "London Maori Club" but also readable as "London's group" or "London's offspring") is like and unlike *kapa haka* performance groups in Aotearoa New Zealand. They perform at cultural events but have also become the heart of a fluid diaspora community. Once a year, Ngati Ranana's *Kohanga Reo* ("language nest" for the teaching and learning of Maori language) hosts an event that is a Maori-style picnic, with food cooked in pits in traditional style and a celebration of the wider Maori and Pacific Islander diaspora community and their cultures. It takes place in the presence of Hinemihi, a Maori *wharenui*, meeting house, brought to England in the mid-nineteenth century and reconstructed in the grounds of Clandon House near Guildford, then home of Lord Onslow, the retiring governor of New Zealand.

It is possible to say of Clandon House, like many other buildings, that "she" is attractive and "has character." But this is, for the most part, a deliberately metaphorical way of talking, and projects human likeness or attributes on to human dwellings. It can be said as casually as a French speaker might assign feminine gender to *la table*, and with as little insistence that the attributed gender is precisely equivalent to that of human female persons. However, when Maori say that Hinemihi participates in ceremonies or that she welcomes guests, they mean something quite different. Hinemihi o te Ao Tawhito (to use her full name) is an ancestor. She is pleased to see her descendants. She welcomes respectful visitors and works with Maori to turn respectful visitors into guests. Maori introduce others to Hinemihi in a personal way. They can point to Hinemihi's welcoming arms, visible as the bargeboards that descend from an apex where the ancestral face observes those who come to visit her. Inside the carved house, Hinemihi's spine and ribs are visible in the roof beam and rafters. It is possible to hear these statements as metaphors, or interpret them as meaning that rafters *symbolise* arms, face, spine and ribs. But something about the way Maori say these things, and something about the way they move towards and within Hinemihi, demonstrates they are saying something quite different. By attention to the host's words and movements, visitors learn to be(come) guests. Explanations are rarely if ever offered as explicit teaching, but knowledge can be caught.

Learning to be a guest of Maori involves responding appropriately to being invited to approach and eventually to enter the host community's *wharenui*. It might not be completely evident to all such visitors in the process of becoming guests that these "meeting houses" are also *whare tipuna*, ancestor-houses, or that a guest is someone brought into the body of the ancestor. But part of learning to appreciate the full implications of guest-making protocols and ceremonies (*powhiri*) is learning that each *wharenui* is an ancestor *and* a meeting place. The ancestor lived in the past in human form, and continues to exist in a human but post-mortem form.

"Ancestor" in most indigenous contexts does not simply point to someone having died. An ancestor is a person who, though transformed in the processes of dying, is still actively involved in the community formed by her or his descendants. The "living face" of the ancestor can be recognised in the form of descendants in each successive generation (Henare 2007: 57). At the same time, in yet another form, an ancestor can exist in various other physical modes, one of which is as a meeting house like Hinemihi. She is a *whare tipuna*, not only an "ancestral [style] house" but also a "house ancestor".

However, this description remains static as long as it points only to the objective materiality of the house. What Amiria Henare says of genealogy, *whakapapa*, is relevant here: it is "[n]ot simply a static record of lineages, it is an inherently dynamic cosmological system for reckoning degrees of similarity and difference, determining appropriate behaviour, and manipulating existing and potential relationships to achieve desired effects" (2007: 57). Hinemihi and genealogy are intimate participants in performed practices that familiarise people with their ancestor and other people with their (potential) guesthood. Indeed, people become guests in the presence of, with the full participation of and by entering into the body of Hinemihi, the ancestor. Taking a strongly relational approach, Hinemihi is technically always an ancestor but requires an opportunity to greet descendants and guests to show what being an ancestor is all about. The acts of being an ancestor and becoming guests of the ancestor and her descendants are about becoming increasingly familiar and personable towards and to others.

There is considerably more that could be said about Hinemihi, other *wharenui* and the social and material processes surrounding their construction, interactions and significance. Indeed, as *wharenui* are at the heart of the Maori relations and processes called *tapu* (taboo) and *mana* (prestige), they are central to Maori culture. Significant elements of Maori performance culture also circulate around *wharenui*, including the employment of traditional knowledges and ceremonies (the "myths and rituals" of scholarly vocabularies) (Tawhai 1988). In turn, since these terms have played important roles in academic theorising about religion(s), they reward further thought (e.g. Harvey 2013a). However, for the purpose of understanding Maori contributions to rethinking materiality and relationality, it is important to hold two seeming opposites in mind. Maori can talk about and act towards Hinemihi as they would about and towards a person. At the same time they can talk about her as a human artefact.

Not only do the descendants of Hinemihi's builders and carvers visit sometimes, but also they have actively participated in the restoration projects that have kept Hinemihi secure, attractive, functional and alive to new possibilities. Maori artists and crafts-people like George Nuku and Rosanna Raymond have also made meeting spaces and other *Taonga* (treasured things) in London, Paris and elsewhere in the diaspora. Maori have plenty of ways of talking about buildings, construction, craft, decoration, labour and artefacts. These "objective" means of labelling materiality and its manipulation do not, however, exhaust Maori discourse about "things" like Hinemihi. Multiple layered, fluid and dynamic understandings and appreciations are regular features of Maori and other indigenous knowledge systems.

Hinemihi is constructed to play significant roles in these multiple discourses. She is ancestor, meeting house, cultural artefact, heritage, (re-)construction and more. Some of these ways of seeing and knowing Hinemihi seem entirely familiar in Western or modernist frames. As a construction, for example, Hinemihi is a praiseworthy exemplar of Maori heritage. However, she remains an object until she is engaged. This is equally true in Maori understanding. Hinemihi needs her descendants and their visitors in order to interact as a personal being, an ancestor and host. For this reason, I have woven thoughts about both Maori performance culture and Maori material culture together. They are inseparable because materiality is an element of relationality, and vice versa.

Grandfather stones

In the Anishinaabe or Ojibwa language, the word for "stones," *asiniig*, belongs to the animate rather than inanimate gender. In an attempt to understand whether this was any more than a grammatical distinction, the anthropologist Irving Hallowell asked an unnamed old Ojibwa man, "Are *all* the stones we see about us here alive?" (1960: 24; emphasis original). Had he been talking with a French speaker he might have asked, "Are all these tables female?" However, it seems likely that to ask this question would invite people to treat one as mad or foolish. French linguistic gender assignment is a figure of speech, and probably has no other sense or significance (see Sedaris 2001: 185–191). However, Hallowell's question about stones received a more helpful (if still enigmatic) response.

Hallowell's question, unpacked, is whether the Ojibwa treat grammatically animate stones as animate persons. Do they speak with stones or act in other ways that reveal intentions to build or maintain relationships? If all stones everywhere are grammatically animate, did the old man actually think that *particular* stones around him were alive? Did he treat them in some way that showed them to be alive? The old man answered, "No! But *some* are" (Sedaris 2001: 185–191). He claimed to have witnessed a particular stone following the leader of a shamanic ceremony around a tent as he sang. Another powerful leader is said to have had a large stone that would open when he tapped it three times, allowing him to remove a small bag of herbs when he needed it in ceremonies. Hallowell was told that when a white trader was digging his potato patch he found a stone that looked like it may be important. He called for the leader of another ceremony, who knelt down to talk to the stone, asking if it had come from someone's ceremonial tent. The stone is said to have denied this. Movement, gift-giving and conversation are three indicators of the animate nature of relational beings, or persons, of whatever species.

In the old man's full response and in the other narratives Hallowell includes, it becomes crystal clear that the key point is that stones engage in relationships – not just that they might do things of their own volition (however remarkable this claim might seem). For the Ojibwa the interesting question is not "how do we know stones are alive?" but "what is the appropriate way for people, of any kind, to relate?"

This is as true for humans as it is for stones, trees, animals, birds, fish and all other beings that might be recognised as persons. Persons are known to be persons when they relate to other persons in particular ways. They might act more or less intimately, willingly, reciprocally or respectfully. Since enmity is also a relationship, they might act aggressively – which is the chief reason why animists employ shamans (Harvey 2005). The category of "person" is perhaps properly applicable only within such thoroughly relational worlds when beings are actively relating with others. There, "person" is not a nominal category but a performance, and one that is both corporeal and corporate. This is quite different to the understanding of most European-derived cultures in which personhood is an interior quality, a fact about an individual (human) who is self-conscious. Hallowell recognised this by insisting that we are not talking here about different "belief-systems," epistemologies, but about different ontologies, different ways of being in the world. Indeed, we could say that the Ojibwa elder lived in a different world from Hallowell's until the latter learnt to see the world as his teacher showed it to be.

Once he saw the world in which Ojibwa elders and local stones might actively relate together, or share gifts and ceremonies, Hallowell had to find new ways to use the English language to write about what he had learnt. To talk of animism may have suggested a discussion of life (animation) versus death. To talk of persons may have implied notions about human interiority (belief, rationality or subjectivity). He has, in fact, been misread in both these ways. However, the "animate persons" Hallowell introduced were relational beings, relations and interactive beings in a participatory world. Indeed, his question is phrased in a way that indicates he had already appreciated some, at least, of what it meant to live in the old man's world: he did not ask "are all stones (universally) alive?" but inquired about nearby stones, "are these stones alive?" Hallowell was already recognising the importance of relationship and participation. Then, having learnt from his Ojibwa hosts, Hallowell coined the phrase "other-than-human persons" (which has entered the vocabulary of many other scholars, some already cited) to refer to the animate beings with whom humans share and co-create the world/community. He was not privileging humanity or saying that what makes something a person is its likeness to humans. He is clear that "person" is not defined by putatively human characteristics or behaviours. The term is a much larger umbrella than "human." His is not an anthropomorphic or anthropocentric notion of personhood.

All beings (according to this and many other indigenous ontological knowledges) communicate intentionally and act towards others relationally: this makes them "persons." All persons are expected to give and receive gifts, and to act respectfully (to mutual benefit or communal well-being) and, if they do so, this makes them "good persons." It is useful for us (humans) to speak about "human-" and "other-than-human" persons only because we are humans talking to humans (if we were bears we might speak of "other-than- bear persons"). This is also useful for speakers of English because we are preconditioned to hear the word "person" as a reference to other humans. The word "person" should be enough, without the additional "other-than-human," and it would be if English-speakers had not learnt to privilege humanity above other beings.

Expanding our vocabulary and analysis

Some words work excessively hard, carrying the weight of entire cultures, religions, histories, epistemologies and/or ontologies. Some suffer the indignity of being made to mean "just what I choose it to mean – neither more nor less" without regard to intelligibility or communicability, and without being rewarded with "extra pay" as Lewis Carroll's Humpty Dumpty would say (Carroll 1962 [1872]: 274–275). Among many indigenous peoples, "respect" is a well-paid, respected, hard-working word. "Persons" has become a similarly well-respected and rich lode/load-bearing term in what has become known as the "new animism" – that is studies of the understanding that the world is a community of persons, only some of whom are human (Harvey 2005, 2013b). "Animism" too is a hard-working term, meaning more than a few different things and often used within contradictory discourses. I noted earlier that "is" carries a significant burden. Straightforwardly it indicates some sort of equivalence between this and that – for example "this [bread] is my body" and "this mask is a Zuni kachina." But "is" can also indicate the kind of difference-and-similarity implied by words like "represent" or "symbolise." Again, for particular speakers and/or hearers/readers "this is my body" and "this is a kachina" provide good examples of these dynamics.

The key challenge here is thinking about "things." Many engagements with indigenous knowledges (regardless of whether they are understood to be such) take place in museums and galleries. Displays present things. Their curators (and perhaps the displayed things) expect some kind of message to be conveyed. Victorian museums might have been satisfied with presenting "curiosities," odd objects extracted from events and interactions, removed from ritual and other relations and re-embedded as spectacle or entertainment. More recently museums have made considerable efforts to employ things as mediators of cultural encounter. A single object or a group represents complexes of actions and thoughts. Museum displays may also speak about relations between cultures (e.g. those of makers and collectors, donors and viewers). They are, therefore, entangled or embroidered in tensions between object and subject, observation and participation, distance and presence, inertness or interaction, and between the individuality of separated and interiorised personhood and the "dividuality" of relational personhood (Strathern 1988; Vilaça 2005: 453; Halbmayer 2012: 110).

The analytical and engaged trajectory that I envisage here is summed up by Manuel Vásquez and those he cites:

> With Spinoza, Nietzsche, Bergson, Deleuze, and now the so-called 'new materialists,' such as Jane Bennett (2010) and Diana Coole and Samantha Frost (2010), we can recover the unicity, potency, and vibrancy of matter. A well-conceptualized materialism allows us "to raise the status of the materiality of which we are composed. Each human is a heterogeneous compound of wonderfully vibrant, dangerously vibrant, matter. If matter itself is lively, then not only is the difference between subjects and objects minimized, but the status of the shared materiality of all things is elevated. All bodies become more than mere objects, as the thing-powers of resistance and protean agency are brought into sharper relief" (Bennett 2010: 13). Materialism, thus, offers the possibility of a radically different, thoroughly relational, dynamic, non-dualistic ontology.
>
> (Vásquez 2012: 659, also see Johnson 2012)

As we move through buildings and spaces we interact. By thus enacting our implicit relationality with the "lively immanence of matter" – that is with materials and other species of embodied existence – we and they become persons to each other (Coole and Frost 2010: 9). In this scenario of being "in life," personhood is always and only a relational interactivity, a moving together in and in between others whose relations are more or less dynamically activated (Ingold 2011: 29). If some of these things (both animated non-objectified but relational materials and communities of persons) are more intimately related than others, so too some things are more esteemed, more prestigious, more powerful or more motivational than others. Some things, like some humans, are more excluded, more restricted and/or more subjected to objectification than others. To echo Amiria Henare, Martin Holbraad and Sari Wastell (2007) we (scholars interested in materials, bodies and other things) need to "think through things" rather than merely about what they "represent" or stand in for.

We (conflicted "moderns" in Latour's terms) may be less aware of it than medieval Christians but for us too "matter [is] a dynamic substratum" (Bynum 2011: 250). Wood or wafer (statues or Eucharistic host) might not bleed for all of us, but we name our cars, swear at our computers, show others photographs that are (in some senses) our loved ones, become upset if we lose our wedding rings, treat books with reverence or disdain, become "engaged" by art (Latour 2013: 241), change our thinking about ourselves under the impact of religious symbols (reassembled as articulations of relations; Ezzy 2015) and sometimes fail to distinguish costumes from their wearers (or vice versa). We are both cyborgs (Haraway 1991) and hybrids (Vásquez 2011: 291–302), dynamically and fluidly fused with technologies and other artefacts that enable our moving through life. It is perhaps time that our thinking through things matched the realities of these modes and relations in which we move through life.

Note

1 I am grateful to Molly Kady, Amy Whitehead, Doug Ezzy and Tasia Scrutton for suggesting improvements to a draft of this chapter; and to the editors for further improvements.

Works cited

Altieri, Pia. 2000. 'Knowledge, Negotiation and NAGPRA: Reconceptualizing Repatriation Discourse(s)'. In *Law and Religion in Contemporary Society: Communities, Individualism and the State*, eds. Peter Edge and Graham Harvey, 129–149. Aldershot: Ashgate.
Baudrillard, Jean. 1988. 'Simulacra and Simulations'. In his *Selected Writings*, ed. Mark Poster, 166–184. Palo Alto, CA: Stanford University Press.
Benjamin, Walter. [1936] 1968. 'The Work of Art in the Age of Mechanical Reproduction'. In *Illuminations*, ed. Hannah Arendt, 217–251. New York: Schocken.
Bennett, Jane. 2010. *Vibrant Matter: A Political Ecology of Things*. Durham, NC: Duke University Press.
Bird-David, Nurit. 1999. '"Animism" Revisited: Personhood, Environment, and Relational Epistemology'. *Current Anthropology* 40: S67–S91.
Bowker, John. 1987. *Licensed Insanities: Religions and Belief in God in the Contemporary World*. London: Darton, Longman and Todd.
Bynum, Carolyn W. 2011. *Christian Materiality: An Essay on Religion in Late Medieval Europe*. New York: Zone Books.
Carroll, Lewis. 1962 [1872]. *Alice's Adventures in Wonderland and Through the Looking Glass*. London: Puffin.
Cavanaugh, William T. 1995. 'A Fire Strong Enough to Consume the House: "The Wars of Religion" and the Rise of the State'. *Modern Theology* 11(4): 397–420.
Chidester, David. 2000. *Christianity: A Global History*. London: Penguin Books.
Coburn, Elaine, Makere Stewart-Harawira, Aileen Moreton-Robinson and George Sefa Dei. 2013. 'Unspeakable Things: Indigenous Research and Social Science'. *Socio* 2: 121–134.
Coole, Diana and Samantha Frost. 2010. 'Introducing the New Materialism'. In *New Materialisms: Ontology, Agency, and Politics*, eds. Dianna Coole and Samantha Frost, 1–43. Durham, NC: Duke University Press.
de Brosses, Charles. 1970 [1760]. *Du Culte des Dieux Fetiches, ou Parallele de l'Ancienne Religion de l'Egypte avec la Religion Actuelle de Nigritie*. Farnborough: Gregg.
Ezzy, Douglas. 2015. 'Reassembling Religious Symbols: The Pagan God Baphomet'. *Religion* 45(1): 24–41.
Graeber, David. 2005. 'Fetishism as Social Creativity: Or, Fetishes Are Gods in the Process of Construction'. *Anthropological Theory* 5(4): 407–438.
Halbmayer, Ernst. 2012. 'Amerindian Mereology: Animism, Analogy, and the Multiverse'. *Indiana* 29: 103–125.
Hallowell, A. Irving. 1960. 'Ojibwa Ontology, Behavior, and World View'. In *Culture in History: Essays in Honor of Paul Radin*, ed. Stanley Diamond, 19–52. New York: Columbia University Press.
Haraway, Donna. 1991. *Simians, Cyborgs, and Women: The Reinvention of Nature*. London: Free Association Books.
Harvey, Graham. 2005. *Animism: Respecting the Living World*. London: Hurst.
———. 2013a. *Food, Sex and Strangers: Understanding Religion as Everyday Life*. London: Routledge.
———, ed. 2013b. *The Handbook of Contemporary Animism*. Durham, NC: Acumen.

Henare, Amiria. 2007. 'Taonga Maori: Encompassing Rights and Property in New Zealand'. In *Thinking through Things: Theorising Artefacts Ethnographically*, eds. Amiria Henare, Martin Holbraad and Sari Wastell, 47–67. London: Routledge.

Hornborg, Alf. 1992. 'Machine Fetishism, Value, and the Image of Unlimited Good: Towards a Thermodynamics of Imperialism'. *Man* 27: 1–18.

———. 2006. 'Animism, Fetishism, and Objectivism as Strategies for Knowing (or Not Knowing) the World'. *Ethnos* 71(1): 21–32.

———. 2013. 'Submitting to Objects: Animism, Fetishism, and the Cultural Foundations of Capitalism'. In *The Handbook of Contemporary Animism*, ed. Graham Harvey, 244–259. Durham, NC: Acumen.

Ingold, Tim. 2006. 'Rethinking the Animate, Re-Animating Thought'. *Ethnos: Journal of Anthropology* 71(1): 9–20.

———. 2007. *Lines: A Brief History*. London: Routledge.

———. 2011. *Being Alive: Essays on Movement, Knowledge and Description*. London: Routledge.

Johnson, Paul C. 2000. 'The Fetish and McGwire's Balls'. *Journal of the American Academy of Religion* 68(2): 243–264.

———. 2012. 'Bodies and Things in the Forest of Symbols'. *Religion* 42(4): 633–642.

King, Richard. 2007. 'The Association of "Religion" with Violence: Reflections on a Modern Trope'. In *Religion and Violence in South Asia: Theory and Practice*, eds. John R. Hinnells and Richard King, 226–257. London: Routledge.

Latour, Bruno. 2005. *Reassembling the Social: An Introduction to Actor-Network-Theory*. Oxford: Oxford University Press.

———. 2010. *On the Modern Cult of the Factish Gods*. Durham, NC: Duke University Press.

———. 2013. *An Inquiry into Modes of Existence: An Anthropology of the Moderns*, tr. Catherine Porter. Cambridge, MA: Harvard University Press.

Latour, Bruno and Peter Weibel, eds. 2005. *Making Things Public: Atmospheres of Democracy*. Karlsruhe: ZKM.

Masuzawa, Tomoko. 2000. 'Troubles with Materiality: The Ghost of Fetishism in the Nineteenth Century'. *Comparative Studies in Society and History* 42(2): 242–267.

Mauss, Marcel. 2006 [1923]. *The Gift: The Form and Reason for Exchange in Archaic Societies*. London: Routledge.

McGuire, Meredith B. 2008. *Lived Religion: Faith and Practice in Everyday Life*. Oxford: Oxford University Press.

Olsson, Tord. 2013. 'Animate Objects: Ritual Perception and Practice among the Bambara in Mali'. In *The Handbook of Contemporary Animism*, ed. Graham Harvey, 226–243. London: Routledge.

Orsi, Robert A. 2012. 'Afterword: Everyday Religion and the Contemporary World'. In *Ordinary Lives and Grand Schemes: An Anthropology of Everyday Religion*, eds. Samuli Schielke and Lisa Debevec, 146–161. Oxford: Berghahn Books.

Pels, Peter. 1998. 'The Spirit of Matter: On Fetish, Rarity, Fact, and Fancy'. In *Border Fetishisms: Material Objects in Unstable Spaces*, ed. Patricia Spyer, 91–121. New York: Routledge.

———. 2008. 'The Modern Fear of Matter: Reflections on the Protestantism of Victorian Science'. *Material Religion: The Journal of Objects, Art and Belief* 4(3): 264–283.

Pietz, William. 1985. 'The Problem of the Fetish I'. *Res* 9: 5–17.

———. 1987. 'The Problem of the Fetish II'. *Res* 13: 23–45.

———. 1988. 'The Problem of the Fetish III'. *Res* 16: 105–123.

Primiano, Leonard N. 2012. 'Manifestations of the Religious Vernacular: Ambiguity, Power, and Creativity'. In *Vernacular Religion in Everyday Life: Expressions of Belief*, eds. Ülo Valk and Marion Bowman, 382–394. London: Equinox.

Ruel, Malcolm. 1997. *Belief, Ritual and the Securing of Life: Reflexive Essays on a Bantu Religion*. Leiden: Brill.
Sedaris, David. 2001. *Me Talk Pretty One Day*. London: Abacus.
Smith, Jonathan Z. 1998. 'Religion, Religions'. In *Critical Terms for Religious Studies*, ed. Mark C. Taylor, 269–284. Chicago, University of Chicago Press.
Strathern, Marilyn. 1988. *The Gender of the Gift*. Berkeley: University of California Press.
Tawhai, Te Pakaka. 1988. 'Maori Religion'. In *The Study of Religion, Traditional and New Religion*, eds. Stewart Sutherland and Peter Clarke, 96–105. London: Routledge.
Vásquez, Manuel A. 2011. *More than Belief: A Materialist Theory of Religion*. Oxford: Oxford University Press.
———. 2012. 'On the Value of Genealogy, Materiality, and Networks: A Response'. *Religion* 42(4): 649–670.
Vilaça, Aparecida. 2005. 'Chronically Unstable Bodies: Reflections on Amazonian Corporalities'. *Journal of the Royal Anthropological Institute* 11: 445–464.
Whitehead, Amy. 2013. *Religious Statues and Personhood: Testing the Role of Materiality*. London: Bloomsbury.

7 Im/material objects

Relics, gestured signs and the substance of the immaterial

Timothy Carroll

During the course of ethnographic research, anthropologists are often met with phenomena that do not easily fit into categories with which they are already acquainted. In fact the process of critically engaged anthropological research is often characterised by a radical realignment of analytical classification; a thing that one might think is like another is in fact most like something with which it shares little apparent similarity. This process of honing one's understanding of cultural artefacts and indigenous ways of knowing is a critical, and often dialogical, aspect of research in the field. This chapter unpacks one such example of a material thing – in fact a thing that can hardly be said to 'exist' as a material at all – and, by comparing it to a class of things apparently distinct, demonstrates a much richer sense of how an indigenous community understands the world.

During the summers of 2011 and 2012 I conducted research in the Holy Great Monastery of Vatopedi, on Mt Athos, Greece. I was studying the devotional uses of fabric in Eastern Orthodox Christianity, and, while I had originally gained access to the monastery in order to study items in their extensive collections, a series of unfortunate events prohibited access to these collections. Instead I spent my days praying, working and speaking with the monks and pilgrims of the monastery. This simple method of participating alongside my informants opened up a wide range of insight into how Orthodox Christians understand and use different material objects in their daily devotion. Of particular relevance to this chapter, a considerable amount of my time was spent discussing and practising the veneration of holy relics.

Relics

Relics are usually spoken of as objects, solid, but old and fragile. For the most part these include bones of dead saints, and sometimes, such as with the chains of St Peter, metal or other enduring materials. Art historian Cynthia Hahn identifies a relic as 'a physical object that is understood to carry the *virtus* of a saint or Christ, literally the virtue but more accurately the power of the holy person' (2010: 290). Much academic discourse borrows a Roman Catholic classification of relics (Geisbusch 2008; Hooper 2014). This system makes a distinction between 'primary relics,' which are bodily remains of the holy person;

'secondary relics,' objects used by or touched by said person; and 'tertiary relics,' an object touched to one of the former, after the mortal repose of the saint. By the relics' 'contagious' (Hahn 2010) quality, the tertiary relic is said to gain that *virtus* from this contact. While these categories are helpful analytically, I have seen no evidence that Orthodox Christians classify types of relics in any sort of hierarchical order. For my informants a relic is a relic; people spoke of bones, wood and things blessed off of these items interchangeably as 'relics of Christ' or a given saint. However, the terms can be useful to designate the kind of object spoken of, and so I do, at times, employ these terms.

Within Eastern Orthodox Christian practice, it is not uncommon to have the bodies of the incorruptible saint, wherein through a sort of accidental (read: miraculous) mummification process, the body of the dead saint is found not to decay. It is with this sort of relic that I will start my argument, but I will then move to ephemeral objects, such as clothing, before moving to an object so insubstantial as hardly to constitute an object at all: a gesture. By looking at objects along a continuum of materiality, I extrapolate some of the technical qualities of relics that are easy to observe in material relics towards the immaterial. Once at that side of the continuum, I then interpolate qualities of the gestured sign back to bones, allowing each to inform the other.

The monastery of Vatopedi, on Mt Athos in northeast Greece, was founded in the tenth century by three aristocratic brothers and has enjoyed imperial benefaction throughout its history. In 1979 a new brotherhood moved into the monastery, and under the guidance of the new abbot there has been a steady plan of growth and development (for a fuller history see Carroll 2014). At the time fieldwork was conducted during the summers of 2011 and 2012, there were about 115 monks, and each day they welcome between 100 and 150 pilgrims. This number grows for great feasts, to between 500 and 600 guests. Around the walls of the monastery, spilling down to the small bay, is a 'fishing village' populated by men who, though not monastic, live there at least part-time, working for the monastery. All told, Vatopedi, set on the shores of a fertile valley against the Aegean, looks like a mediæval village teeming with between 200 and 700 men – they allow neither women nor children within the monastery grounds.

During the regular daily schedule, the monks of Vatopedi spend roughly eight hours in communal, liturgical prayer. Of this, pilgrims are welcomed to join in about six hours that take place in the main church, the katholikon, or one of several chapels. The remaining two hours are spent in communal recitation of the hesychastic prayer[1] said in the monastic quarters. Each morning, starting from 4:00 a.m., Orthros (Matins) and the Divine Liturgy are sung. On most evenings, from about 4:30 p.m., Vespers is sung, and then towards night Compline is sung. Fitted into this regime of prayer are times of eating, working and rest. Two meals are served each day, the first directly after the end of Liturgy, the second directly after Vespers. Following the morning meal, the monks and pilgrims head out to work at their various assigned duties. After the evening meal, again the monks and pilgrims join in work; this time, however, it is communal work – often preparing vegetables for the kitchens or other 'light' work.

In preparation for feasts, the evening services are replaced with a Vigil, which leads into Orthros. The lengths of these services vary with relation to the magnitude of the feast. For the feast of the Holy Cincture of Mary, for example, roughly seventeen hours of liturgical worship are conducted in preparation for the celebration of the feast.

It is not uncommon for these Vigils to correspond with feasts in honour of saints of whom the monastery has relics. On these occasions, a priest exits the Altar with the reliquary, blesses the congregation with it by making the sign of the cross over them with the box, and then places the box on a small table that is set up for it. With well over 200 relics in the monastery's holdings, the presentation of relics in this manner is quite regular. There are more days of the year for which there is a relic corresponding to a saint that is remembered that day than those for which there is not.

Take for example St John the Forerunner. The monastery holds part of one of his fingers, and for the feast of his beheading a small table was arranged just to the south of the ambon.[2] As Orthros proceeds, the priest exits from the Altar and lifts the reliquary that holds the finger towards the congregation. While the choir chants the troparia (sg. troparion, a short triumphant hymn) of the saint, the priest blesses the congregation, then turns and sets the relic on the small table. He then crosses himself, performs a prostration (bowing, on all fours, touching his forehead to the ground) before the relic, and then bends forward to kiss it. The brothers of the monastery follow suit, forming a queue according to their seniority within the brotherhood. Each comes forward, performs a prostration before the relic, rises and kisses it before moving on to venerate other ikons. On this occasion the abbot is also present for the feast, and they each go to venerate the abbot with a low bow, what is called a metanoia,[3] asking his blessing. He makes the sign of the cross over them with his right hand, and they kiss the hand – much as they just did to the relic of St John and the ikons of the saints arranged throughout the katholikon. After the most junior of the novices, the pilgrims join the queue and likewise prostrate before the relic, venerate the ikons and seek the blessing of the abbot.

Such is the start of a fairly typical day in Vatopedi. It is so usual to have relics that visitors begin to lose track of which mornings they have been present. Monks likewise are not always even certain who a relic is. There is a book, the *Synaxarion* ('bringing together'), that catalogues the saints according to the calendar, but many do not have the time to read it and so have to ask around in order to find out whom they are about to venerate. Pilgrims often have no idea. Sometimes they might be able to pick out the name from the troparia, but since these are sung in various periods of Ancient Greek, few could actually understand what is being said. Also, many names are common, like 'John,' and identifying *which* 'John' they are about to venerate may be impossible. The relative unknowing parallels the darkness within the katholikon, which, well before dawn, is lit by only a few candles.

Towards the end of the day, a second display of Holy Relics forms a very different encounter. Directly after the evening meal, when the monks go to communal work, while the sun is casting long shadows through the doors into the katholikon, a long table is set up across the front of the katholikon. On the table are arranged five relics of particular note: the Holy Cincture of the Mother of God; a piece of the Cross; the reed used by the centurion to give Christ vinegar; the head of St John Chrysostomos; and another head, usually that of St Evdokimos (a monk of Vatopedi), though sometimes another apropos to the feast is brought out instead. Spaced along the long table, these relics are made available to pilgrims. Dozens of pilgrims, broken into groups according to language, are led around the katholikon on tour by monks appointed the duty. In shifts they are brought to the relics, and the monk explains who each are for those who may not recognise them. Most push forward to kiss them; some do prostrations in front of each. Most men also pass handfuls of prayer ropes, crosses and other small trinkets to a guarding priest to have them blessed. Rubbing the handful of items over each relic, the priest blesses the trinkets, which in turn are taken home by the pilgrims as gifts, or to help heal loved ones who cannot come to the monastery themselves.

During one tour of the katholikon, a Catalonian father and son were also present. As nominal Catholics they understood generally the concept of relics, but the son expressed confusion as to how they worked. The monk guiding the tour explained that the human person is both body and soul, and one cannot be considered without the other. They work together, he said, and here he enmeshed his fingers trying to think of the right word. After flexing his interdigitated hands, he finally settled on the word 'synergy.' There is a synergy between the body and soul, he explained, and then glossed it as 'cooperation.' A man or woman leading a holy life, he continued, does something spiritual, but it cannot be spiritual alone. The body must also take part in the ascetic struggle, and so the body, too, becomes holy. Likened to the struggle of an athlete, such an ascetic struggle is routine and continuous. The godlike quality of saints makes their bodies holy *things* because the connection between the body and the soul works a lasting effect on the physical body, something which lasts even past death.

A 'thing,' as Tim Ingold points out, is 'a place where several goings on become entwined' (2010: 96), or as Heidegger argues, is 'a gathering specifically for the purpose of dealing with a case or matter' (1971: 173). In this light, the Orthodox relic can be seen as a place of coming-together, an aggregation of various qualities towards a specific purpose. As such the continual dedication to a holy way of life, coupled with a life of prayer, is seen to produce holy objects/things as a by-product of producing holy subjects.

In the examples of the two Sts John so far mentioned – St John the Forerunner's finger and St John Chrysostomos' head – two uses of relics can be seen. Presented in the context of the night Vigil, the Forerunner's finger served as a point of liturgical focus; set on the table in the evening light, Chrysostomos' head served as an aim of pilgrim's devotion. As bodies of saints, they copresence – that is allow 'the conditions in which human individuals interact with one another face to face from body to body' (Zhao 2003: 445) – the saints themselves. St John, as a living person, is present via his remains of his dead body; this copresence with the saint via the relic's *vitus* allows for the formation of intersubjective communication in a highly sensual context.

The anthropologist João de Pina-Cabral, discussing Lucien Lévy-Bruhl's term 'participation' as akin to 'copresence,' observes how this phenomenon may exist 'with other persons, with collectives, with supernatural forces, and even with material aspects of their world (things)' (2013: 266). Similarly, geographer and historian David Lowenthal points out that an object from the past as 'a tangible relic seems *ipso facto* real' (1985: 244), and as such allows 'participation,' becoming conduits of prayer and devotion in the expression of religious devotion and supplicatory appeal. The copresence of and with the saint spiritually through the materiality of the relic and the role of liturgical and supplicatory prayer requires an expanded view of the relic as a participant in the liturgy of Orthodox prayer.

Hahn points out that relics need an audience, saying that 'An audience is essential. Its attention authenticates the relic' (2010: 291). It is in the often highly curated space of devotion, that, Hahn argues, a saint's cult is able to authenticate the *virtus* of the saint (Hahn 1997). In Hahn's understanding there is a kind of mutual constitution between the relic as a holy and powerful object and the supplicants as devotees.

What is seen in the monk's account of relics is a different sort of mutual constitution. For the Orthodox Christian the validity of the relic rests in its *virtus* – its life – being able to bring together the saint and the supplicant. The relic joins with the people and the clergy into an intersubjective 'together with,' like Ingold's (2010) notion of being caught up together in action. So while, analytically, we could simply agree with Hahn, doing so does little to explain *what* the presence of an audience actually does for the relic and for the audience. It is in this notion of copresence, or 'together with,' that the answer can be found. The production of relics, and the effective use of relics, rests on an understanding of bodies and persons as being porous. I have written elsewhere (Carroll 2014) concerning this ethnographically; here I offer a shorter formulation, working from the writings of Clement of Alexandria (c. 150–215 CE). A similar description of Orthodox understanding of persons could be gained from any number of sources; I choose Clement as I think his writing is particularly clear.

The soul, the body and external things

Among Clement's writings, there stand three works of instruction for the beginner, intermediate and advanced Christian. The first, a very direct work of practical theology, is called *The Instructor*. Clement uses Christ's instruction in Luke 12 to devise a tripartite classification for what relates to the person. He argues that 'The Lord Himself [divided] His precepts into what relates to the body, the soul, and thirdly, external things' (Clement of Alexandria 2004: 263). Much of Clement's teaching proceeds from this, focusing on the relationship between the soul, the body and external things. In so doing, Clement's category of 'external things' is seen to include things distant (e.g. household furniture) and close (e.g. unctions and ointments). Throughout *The Instructor* several qualities come to the fore. In discussing effeminate men, who like fine clothes, for instance, and put flowers in their hair, Clement sees direct correlation between the exterior of the person and his or her soul (Clement of Alexandria 2004: 255). The parallelism understood to lie between the exteriority and interiority in relation to the true quality of the person stands in contrast to many contemporary notions of fashion and identity; the typical stance in western societies places the weight of identity in the interior, typified by expressions such as 'it's what's on the inside that counts.'

Siting the true locus of being in the interiority is something Daniel Miller, in his work on Trinidadian persons, terms a 'depth-ontology' (1994). He contrasts this interior essence of being with what he argues is true for Trinidadians, for whom the surface is the true site of the self – what he terms a 'surface-ontology.' For them, what lies beneath is simply shadows: not to be considered in social praxis (1994).

What emerges in Clement's writings and in wider Orthodox social practice today fits neither framework. Rather, Clement offers what might be called a 'depth-to-surface ontology,' wherein the diseased state of the soul is manifested in practices such as manscaping, perfumery and dainty dress. What is true about the essence of the self is in the interior, and seen in the exterior. Clement gives a number of other exteriorising causalities, such as the modesty of speech, manner of eating at a banquet, the governance of belching and other bodily perfusions, and the mien and comport of individuals, which are all direct denotation of the modesty and harmony resident or absent in the soul. But these relationships of similitude from depth to surface also run causally from surface to depth.

In his teaching on ointments, for example, Clement warns that 'The use of crowns [of flowers] and ointments is not necessary for us; for it impels to pleasures and indulgences, especially on the approach of night'; and argues that such smooth oil 'is calculated to render noble manners effeminate' (2004: 253, 255). In this view, the human is something of a porous vessel, and as such certain things external may cause harm to the interior. Unsuitable external things, being applied to the body, create a disharmony in the person, and so Clement urges his reader to use external things as befits the person. Clement asserts that unguents are not to be completely done without, and the surface-to-depth ontology can be seen in the benefits of ointments, too. He recognises the medicinal qualities of ointments that 'help in order to bring up the strength' (2004: 255). These material resources, when applied rightly, are good and helpful to the health of the body. And while not an end in itself, Clement does link the health of the body with the well-being of the soul. On one hand the interior quality of the soul shows forth through the body into the external things. On the other, external things have an effect on the soul through the manipulation, either beneficial or harmful, of the body. As such, soul, body and external things have a double-reciprocal relationship whereby each is bound to and affected by the other two.

With such an understanding, the monk's explanation makes more sense. The synergy, or coaction, of soul and body means that even as the soul becomes holy – and the saint glorified – so too does the body become holy. The quality of the immaterial soul is the same quality of the material body.

Materials of holiness

In this way the synergistic coaction of the material and immaterial connects the two extremes as continuations of each other. In fact, the coaction of material is not limited to the physical body. The first three relics on the table, as described earlier, are composed of non-human biomatter. Two are associated with the crucifixion of Christ; the other is a camel hair belt, which is understood to have been woven and worn by his mother throughout her life. As such, it was in cooperation with the Mother of God until her death and her subsequent translation into heaven. As she was taken up, Mary is said to have given St Thomas her belt. This camel hair belt is interpreted to be something that would have been given to her husband at the consummation of their marriage. This never happened, and instead it was given to the Church. As a great relic, this belt is brought out each evening for the veneration of the pilgrims, and bolts of ribbon are blessed over the relic in order to produce items that, once given to the faithful, they may take home with them on their return.

These ribbons, which following the classification scheme outlined earlier can be called tertiary relics, are sought in order to secure various miracles. Through these ribbons, I was told, the Panagia Theotokos has healed numerous cases of cancer, brought children to countless barren women and protected individuals from harm. One, I was told by a senior hieromonk, was in the breast pocket of a police officer, and had stopped a bullet to the heart.

In the same way that the finger of St John the Forerunner is sufficient to impart presence to the entirety of St John, the tertiary relic of blessed cotton ribbon is spoken of as the belt. It takes on a sort of holographic relationship, such that the whole is present in each part. The ribbon is a relic of the relic, but in no way is that considered to diminish the potential wonder-working capacity – as Victor Buchli (2010) points out in his work on prototypicality in the context of early Christian use of ikons, the distinction between original and copy is hard to make, and as such, one may venerate the cotton ribbon as one would the camel hair original. The ephemerality of such objects does not inhibit the affective power; rather the flexible, soft, manipulability of the fabric heightens the effectiveness. Whereas solid relics require boxes or wall mountings, fabric can be wound, tied or folded around a body or into a pocket. Thus the indexical qualities of the material foster a more overt synergistic coaction of the small, mutable relic with the body.

We have already mentioned the synergy of body and soul towards the production of relics. Now two other synergistic relations have subsequently emerged. The first is that of external things produced as relics. The Holy Cincture, for example, is a relic of the Virgin Mary because, though she is understood to have died, no body remained on earth, as she was raised on the third day. Her items of clothing, however, she gave to the Church. These are holy through their association to her holy life. To put it another way, in Orthodox Christianity, things (as places of goings-on), as well as people, may become holy, if the social life of those things is a holy one. The next synergistic relation flows from this. Through cooperation in the Virgin's ascetic struggle, the belt was made holy. And while the Panagia was materially removed from the world in her person, her belt (as well as her tunic) remained. These, being given to the Church, are used within the liturgical and pilgrimatic ascesis of Orthodox faithful. By aligning the flow (in Ingold's use) of the body and soul to the Holy Cincture, a synergetic cooperation is understood to function between the sacred materiality of the Virgin's belt and the aspiring (im)materiality of the penitent's soul and body.

The affective cooperation of things and the coactive affect of holy things towards Orthodox persons in their effort to be holy are something I have come to think of in terms of holy contagion. Earlier I described how pilgrims pass mundane trinkets to the priest to render them holy objects, through touching and tracing the sign of the cross over something that is sacred. Likewise, ikons can be blessed by turning them face to face with older ones and making the sign of the cross – something pilgrims do regularly over the many miracle-working ikons in Vatopedi. In this way the contagious qualities of the sacred contaminate the mundane and make it likewise something that can bestow blessedness.

Jan Geisbusch, in his discussion of Roman Catholic relics, makes space for a fourth category of relics – 'the paraphernalia of Catholic devotionalism such as images, prayer cards, statues, books, or rosaries' (2008: 60). In an Orthodox setting these are much more appropriately called *eulogia* or 'blessings.' *Eulogia* are regularly given and come in a multitude of forms, though they are usually consumable (e.g. bread blessed at the altar) or a trinket (e.g. a vial of oil, or a paper ikon given to a traveller). Giving an *eulogia* – that is giving a blessing – imparts grace upon the recipient. By using the idiom of contagion in order to understand this kind of transaction, I bring to mind something which cannot be seen with the naked eye, but nonetheless is still something. If a person is contagious, it is not always through a material embrace that a disease passes from one to another; it can pass through the air – particle moisture is sufficient to carry microbials. These we know about, however, by the ocular magic of microscopes. From the perspective of the naked eye, contagion moves from substance to substance through insubstantial mediation. In the same way that the soul, the body and external things enjoy a permeability through which each may affect the other, substances of blessing may confer blessing from a distance. The priest, before placing St John's finger on the table, holds it aloft and blesses the congregation, making the sign of the cross over them.

As such, the affective cooperation of and coactive production of holy things in relation to Orthodox persons is markedly similar to Ingold's idea of the textility of making, the joining in of what he calls the flow in the making of art. He says,

> A work of art, I insist, is not an object but a thing and, as [Paul] Klee argued, the role of the artist – as that of any skilled practitioner – is not to give effect to a preconceived idea, novel or not, but to join with and follow the forces and flows of material that bring the form of the work into being.
> (2010: 97)

It is this, being 'swept up in the generative currents of the world', which Ingold identifies as the productive mechanism of making art (2010: 95). Ingold's main point, that artefacts are things with their own generative flow, is helpful in considering the productive cooperation of Orthodox relics and people. However, there is one significant departure and one curious alteration presented by the ethnography of relics detailed earlier.

The first is the issue that Orthodox people do hold something of a preconceived idea in their mind when engaging with relics. For some it is very clear: one man passed a white onesie to the priest to have it blessed over the relics; he took it home to heal his sick daughter. For some it is slightly less clear, but still a preconceived idea: one young man came regularly to the Holy Mountain, to visit the monks and pray before the miracle-working ikons and relics. He told me he was doing so to be close to the Theotokos and learn how to be holy – something he expressed as 'becoming Orthodox' and 'becoming human.' While this may not be the preconceived design model Ingold (2010: 92) tries to dismiss, it is nonetheless purposeful, and modelled after specific ends in mind.

The other aspect to each of these accounts outlined so far is that the end result is not the production of the thing – in this case the relic – but the production of the people. In the passing of the white onesie, the man passes an object and asks the priest to make it an index of the relic. The priest blesses it over each relic, making the cotton clothing item an index of the sacred (a tertiary relic), and a conduit of the blessing to be conferred onto the man's daughter. For the young man, and many like him, who came to the mountain to venerate the holy ikons and relics, to visit a renowned spiritual father or to learn how to pray, the various techniques of joining into the generative flow of Mt Athos and the sacred objects therein contained were an explicit making (becoming) of the self as Orthodox and human. This iterative transformation of the self is most visible in those who come as pilgrims and stay as monks, as their whole way of life is crafted into the production of themselves as saints. But the same modes of life (characterised by humility, repentance, self-denial) can be seen in others, too. The practice of joining the productive flow of material in order to produce the self raises the issue of human materiality. The Orthodox person is seen to be an ikon of God (a relation taken to be innate of all human beings) and of Christ (a relation cultivated through ritual practice, particularly baptism). Here, in the monk's explication of how relics come into being, it can be seen that the art-like formation of the human subject (Ugolnik 1989: 188) in the likeness of Christ works on the premise of inter-permeability of people and things – the coaction of soul, body and external things – along lines of flow.

Thinking through the tripartite distinction from Clement's writing to the novice Christian, and thinking through the celebration and use of relics in Vatopedi, it can be seen that the material ecology of the person (body and external thing) is inalienably linked with the immaterial ecology of the person (soul, spirit and, I would add, mind). The dividing line, however, between im/materiality is difficult to identify. This next section addresses one final relic, the sign of the cross, in order to trouble this distinction further. The distinction may, in fact, not exist; im/materiality is, then, best understood as a continuum.

The sign of the cross

In the same way that the soul, the body and external things enjoy an inter-permeability through which each may affect the other, substances of blessing may confer blessing from a distance. As mentioned earlier, the priest, before placing the relic on the small table for veneration, holds it aloft and blesses the congregation using the reliquary to make the sign of the cross over the people.

At the far end of the spectrum, now, is the sign of the cross. Already in this chapter I have mentioned this to be made with relics over people, with trinkets over relics, with ikons over ikons, with the abbot's hand over those greeting him. Within the compound of Vatopedi the sign of the cross is made in more ways than I can enumerate here. The sign of the cross is a thing that is deployed everywhere at Vatopedi – upon entering, upon leaving, if something is broken, if something is working, when one yawns, when one goes to sleep, when one wakes, when one eats. There are different ways to hold the fingers of the hands depending on if the person is episcopal, clerical or lay, but all Orthodox Christians are expected to make the sign of the cross over themselves as well as any number of other people and things.

Analytically, I would not be inclined to speak of the sign of the cross in a chapter on relics. Earlier I mentioned a piece of the Sacred Cross – this certainly is a relic, but I was assured by informants that the sign of the cross, too, is a relic and must be thought of as one. The gestured motion, with the first three fingers pinched together, and the last two flush against the pad of one's palm, makes a relic. It is not that the layperson's hand is a relic. A bishop's or priest's hand may be considered a relic, as it is the material remains of the incarnational act of consecrating the Eucharist. But this is not true of the layperson's hand, although this hand, tracing in the air an entirely insubstantial gesture, makes a relic. By participating in the formal quality of the crucified Christ, the gestured cross is understood to make presence and endow the blessing of the crucifixion within the situation. As in the production of other *eulogia*, the contagion with the holy object produces something that can be taken away with the pilgrim.

Here, however, it is apparently an immaterial object and the *eulogia* is likewise immaterial.

Having worked as a tailor before returning to academia, I received a blessing (given with the sign of the cross) from the abbot to work with the tailors while at Vatopedi. The Romanian monk under whose guidance I was to work showed me the various machines and their temperaments. Pulling up the chair, he gathered his skirts and sat down, flicked on the power switch, and then with his right hand he made a small cross over the space of the sewing needle. Throughout the weeks working alongside him, this was routine. Each time he or the other tailors sat down at a sewing machine, or turned on the iron, a sign of the cross was made over the mechanism. Each time a bobbin needed re-threading, the sign of the cross. These were not large motions, no attention was drawn to the making of such a sign, but as routine as turning on the power, so was the making of the sign of the cross.

In this gesture we have a case of what appears to be an entirely immaterial relic. While fragile materials may last only a short time, the gestured thing is fleeting. It is not just ephemeral; it is fugacious, gone even as it is made. It is even less durable than fabric and ribbon relics; as such it is also even more deployable. It may be used everywhere to bless everything. With normal relics, it is the very material of the saint through which the contact is made. With the sign of the cross, the representational form is enough to make the same contact through which grace is conferred. In both cases, and indeed also with ikons, the coaction of grace, efficacious towards the holiness of the supplicant, is because of 'the truth of the person', revealed through personal relationship (Yannaras 1975), present in the relic.

It is tempting to say that the gestured object – not the embodied gesture but that thing produced out of the gesture – is immaterial, and simply leave it at that. The idea of an immaterial object, however, troubles some analytical gazing pools. Earlier I suggested that the saint's holy life renders his or her body a 'thing' which is produced by a subject, a bundle of 'goings-on' in Ingold's sense. But it is also 'real' following Alfred Gell's use of 'object' and 'objectification' (1998: 13). Gell, in his use of 'objectification', identifies it as a process of 'externalizing' the mind, emotion or social relations in an index (1998: 236, 31, 62). Contrast this to Foucault, whose use of 'objectification' is predicated on the making of distinction – between the self and others, within the self and between others (1982). Whereas Gell's use is concerned with the concretisation of abstract or immaterial things into objects (or, better, indices), Foucault's use concerns the making of objects – out of anything. Within the process of making a distinction is the making of an object and a subject. People, for Foucault (1977; 1982), are objects of other people's (and their own) subjectivity. For purposes here, Gellian objectification will be followed, calling it the concretisation of the prototypic relations into the art index; however, as the index is the body of the saint, it is fruitfully compared to Foucault's objectification of the self (Foucault 1988). The critical difference, however, between a Gellian and Foucauldian stance regarding the objectification of the self-as-relic is that Foucault's subjects are such because of self-division, not because of achievement (Warnier 2007: 23). In the Orthodox context, there is a strong emphasis on achievement – more aptly called 'becoming.'

As such, the Gellian process of intentional externalisation of the mind into something physical bears a certain marked resemblance to Orthodox usage of the sign of the cross – save that there is no physical substance to it. Yet throughout my research I saw evidence to suggest it must be considered as a material object and indication from interviewees that they thought of it as somehow material, too. People described it as something *made*, *given* and *received*; it comes with a blessing that is always worth *having*, and is something *sought* and *gained*. This expanded materiality allows us to consider bone, cloth and the unseen fugacious simulacra of gestured prayer all within the same panorama of material substances. And while on one hand it expands material out to the insubstantial, it also suggests that our current understanding of materiality, in its hard durable substantial form, is likewise only half the picture. In the space between spiritual religion and material religion, there may need to be made room for continua of immaterial substances and insubstantial materials.

In examining the fugacious material at this far end of the spectrum, it can be seen, as mentioned earlier, that *eulogia* is understood to be imparted to the Orthodox Christian even in settings where there is no *physical* object being conveyed. Taking this distilled quality back into the context of the relics of bone and wood and the blessings gained from them, there is the certain implication that *eulogia* such as bread may be best understood as primarily an insubstantial material. While these objects are 'real' and 'physical' in Gell's sense, they are also 'things' in Ingold's sense: sites of 'goings-on.' Such material seems to have immaterial qualities that must be examined in order to understand the social uses of these object/things.

The argument here is that the affective qualities of material properties within things, as sites of 'goings-on,' offer an analytic model to understand the formation and coactive abilities of such sacred objects. As I argue elsewhere (Carroll 2014), the materiality of fabric facilitates the production of sacred space. Fabric is a pliable material that can fold and open, hide and reveal – even at the same time; it can take on colour and odour, can flutter and – if in the right material and the right light – shimmer. All of these qualities are highlighted by informants as they seek language to describe the action they perceive the fabric to facilitate. The sign of the cross (as a thing) has fewer constraints, and is thus even more versatile.

In many studies within material culture that touch on religious subjects, the investigation is one of how the material engages the mind and body towards the creation or negotiation of imagined worlds and religious cosmologies. What I would like to do now is turn that question back on the material. That is to say, what happens to the material when it is engaged with the mind in the creation of such imagined worlds?

Discussion

Working from accounts like that mentioned earlier about Mary's Cincture, Orthodox Christianity has, over the centuries, come to understand a succession of productive images of Mary's closeness to the Church, her chastity, monastic virginity, betrothal and marriage, childbirth, the giving of wanted growth, and ending of unwanted growth, the healing of cancer. In Mary's translation into heaven, her belt took on an affective quality linked to her and all with which she is associated. The Holy Cincture is a material thing linked, by its folk narrative and the indexical qualities of its material, to the body and spirit of the Virgin Mary. As such, it carries the coactive subjectivities of Mary in the material indexicalities of fabric.

Relics, such as the finger of St John and the belt of Mary, have, then, the *virtus* of the saint because of their association with that saint. But what that *virtus* is and how the *virtus* may be enacted rely to a great degree on the material qualities of that relic. In some cases, such as with skulls and fingers, the relational link between the subject and the object is quite clear, and the Orthodox understanding of the synergistic coaction of body and soul allows for the body to become a thing of great potency and a site of intersubjectivity. For other objects, such as the belt, the sensuous proximity of the item to the body of the saint does similarly.

The thing-like qualities of these objects – that is understanding the material objects as places of goings-on with a purpose, and understanding those goings-on and purposes – become clearer when looking at the increasingly non-material relics. For the tertiary relics, such as the ribbon blessed over the belt, the flexibility of the cotton threads to wrap and coil about anyone or within anything enables Orthodox Christians to have, as it were, Mary (via her *virtus*) in their pocket protecting them. At times this protection may be counted through her blessing – in the begetting of children, for example. But, as mentioned earlier in the account of the police officer, her protection may also be experienced clearly through the material presence of the relic.

Conclusion

Thinking about the impact on the material within the production of religious subjects allows us to consider objects as diverse as skulls, belts, ikons and gestured signs as things, each of the same class. These are things produced in inalienable relation to specific saints such that even when *which* John is not known, he can nonetheless be participated with through the copresencing of his self within his remains. The porosity of persons, such that souls, bodies and external things all are part of the true self, renders objects – because of their thingness – subjects.

Acknowledgements

I want to thank the Abbot Geronda Ephraim for granting me access to live and conduct research at Vatopedi, and the monks for making research truly pleasurable. I also thank Alex Pillen and Alexandra Antohin for their helpful comments and critiques on this chapter. Funding for the research on Mt Athos was provided by the Pasold Fund and the Paleologos Graduate Scholarship. All errors are my own.

Notes

1 'Lord Jesus Christ Son of God, have mercy upon me.'
2 The ambon is front and centre within the temple from where the priest addresses the congregation.
3 Pronounced me-**ta**-nʲa, meaning 'to turn' or 'to repent.'

Works cited

Buchli, Victor. 2010. 'The Prototype: Presencing the Immaterial'. *Visual Communication* 9(3): 273–286.
Carroll, Timothy. 2014. *Becoming Orthodox: Of People and Things in the Making of Religious Subjects*. Unpublished doctoral thesis, University College London.
Clement of Alexandria. 2004 [1885]. 'The Instructor'. In *Ante-Nicene Fathers, Vol 2*, trans. Philip Schaff, 207–299. Grand Rapids, MI: Christian Classics Ethereal Library.
Foucault, Michel. 1977. *Discipline and Punish: The Birth of the Prison*. New York: Vintage Books.
———. 1982. 'The Subject and Power'. *Critical Inquiry* 8(4): 777–795.
———. 1988. 'Technologies of the Self'. In *Technologies of the Self: A Seminar with Michel Foucault*, eds. Luther H. Martin, Huck Gutman and Patrick Hutton, 16–49. London: Tavistock.
Geisbusch, Jan. 2008. *Awkward Objects: Relics, the Making of Religious Meaning, and the Limits of Control in the Information Age*. Unpublished doctoral thesis, University College London.
Gell, Alfred. 1998. *Art and Agency: An Anthropological Theory*. Oxford: Clarendon Press.
Hahn, Cynthia. 1997. 'Seeing and Believing: The Construction of Sanctity in Early-Medieval Saints' Shrines'. *Speculum* 72(4): 1079–1106.
———. 2010. 'What Do Reliquaries Do for Relics?' *Numen* 57(3–4): 284–316.
Heidegger, Martin. 1971. 'The Thing'. In *Poetry, Language, Thought*, trans. Albert Hofstader, 163–180. New York: Harper and Row.
Hooper, Steven. 2014. 'A Cross-Cultural Theory of Relics: On Understanding Religion, Bodies, Artefacts, Images and Art'. *World Art* 4(2): 175–207.
Ingold, Tim. 2010. 'The Textility of Making'. *Cambridge Journal of Economics* 34(1): 91–102.
Lowenthal, David. 1985. *The Past Is a Foreign Country*. Cambridge: Cambridge University Press.
Miller, Daniel. 1994. 'Style and Ontology'. In *Consumption and Identity*, ed. Jonathan Friedman, 71–96. Chur, Switzerland: Harwood Academic. [Original publication lists author as 'David'].
Pina-Cabral, João. 2013. 'The Two Faces of Mutuality: Contemporary Themes in Anthropology'. *Anthropological Quarterly* 86(1): 257–275.
Ugolnik, Anthony. 1989. *The Illuminating Icon*. Grand Rapids: William B. Eerdmans.
Warnier, Jean-Pierre. 2007. *The Pot-King*. Leiden: Brill.
Yannaras, Christos. 1975. 'The Distinction between Essence and Energies and Its Importance for Theology'. *St. Vladimir's Theological Quarterly* 19(4): 232–245.
Zhao, Shanyang. 2003. 'Toward a Taxonomy of Copresence'. *Presence* 12(5): 445–455.

8 'An altar inside a circle'

A relational model for investigating green Christians' experiments with sacred space

Maria Nita

Introduction

How do participants in ecological rituals engage with and relate to place? How do they draw on their respective religious traditions and existing green practices in their perceptions of sacred space and ritual place? How do religious and non-religious green activists relate to the planet, given its prominence as a central symbol in climate change discourse? The present chapter aims to address these three questions by taking a relational approach to the understanding of ritual place or by applying a relational model of sacred space to my own empirical findings from a research project examining the involvement of Christian networks in the climate movement in Britain (2008–2012). I will attempt to show that ritual or sacred space both reflects and affects participants' relational identities, which can be challenged, disassembled and redefined by their engagement with place and materials.

Climate activists based in the UK are involved in a great diversity of networks, both local and global. Climate days of action are often synchronous in many countries around the world and presented on the Internet as a global event. The scope of the movement is global, since climate change is a global issue. The specific focus on the Earth's globe during marches and protest events reflects a new concern with the fate of the planet and a realisation that conservation of a locality is no longer possible in the light of a global climate system. To understand this shift, a contrast can be made between the road protests of the 1990s and recent climate campaigns, focused broadly on legislation concerned with the sourcing of fossil fuels, carbon trading and air travel. Protests in the 1990s were led by eco-Pagans – for example the protests on Solsbury Hill (1994 and 1996) – and were often preoccupied with preserving and protecting land and localities that were considered sacred, often by reclaiming an animist and indigenous understanding of nature (see Letcher 2003: 73). Climate protests on the other hand place at the forefront of their campaigns the destruction of the planet as a whole, through such imagery as the rising sea levels, the sick and feverish planet affected by raising temperatures or the destruction of the Amazon, often represented as the decimated lungs of the planet.

The emphasis on the planet, as one entity, in the broader green movement is certainly not new since the early images of the Earth photographed from space in the late 1960s represented important sparks in the emergence of the environmental movement. Andy Letcher (2003) persuasively shows in his '"Gaia Told

Me to Do It": Resistance and the Idea of Nature within Contemporary British Eco-Paganism' that environmental protestors in these earlier anti-road protest movements were engaging with many different and developing ideas of nature, from conceptualising nature as ancient, forgotten, premodern, separate and distinct from humans, all the way to the more unified concept of Gaia (Lovelock 1972), of nature as *one* self-regulating organism which includes humans (69). Yet, while activists in earlier protest movements seemed to more readily invoke elements of *topophilia*, love and attachment for a particular place (Yi-Fu Tuan, 1974), climate activists appear to be far more oriented towards the planet as a whole, which is also reflected in their increased mobility and global political interests, travelling to Paris or Copenhagen to take place in global protest activities for example.

At the time of my research the Christian activists in my study were situated at a confluence of many conflicting discourses about nature and the planet, the most significant of these being the anthropocentric versus biocentric positions derived from their Christian tradition on one hand and that of the green movement on the other. While for many Christians the biblical stewardship model, by which humans were made stewards of the Earth, still represented the main or rather the official platform for their environmentalism, the darker shades of green Christian networks in my study critiqued this model by breaking it down and asking during workshops and in interviews, 'Where was Man when God created the Earth?', thus reclaiming a hegemony and sovereignty on behalf of the planet in its relation to humans. This critique was not always spelled out but sometimes tacitly implied by the material organisation of place. As I will show here, rituals and performances have the role of reorienting space, asking participants to perceive our planet and its inhabitants from a different perspective while often critiquing the anthropocentric position, which is seen as the root of the ecological crisis.

Sacred space is often understood by scholars to have a role in reinforcing and transmitting collective beliefs, values and identity (Smith 1982; Hervieu-Léger 2000; Knott 2005). I will enquire here into what happens in the case of syncretic encounters between people or values that have not yet been amalgamated or integrated into a coherent whole or where ideological divisions and tensions persist, such as is the case with the Christian networks in my research (see Nita 2014). One way of addressing this question is to look at ways in which new syncretic values and beliefs translate into place-making practices. I will specifically discuss how the Christian activists in my study engaged with sacred space in the context of the climate movement as a way of representing their Christian identity while experimenting with new models of organisation.

In the first part of this essay I will examine some key theoretical positions regarding 'sacred space' and enquire into the role sacred space plays in ritual encounters by discussing two important green rituals: the Council of All Beings and the Cosmic Walk. These rituals are performed in a variety of contexts and have been adopted and adapted by some of the green Christians in my research. In the second part of this chapter I will draw on my own empirical research at a climate camp (2008) and Christian eco-retreats (2009 and 2012) to discuss how activist groups construct different places for ritual and worship, outside their traditional settings or churches. I will end this chapter with an examination of how green Christians and climate activists relate to the planet through ritual, drawing out the role of the material objects used in the construction and performance of sacred space.

A relational model for sacred space: ritual, relationships and identity

The construction or organisation of space, regardless of whether it is considered 'sacred', is a social and political process that reflects human and non-human relationships. The story behind place is dependent on the collective meaning making of the people who build it. In his seminal essay 'Language and the Making of Place: A Narrative-Descriptive Approach', the cultural geographer Yi-Fu Tuan reminds his readers that a constructed material place, be it architecture, landscape art or a garden, tells a story about the people who created it through its very shapes, structures and colours: 'it is not possible to understand or explain the physical motions that produce place without overhearing [...] the speech – the exchange of words – that lie behind them' (Tuan 1991: 684–685).

The actor-network theorist Bruno Latour also emphasises the ecology of social relationships that take place in the construction of space/place. It is impossible, Latour argues, to understand any scientific discovery, either theoretical or technical, without imagining the thousands of people and materials that have made it possible (Latour 1987). By looking at how space is constructed and organised we are promised a better understanding of the human and non-human actors who took part in its construction, as well as their social and political relationships.

Sacred spaces often communicate collective values and beliefs through their architecture (see Holm and Bowker 1994). By providing a sense of communal or collective identity the sacred space becomes a safe space. Thus for a Christian community, the traditional architecture of a church may be understood to provide a harmonious space belonging to a shared cultural, historical and aesthetic outlook. An enclosed place can provide a space of congruence for language/meaning, ritual and participants. A church for example is not just a building but a constructed place that reflects and re-enforces a particular cosmology and collective coordinates for meaning making and where participants' personal and social values are in harmony with each other. Relatively little effort or anxiety is required in such a place to interpret reality in terms of collective meaning.

Sacred space is a place where the relationships between participants are performed, reinforced or even changed through ritual. Numerous interpretations of the ritual process point to 'a recovered unity' (Turner 1969: 93), 'a [re]incorporation' (van Gennep 1960: 191) or 'an assemblage' (Durkheim 1995 [1915]: 465). Recent approaches to ritual and entrainment (Grimes 2003, 2005) suggest that ritual provides the opportunity to stop as an individual and begin again or synchronise together. The organisation of sacred space is crucial to creating

136 *Maria Nita*

and reflecting a new order, allowing participants to leave the space with newly acquired identities (see also Nita, 2016: 65–95).

The present chapter investigates how sacred space comes to reflect a new, desired order and what role it plays in creating new relationships and new collective identities. I will first look at how green activists seek to create new relationships between humans and non-humans by constructing new types of sacred spaces.

Novel ways of organising space: the circle and the spiral in green rituals

To understand how these new models of sacred space can deconstruct and reconstruct relationships and modes of relating, it is important to first look at two key ecological rituals – namely the Council of All Beings and the Cosmic Walk ritual. Both rituals were created around 1980 and have since been adopted by ritualists across the world (see Edwards, 1999; Barlow 2005), partly because of Joanna Macy's missionary activities in green networks, as a key protagonist in their creation and propagation (Macy 2005). Both rituals focus on the planet, attempting to unite or relate participants to a planetary community and to reassemble participants and the planet as one.

The rituals themselves have a unique status insofar as their performance is often regarded with a solemnity that is somewhat unusual in the more countercultural, irreverent and playful ethos of the green movement. I attempted to conduct research via participant observation at one Council of All Beings ritual but this was refused by the gatekeepers of the group, who told me that members would not want to be observed while taking part in the ritual. Since the ritual aims to allow a change of perspective from human to non-human, the presence of a human observer might indeed disrupt its purpose.

The Cosmic Walk ritual was inspired by Thomas Berry and Brian Swimme's *Universe Story: From the Primordial Flaring Forth to the Ecozoic Era – A Celebration of the Unfolding of the Cosmos* (Swimme and Berry 1992). Berry understood the evolution of the universe and the Earth as an epic story, 'the greatest story ever told'. The Cosmic Walk attempts to tell this great story through a symbolic walk that represents the evolution of the universe and our planet. Participants re-enact this journey by walking a marked spiral and pausing at important milestones in the development of the universe. The ritual is enacted both indoors and outdoors, while the spiral can be marked by white stones or candles, drawn with chalk or marked with rope. The spiral represents a timeline of the evolution of the universe, beginning in the centre with the 'great emergence' and continuing all the way to the present moment.

The focus of this ritual is, however, not so much the universe, symbolically placed at the centre of the spiral, but the Earth. A narrator reads the story of this evolution of the universe, which is accompanied by meditative music and poetic metaphors that focus the attention of the participants: 'Step 14 – 330 million years ago insects take to the air. The Earth learns to fly', or 'Step

29 – 30 years ago the Earth is seen as whole from space. The Earth becomes complex enough to witness its own integral beauty' (Edwards 1999: 15). As participants complete the walk slowly and contemplatively, they pause and reflect on some final significant landmarks in the Earth's personal story, such as the publication of Rachel Carson's *Silent Spring* in 1962 or the first Moon landing in 1969. When the walkers reach the end of the walk, on the outer edge of the spiral, the narrator ends by saying, 'This flaring forth continues as this moment, with us, as one' (Edwards 1999: 15). This merger between the two stories both extends the individual's identity to incorporate the collective story and makes the story of the Earth personal to the individual.

Like the Cosmic Walk, the Council of All Beings also extends the participants' identity, this time to the non-human world, while making ecological concerns personal to the individual participants, by asking them to give voice to the plight of the non-humans. Joanna Macy (2005: 425) describes the Council of All Beings as having three consecutive stages: 'The Mourning', 'the Remembering' and 'Speaking for Other Life Forms'. Following the first stage, where participants lament the abuse and mistreatment of the non-humans, 'the Remembering' is in essence a version of 'the Cosmic Walk', which helps participants 'remember the last four and a half billion years' (Macy 2005, 427). Finally during the last stage participants, wearing animal masks they have made themselves and thus taking on their non-human identity, speak for 'the other life forms', decrying the 'changes and hardships they are experiencing in these present times':

> The shells of my eggs are so thin and brittle now, they break before my young are ready to hatch. . . . I am crowded in a dark place, far from grass and standing in my own shit. My calves are taken from me, and instead cold machines are clamped to my teats. I call and call for my young. Where did they go? What happened to them?
>
> (Macy 2005: 427)

Since this is a Council of All Beings, humans must be present, and so participants take turns to sit, in silence, in the middle of the circle, remove their masks and represent humanity. Yet this movement to the inside of the circle does not provide participants an opportunity to experiment with a dual identity because they never give voice to the human being. This is in fact an opportunity to relinquish their human identity; hence at the end of the ritual, Macy writes, participants, now fully transformed, put on 'human masks' 'as we re-enter the world of the two-legged' (Macy 2005: 428).

An important feature of these two rituals is the way space itself is organised. In the Cosmic Walk, the participants walk contemplatively in a spiral, reaching their destination or receiving their initiation on the outer edge of the spiral. Although the story of the universe appears to be the focus of this ritual, since the centre of this space is marked by 'the great emergence', the story of the universe is just a grand canvas for observing the beauty and uniqueness of the

Earth. Thus the spatial model of the Cosmic Walk privileges the outer edge of the ritual space and not the centre, which is an important reversal if we consider the significance of the centre in traditional ritual practices and organisation of sacred space, captured by Mircea Eliade's concept of the *axis mundi* and his discussion of the relevance of the centre in the construction of sacred space (Eliade 1963: 42–65).

The Council of All Beings similarly privileges the edges or margins of ritual space and changes the polarity of the centre from a celebratory place to one of lamentation and disempowerment. Thus both these rituals use the spiral and circle to invite an equal distribution of power, constructing an arrangement in which no one place is more powerful or more privileged. In the Council of All Beings the place in the centre where 'the human' stands at the end of the ritual is not a place of power but the exact opposite, a place where the human participant is stripped of his or her power and isolated. This particular performance inside this sacred space is a critique of anthropocentrism and we can talk here of a physical, material deconstruction of the anthropocentric position: 'the human in the centre' is silenced and surrounded by animal masks that are given voice by the other participants.

I will now turn to how the Christian activists in my study made use of ritual space to perform their hyphenated identities, as green Christians or eco-Christians.

Christian climate activists and the climate community

The climate camp movement and the transition towns movement both started in 2005 in Britain, and both are still very much influencing the green activist networks there today. The two movements intersect in their aims and values but are centred on protest and community building respectively. Transition towns focus on adapting green community ideas to the realities of urban living, while the climate camp – my focus in this section of the chapter – advocates or models a rural community. Christian activists in both movements experiment with novel ways of engagement with space which differ from traditional Christian settings.

Green Christian activism is an important fringe movement that demands scholarly attention, because it represents the syncretic encounter between two opposing ideologies: anthropocentrism and biocentrism. Lynn White (1967) famously placed the blame for the ecological crisis on the Judeo-Christian roots of the West and many eco-theologians responded to this challenge by eco-reforming the Christian tradition. Grassroots Christian organisations such as the ones studied in my research are accepting this task of greening their faith in practical ways, such as making lifestyle changes, protesting the current climate legislation, praying and fasting for the planet.

My research with climate activists suggested that only a small section identified as religious. Half of the participants in my surveys self-identified as atheists or not religious, and only 16% of respondents stated a specific religious affiliation.[1] Half of those who identified as religious were represented by Pagans and Buddhists, a finding which indicates that inside the green movement Christians are a minority, with only 16% identifying as Christians in my study (see also Nita 2016: 102–104). The rest of the participants identified as 'partly religious', 'spiritual but not religious' or as 'poly-religionists', listing a number of religious traditions from which they drew inspiration. However, many green Christian organisations are beginning to take a more active or political role in the fight against climate change, from smaller organisations, such as the Forest Church, Operation Noah, Christian Ecology Link, Green Spirit and SPEAK,[2] all the way to the bigger players, like Christian Aid, A Rocha, Student Christian Movement and CAFOD (The Catholic Agency for Overseas Development). The wide endorsement in green Christian circles of the recent papal encyclical *Laudato Si: On the Care of our Common Home* (May 2015), as well as their cooperation and renewed presence during collective events, such as during climate marches or the Greenbelt festival, where these distinct networks get together to hold vigils or workshops for example, demonstrates the unity and ecumenism of the green Christian movement in the UK.

Experimenting with living space

Climate activists, including the groups of Christian activists who attended the protest camps, often experiment with green communes during their annual climate protest camps across England and Wales. Eco-communes often involve rules for all participants, usually including a vegan or vegetarian diet, common transport (e.g. no individually owned cars) and consensus decision making – whereby activists make decisions while sitting in a circle without a designated leader or central authority.[3] During climate camps, climate protestors live in a temporary version of this kind of commune for as long as two weeks.

A commune is a moral experiment in 'an imaginary community' (see Tremlett 2012), with a long history. These green communes build on the communes of 1960s counterculture and the nineteenth-century socialist ideals of community. At a climate camp most of the core campers are already living in an eco-commune or would be looking to join one, and workshops are often held on the theme of buying land or starting a commune. Often climate camps are opportunities to both experiment with green ideals and demonstrate these experiments to a wider audience (see Figure 8.1), particularly to first-time campers but also to the diversity of networks taking part in this experiment whose models of living and ritualising could thus be synchronised.

This utopian space is very strongly delimited by 'the gates', like other festival spaces that are erected periodically and begin to have a 'tradition' in their punctuated ephemeral existence (Bowman 2004). The boundary is continuously maintained by protestors on one side and police on the other. The police can be seen as an audience, with the camp as a theatre stage and a deeply liminal space. The enthusiastic solidarity that Victor Turner called 'communitas' (Turner 1969) is very easy to form within the camp, provoked by isolation from society

Figure 8.1 Climate campers cooking together at the Kingsnorth climate camp in 2008. Photo by Maria Nita.

and direct confrontation with the surrounding police. The motto of the camp I attended in 2008 was 'They are building fences – we are building a movement.'

In their experiments with living space, these climate activists modelled a way of living that could be carbon-neutral not only for themselves but also for the police, the media and mainstream society more widely. While the campers performed their activist identities inside this ephemeral, liminal and powerfully charged space, the gates allowed them to maintain a window to the very world they set themselves in opposition to: the consumerist culture outside. Similar to sacred space, the spatial organisation of the whole camp reflected new desired relationships, abounding in communal spaces that encouraged performances and expressivity.

The gates represent an important ritual space, highly charged by the real or symbolic confrontation with the police. My Christian informants often prayed for the gates and for those who were going to spend their night in vigil at the gates. One Christian informant told me that when biscuits were being passed along the line of protestors who were defending the gates, she experienced this as 'taking communion', which raises an interesting point about individual perception of sacred space and the fact that Christians are engaged in a continuous emotional translation or calibration of their Christian and 'dark green' identities (Nita 2014). The emphasis on the gates can be considered once again a privileging of the outer limits of the sacred space, which may symbolically reflect a postcolonial and countercultural focus on marginalised humans and non-humans and a critique of the centre and the implicit power relationships denoted or reinforced by it.

Experimenting with sacred space at the climate camp

At the climate camp the Christian activists[4] lived as a small group (around twenty people), offering a café inside the camp as well as daily worship.

Rituals and sacred space played a role in demarcating the Christian group from the rest of the camp and creating a sense of common identity, but also provoked some discomfort. In one event, the Christian group prayed at the gates of Kingsnorth Power Station, separated from the non-religious activists. This ritual asserted the Christian identity of the group, and took place while the other activists were taking turns to give speeches. One of the Christian activists later told me in an interview that 'I felt quite self-conscious, because I am not usually one of the Christians who is in a group of Christians, being ostentatiously Christian, at something like that.' Yet the group also defended their distinct Christian identity and at times they needed to defend their actions of demarcating themselves from the wider camp. In one instance the Christian group decided to carry a cross during one of the protest activities, a decision which was initially opposed by camp officials on the grounds that other collective symbols, such as a dragon and kites, had already been assigned for this particular action. This is a clear example of the important role material objects have in creating and challenging a sense of identity and belonging.

At the climate camp, the Christian group offered daily worship inside the Christian tent, where they had an opportunity to draw on their own ritual models while also experimenting with new forms of worship. Participants sat in a circle around an altar that had been constructed by putting together two large hay bales, covered by a large green cloth and decorated with stones and flowers. Evening services composed of singing Taizé songs and praying for the camp, for people whose life had been affected by climate change, and sometimes even for political leaders so that they could make difficult decisions concerning climate change.[5] In some cases prayer was a means of asserting disapproval of corporations and politicians, a message that resonated better with the collective voice of the camp. The service would normally end with open/free prayer, which allowed participants to express their personal environmental concerns, and with communion, which was not given by a leader, as might be expected in a more traditional setting, but was celebrated by passing bread and wine around the circle and thus by giving or offering communion to each other.

However, this democratic model of giving communion, which is practised by many green Christians in various ways outside of the church and during protest camps, retreats and festivals, was not upheld when green Christians found themselves in a church building, such as during a night climate vigil at

St-Martin-in-the-Field in London in 2010, when the service was led by a priest and participants received communion from him. Although there are many possible explanations for these variations, it is clear that Christians were more able to experiment with rituals and modalities of relating to each other outside of traditional settings, which demonstrates the 'material' power of place on re-enforcing particular behaviours. It must be said that when this more experimental group of Christians was joined on the last day of the climate camp by an ordained vicar, who also happened to be the mother of one of the organisers, they all received communion from her, a fact that highlighted for me the high plasticity of this syncretic green Christian movement.

In Figure 8.2 the Christian group is sitting in a circle at the actual gates of the Kingsnorth Power Station during a collective day of action. Upon arrival at the gates, the Christian group formed a separate group, distinguishing themselves from the rest of the climate activists, who continued their protest outside of the station. One informant told me,

> We didn't want what we did to be a play. I mean we did think about costumes and things like that, but we wanted to be there praying, in spirit and in truth [...] we wanted to do something that would set us apart and bring Jesus in the situation.

Figure 8.2 Christians praying at the gates of Kingsnorth Power Station, Kingsnorth 2008. Photo by Maria Nita.

By inviting Jesus into the public ritual situation, the Christian group reasserted their own identity and also invoked a spiritual dimension which was otherwise missing for them in secular events, making them less satisfying, as one informant told me. They prayed around an effigy of the power station, on top of which they placed an apple as a symbol of nature growing on the ruins of destruction. This arrangement is particularly interesting because of the material use of space in which we can see reflected the circle and centre model outlined earlier, when I discussed the Council of All Beings. The centre is occupied by the ruins of the power station and so it is negatively charged; it is not a place of power but, like with the Council of All Beings model, a place of lamentation. To some extent the apple places a positive value inside this space, yet this arrangement can be seen as a model for repentance, whereby old meanings and values can be replaced by new ones through a process of reversing the polarity of place through symbolic representation. Another negatively charged material object I encountered during my research was 'coal', which was sometimes placed on the altar, alongside other climate symbols, such as 'polar bears', to represent the crux of the problem, humans' dependence on fossil fuels.

Green Christians represent the coming together of an institutionalised religion and a decentralised movement, and they do not yet have firm shared traditions in the way they organise space. When they find themselves in a church, green Christians will conform to the familiar way in which space is already organised. Their models of organising space at the climate camp were not necessarily free of traditional pressures either, since the group needed to use easily recognisable identity markers that would allow its demarcation from the larger group. Yet green Christians are constructing and using sacred space in novel ways, such as by reversing the polarity of the centre and empowering the outer circle or participants themselves, which points towards a model for transformation for green Christian activists. In the next section of this chapter, I will discuss sacred space in the context of the green Christian retreat. This is an alternative experimentation with sacred space in a place where external pressures, from traditional material settings on one hand and non-religious activists on the other, can be avoided.

Moving mountains during eco-retreats and relating to the planet

One of the Christian networks in my research was the Green Christian (GC), previously called Christian Ecology Link (CEL), a network of Christians that has been in operation for almost three decades, and therefore has today an older membership than the Christian participants in the climate camp.[6] Often focused on spirituality and lifestyle rather than protest, Green Christian holds public conferences, forums and collective worships (often ahead of major green events) as well as private retreats and closed steering committee meetings that are open only to members. As previously discussed when events are held in church halls, the content and form of worship tend to be more traditional, to accord with the wider community which may be attending. During private retreats members experiment with newer, less conventional forms of worship, such as praying through painting, offering communion to each other, doing experimental ecological rituals and contemplating and praying outdoors.

Eco-retreats abound in workshops and commonly involve a high degree of exploration and plasticity. The outcome of these 'workshop rituals' has not been decided yet; the ritual is not finalised – it will be 'worked out' during the workshop. The participants will have a chance to 'remember', 'rediscover' or 'connect' with the aid of a specially trained guide. The 'retreat' also involves an opportunity for transformation, in essence abandoning the world so that one may come back to it with a fresh perspective. These provide opportunities for Christian participants to organise their own sacred space, a praying room or an altar like the one in Figure 8.3.

The 'retreat' provides green Christians with the opportunity to express ecological beliefs which are not represented in more mainstream Christian settings. It also provides an opportunity to organise space in ways that reflect the group organisation; for example in Figure 8.4 the chairs were arranged in a circle around the altar. Often in these settings, as at the climate camp, green Christians would give each other communion rather than receive it from a vicar. As I suggested previously, this informal way of giving and receiving communion reflects an aspiration towards a less hierarchical organisation of the Christian community, in accordance with the central precepts of the green movement.

A shared practice in eco-ritual performed by members of different religious traditions is the use of 'natural' materials, such as acorns, leaves, plants and trees (Kearns and Keller 2007). Here (Figure 8.3) the altar has been decorated with cones, leaves, stones and feathers alongside more traditional altar furnishings, such as candles and prayers. The altar coverings, green and blue, signify earth and water.

Figure 8.4 depicts the room where the altar was placed. This was the main room where participants gathered daily during this retreat, at Ringsfield, Suffolk, in 2009. In the background there is a big poster of the planet Earth. There are chairs all around the room, again with the altar in the centre of this space. Beside the altar there is a pile of stones placed next to a big shoe, and in front of the pile there is a small child's shoe. Children were invited to this Christian retreat, and parents were given the opportunity to take turns with childcare to allow others to attend the workshops. The pile of stones was a symbol of the difficult task of shrinking our carbon footprint.

The picture depicts the setting before the enactment of the 'Moving Mountains' ritual, on the last day of our stay. The ritual followed a day of workshops and discussions, with opportunities for dramatic expression. The two piles break the monadic organisation of the circle-centre model, inserting division and movement inside this sacred space. In a traditional Christian setting participants would walk out towards an altar to take communion and then return to their previous seats. They would take from the centre and return to the margins, thus maintaining the status of the altar as a central source. In contrast in the 'Moving

Climate activists and green Christians 145

Figure 8.3 Altar at eco-retreat organised by Christian Ecology Link (Suffolk, 2009). Photo by Maria Nita.

Mountains' ritual the objects inside the circle are again negatively charged, the stones representing the carbon in the atmosphere, and so just like the ruins of the power station this negative symbol depletes the centre. During the enactment of the ritual participants formed an energetic conveyer belt inside the

Figure 8.4 'Moving Mountains' ritual (Suffolk, 2009). Photo by Maria Nita.

circle, as they shifted the stones from the pile representing the big carbon footprint to the other smaller footprint. The constant movement inside the circle could be understood to transform it into a dynamically charged space, in which participants are asked to take up an active role, symbolising their personal involvement with fighting climate change. When the ritual ended, our host, who was also a vicar, praised the children who took part in this ritual for energetically moving the stones and told us all, in his usual humorous way, that the fight against climate change could not be won if we 'were dragging our feet'.

In other rituals enacted during eco-retreats the central altar was missing all together. For example during a GC retreat in 2012 participants took part in an outdoors Eucharist celebration, forming a semicircle and looking out into the fields that surrounded the house in which we were staying. There was no altar and a row of trees in a nearby field seemed to complete the circle on the other side. Two participants, a man and a woman, stood at the two respective edges of the semicircle and passed bread and wine in small wicker baskets. While the bread and wine were passed around everyone remained silent, staring out into the fields. This organisation of the sacred space suggested both an inclusion of the other-than-human into the 'communion circle' and an equal distribution of power among the human participants, amplified by the absence of the altar and that of a formal officiant; having both a man and a woman passing the bread and wine could also be interpreted in light of recent debates inside the Christian tradition concerned with the ordination of women.

Relating to the planet and developing a planetary identity

Ecological rituals, which include new constructions and organisations of sacred space, are ways in which climate activists perform their opposition to traditional power structures and invite participants to consider a different perspective, to change how they look at the non-human world. For Christian activists this protest is twofold, as they have the added task of reforming anthropocentric values and beliefs inside their own tradition. They have to tread carefully between tradition and innovation and be able to represent or perform both their Christian and their green identities, despite the conflicts that arise from this encounter.

Relating to the planet as a unified whole, the Earth, sometimes referred to by the participants in my research as 'God's creation', is in some respects not very challenging for Christian activists despite the obvious danger of intersecting Pagan and New Age discourses of the planet as 'mother Earth' or 'Gaia'. In some Christian rituals I have observed, the globe of the planet is processed and placed on an altar or simply placed in the middle of the space as a distinct focus for participants. Placing the planet in the centre of a constructed sacred space is a powerful and radical statement, since it invites participants to consider a biocentric viewpoint in a very literal way. Yet it can also be argued that the representation of the globe and the iconography of the planet sustain ideas of transcendence, whereby the planet is outside of us, somewhere in the distance of space, which is why rituals like the Cosmic Walk appear to stress this realisation of our belonging to the Earth: 'this flaring forth continues as this moment, with us, as one' (Edwards 1999: 15). At the end of the ritual the participants can internalise the history and identity of the planet into their own history and their own personal or group identity.

Other ecological rituals integrate the more distant and unseen places or inhabitants of the planet and make them relevant for participants and often for the audience. Arctic inhabitants are usual protagonists in climate rituals and performances, whether activists stage protests in which they dress up as seals and cover themselves in oil (2008) or dress up like penguins (Figure 8.5) and polar bears during direct actions (see Avery 2012). These protest rituals have a role in both making climate change visible for the unengaged public and enabling activists to explore non-human identities, as is the case with the Council of All Beings ritual.

Ritualised processions and events like the Council of All Beings try to enable participants to experience the other-than-human world and then return to 'the world of the two-legged'. This is less transcendent and conversely a more immanent or embodied means of relating to the planet since the ritual can be a way for participants to form a connection or personal relationship to another species and have a lived experience of a biocentric world view. Dressing up, walking, being silent for a few hours and being in the company of

Figure 8.5 Penguins prodding the gates of Kingsnorth Power Station in 2008. Photo by Maria Nita.

fellow human-penguins represent powerful ways of personally relating to the planet and performing the climate crisis. Green rituals are often opportunities to extend the participant's identities by attempting to incorporate or integrate the planet in one's sphere of personal concerns, thus aiming to transform both participants and their audiences in planetary-minded-humans.

Conclusions

The green Christians in my research adopted elements from the green movement and ecological ritual repertoire and performed these syncretic encounters by experimenting with sacred spaces. Using natural materials, such as stones or wood, green Christians physically represented their ecological beliefs by bringing these materials into focus. By placing the altar inside the circle of participants, green Christians combine Christian forms of organising space, in this case the centrality of the altar, with the horizontal relationships in ecological practices suggested by the circle. This new space reflects changes in the relationships of the participants, where leadership can be (temporarily) abandoned in favour of experimenting with new models of organisation.

I suggested here that the organisation of space can represent a powerful critique of traditional structures, as is the case with the Council of All Beings ritual. Humans are in the centre of the circle only when they are being reprimanded by the other life forms or put on trial for their crimes. Anthropocentrism is therefore spatially criticised and deconstructed. Thus ideas can be challenged by challenging material space itself: by dividing space into more than one centre, by neglecting the centre of a sacred space, by reversing the polarity or charge of such a space, by making the central marginal and vice versa, and finally by inserting a dynamic movement into established models of sacred space.

The natural materials that create and adorn sacred space are used to alter as well as challenge what participants consider sacred. If conventionally an altar might have been furnished with more traditional precious objects, such as sacred books or icons, in the examples I discussed here the altar arrangement displayed acorns, leaves and feathers. By placing these natural materials in a sacred setting, they can undergo what David Morgan calls in his introduction a process of 'remediation', whereby they begin not only to reflect new relationships between participants but also, despite their inanimate nature, to carry new meanings that can generate cultural change.

Notes

1 I administered two surveys at climate camps in England and Wales for which I had seventy-eight respondents. One question asked respondents to describe their religious affiliation and these descriptions were later interpreted and classified.
2 SPEAK is Christian activist network preoccupied with global justice. The name 'SPEAK' is inspired by the biblical verse 'Speak up for those who cannot speak for themselves' (Proverbs 31:8), as their literature explains.
3 Consensus decision making is a process of making decisions that represents an alternative to democratic voting. As a process, consensus relies on discussions and creative solutions rather than winning the vote of a majority.
4 Most of the members of this group belonged to a Christian anarchist network called Isaiah 58, a small network with a young age demographic. My last attempt to make contact with the group in 2009 was refused due to the nature of their covert activities.
5 Taizé is a monastic community in the south of France concerned with peace and reconciliation.
6 CEL's core membership is made up of around thirty committed members who form the steering committee. The larger network comprises over 1,000 paying members, with a wider readership of the network's bimonthly magazine, the *Green Christian*.

Works cited

Avery, Catherine. 2012. 'Greenpeace Activist Dressed as Polar Bear Arrested at Petrol Station Protest'. *Metro*, 16 July. http://www.metro.co.uk/news/905344-greenpeace-activist-dressed-as-polar-bear-arrested-at-petrol-station-protest. Accessed 30/07/2012.
Barlow, Connie. 2005. 'The Epic Ritual'. In *Encyclopaedia of Religion and Nature*, ed. Bron Taylor, 612–613. London and New York: Thoemmes Continuum.
Bowman, Marion. 2004. 'Procession and Possession in Glastonbury: Continuity, Change and the Manipulation of Tradition.' *Folklore* 115(3): 1–13.

———. 2005. 'Ancient Avalon, New Jerusalem, Heart Chakra of Planet Earth: The Local and the Global in Glastonbury.' *Numen: International Review for the History of Religions* 52(2): 157–190.

Carson, Rachel. 1962. *Silent Spring*. Boston, MA: Houghton Mifflin.

Durkheim, Émile. 1995 [1915]. *The Elementary Forms of the Religious Life*, tr. Karen Fields. New York: The Free Press.

Edwards, Larry. 1999. 'The Cosmic Walk.' *Epic of Evolution*, Spring: 14–15. http://www.thegreatstory.org/CosmicWalk.pdf. Accessed 12/01/2010.

Eliade, Mircea. 1963. *The Sacred and the Profane: The Nature of Religion*. New York: Harvest Books.

Grimes, Ronald L. 2003. 'Ritual Theory and the Environment.' *Editorial Board of the Sociological Review* 51(s2): 31–45.

———. 2005. 'Ritual.' In *The Encyclopedia of Religion and Nature*, ed. Bron Taylor, 1385–1388. London and New York: Thoemmes Continuum.

Hervieu-Léger, Daniele. 2000. *Religion as a Chain of Memory*. Cambridge: Polity Press.

Holm, Jean and John Bowker, eds. 1994. *Sacred Place*. London: Printer.

Kearns, Laurel and Catherine Keller, eds. 2007. *Eco-Spirit: Religions and Philosophies for the Earth*. New York: Fordham University Press.

Knott, Kim. 2005. *The Location of Religion: A Spatial Analysis*. London: Equinox.

Latour, Bruno. 1987. *Science in Action: How to Follow Scientists and Engineers through Society*. Cambridge, MA: Harvard University Press.

Letcher, Andy. 2003. '"Gaia Told Me to Do It": Resistance and the Idea of Nature within Contemporary British Eco-Paganism.' *Ecotheology* 8 (1): 64: 80.

Lovelock, James. 1972. 'Gaia as Seen through the Atmosphere.' *Atmospheric Environment* 6 (8): 579–580.

Macy, Joanna R. 2005. 'The Council of All Beings.' In *Encyclopedia of Religion and Nature*, ed. Bron Taylor, 425–429. London: Continuum.

Nita, Maria. 2014. 'Christian and Muslim Climate Activists Fasting and Praying for the Planet: Emotional Translation of "Dark Green" Activism and Green-Faith Identities.' In *How the World's Religions Are Responding to Climate Change Social Scientific Investigation*, eds. R. Globus-Veldman, A. Szasz and R. Haluza-DeLay, 229–243. New York: Routledge.

Nita, Maria. 2016. *Praying and Campaigning with Environmental Christians: Green Religion and the Climate Movement*. New York: Palgrave Macmillan.

Smith, Jonathan Z. 1982. *Imagining Religion: From Babylon to Jonestown*. Chicago: University of Chicago Press.

———. 2005 [1987]. 'To Take Place.' In *Ritual and Religious Belief: A Reader*, ed. Graham Harvey, 26–52. London: Equinox.

Swimme, Brian and Thomas Berry. 1992. *The Universe Story: From the Primordial Flaring Forth to the Ecozoic Era*. New York: HarperCollins.

Tremlett, Paul-François. 2012. 'Occupied Territory at the Interstices of the Sacred: Between Capital and Community.' *Religion and Society* 3(1): 130–141.

Tuan, Yi-Fu. 1974. *Topophilia: A Study of Environmental Perceptions, Attitudes and Values*. Englewood Cliffs, NJ: Prentice Hall.

———. 1991. 'Language and the Making of Place: A Narrative-Descriptive Approach.' *Annals of the Association of American Geographers* 81(3): 684–696.

Turner, Victor. 1969. *The Ritual Process: Structure and Anti-Structure*. London: Routledge.

van Gennep, Arnold. 1960. *The Rites of Passage*. Chicago: University of Chicago Press.

White, Lynn T. 1967. 'The Historical Roots of Our Ecological Crisis.' *Science* 155(3767): 1203–1207.

9 The significance of secular sacred space in the formation of British atheist identities

Janet Eccles and Rebecca Catto

Introduction

Work on material, lived and everyday religion has established the significance of these dimensions for a better understanding of what religion is and does in the lives of ordinary citizens. Yet Tiina Mahlamäki (2012) points out that everyday forms of non-religiousness and lived non-religiousness are missing from academic and public discussion. Aston (2015) has made a start at looking at material forms of non-religion and this chapter adds to such work.

We follow Lois Lee's suggestion that non-religion be given a general definition that qualifies it as the 'master or defining concept' for the field; and that the use of 'atheism' be strictly restricted to the task of indicating the explicit rejection of god-centred outlooks and/or individuals and cultures who/which appropriate the term (2012: 130).

This chapter focuses on British adults who identify explicitly as atheist, a conscious position defined by a denial of belief in god(s) (Cliteur 2009). In recent times such a position has been popularised by the so-called New Atheists (Harris 2004; Dawkins 2006; Hitchens 2007, among others), although, as Amarasingam (2012: 2) points out, there is very little that is actually 'new' in their polemics against religion. What is novel, he claims, is the urgency in their message as well as a kind of atheist social revival that their writings, lectures and conferences have produced. The reception of their work in consciousness-raising has been remarkable, catching many people, not only cardinals and theologians, unawares (Bullivant 2012). The seminal claim by the New Atheists and their followers is that belief in G/god is a truth claim about the nature of reality. Hence the nature of religion should be amenable to some kind of quasi-scientific investigation: the 'God Hypothesis' should be testable (Falcioni 2012: 206). Because the New Atheists, and some of our informants, cannot find the kind of evidence for the existence of G/god they would need to be convinced, they find religion lacking, incredible, illogical and irrational.

A non-religious stance has been/is the default option for many citizens in the UK (Connolly 2006; Crockett and Voas 2006; Bagg and Voas 2010; Bullivant 2012: 117). A quarter of the population claimed 'no religion' on the 2011 census (Office for National Statistics 2012), with a considerably smaller number regularly identifying as atheist on surveys.[1] However, as Bullivant (2012) observes, religion has re-entered the public sphere in recent times, with religiously themed stories making the front pages of newspapers and in radio and television news coverage (see also Pasquale 2010: 79; Gledhill 2012: 89; Taira, Poole and Knott 2012: 33; Knott, Poole and Taira 2013; Stringer 2013: 170). This new visibility and interest in religion, Bullivant argues (2012: 118), help us to understand the new visibility and interest in atheism in two ways. The impression is created that religion still matters in some way in the twenty-first century in the UK, which in turn causes a sense of 'panicked urgency' among atheists, such as Dawkins (2006), though this may be misplaced, if one considers the low levels of religious attendance/interest in Britain (Stringer 2013: 170).

Atheism and the material sacred

Is it possible that denial of a belief can be displayed through clothing, ritual, objects and, particularly, space, considering that one young atheist respondent told us, 'I don't spend my life doing things because I don't believe in religion'?

Morgan reminds us that belief

> is not simply assent to dogmatic principles or creedal propositions, but also the embodied or material practices that enact belonging to the group. The feeling that one belongs takes the shape of many experiences, unfolds over time, and is mediated in many forms.
>
> (Morgan 2009: 141; see also Morgan, this volume)

Emotion is integral to the process of reasoning and decision-making and is fundamental to experiences that exert the greatest influence on human behaviour (Riis and Woodhead 2010; Eccles 2012). Philosopher and atheist Alain de Botton observes that atheists don't go on pilgrimages or build temples but are presented with an 'unpleasant choice between either committing to peculiar concepts about immaterial deities or letting go entirely of a host of consoling, subtle, or just charming rituals for which they struggle to find equivalents in secular society' (de Botton 2012: 14).

Drawing on the work of Doreen Massey, Kim Knott (2005, 2010a, 2010b, 2011) sees space as a moment in the intersection of configured social relations. The spaces of religion are dynamic, with events not just happening simultaneously but also acting on each other and with each other. Responding to a podcast by Knott on her spatial methodology for the Religious Studies Project, Aston notes that we can usefully employ this method to investigate forms of non-religion (2012). Body, place and space are all relational, whether religious or non-religious (Knott 2010a: 31).

Lynch claims that we need a sociology of the sacred, which can be but is not *necessarily* religious (2012: 3). The sacred here is understood as a form of special non-negotiable value commitment that religious and non-religious people are equally capable of making. A sociology of the sacred helps us see what is 'sacred' in our lives, to understand where it animates our feelings and our institutional practices and to recognise its role in the formation of subjectivities. Thus, we learn where to locate socially significant sources of meaning and value within increasingly de-Christianised societies, such as Britain. Sacred thought, feeling and practice cannot be understood as abstract entities but are performed through contingent bodies and learned through specific processes grounded in bodily practices associated with particular emotions.

Lynch (2012) delineates three types of lived experience: the mundane, the sacred and the profane. He sees '(t)he reality-constituting sacred' as 'the intersection of symbol, emotion, normative claims, ritual practice and social collective', the profane as 'the evil that threatens this sacred form' and 'pollutes' whatever it comes into contact with and the mundane as 'the logics, practices and spaces of everyday life' (26).

The mundane, then, is that which we experience most of the time: going to work, domestic chores and so forth. But there are occasions and spaces when there can be a significant interruption of this daily round which brings into sharp focus one's deeply held 'sacred' commitments, not consciously or clearly articulated most of the time. This significant interruption occurs when the profane pollutes that which is held sacred. At the micro level of individual social relations, instances of such 'profanations' occur among our respondents' otherwise mundane experiences. Deep bodily emotions are stirred by interactions between those identifying as atheist (Mumford 2015) and those holding different sacred commitments who exist in a different 'community of feeling' (Morgan 2009). We should also note, however, Lynch's (2012: 43) contention that individuals tend to hold more than one sacred commitment and are often influenced by the interplay and multiplicity of sacred forms present in individual and social life.

Sacred space is not confined to buildings explicitly designed for the performance of the rituals of organised religion. It can also exist in cities, homes, schools, hospitals, prisons, museums and malls (Chidester and Linenthal 1995: 43–98). In order to be sacred the space needs ritual context, contestation and a focusing on central human questions.

We follow McKearney's work on ritual in British stand-up comedy gigs as a way of conceiving how 'lived' atheism materialises in the everyday life of our respondents (2010). By ritual he means 'the way people come together in a very particular setting to engage in a very particular form of interaction' (2010: 5). The rehearsal of the conflict between the religious and non-religious features prominently in the gig setting, with, not infrequently, the old order (of religion) being juxtaposed with the new (non-religion), with the former being held up to ridicule. So, proceeding on the basis that the investigation of the (secular) sacred in particular spaces is plausible and productive, we turn now to its application to atheism specifically.

Methods of the studies

Our data were gathered during the Young Atheists Research Project (Catto and Eccles 2013) and Eccles's more recent project focused on atheist women in northern England.[2] These studies were not initially undertaken from a material culture perspective – for example by first considering buildings and objects and then moving on to practice, values and meaning. Rather, we have come subsequently to recognise space, both offline and virtual, as a significant dimension of respondents' narratives. Thus what follows is a post hoc analysis of what respondents reported in interviews rather than based upon systematic observation of their interactions in space and/or with material culture.

We had assumed, initially, for the young atheists that it would be possible to recruit respondents via an established humanist or secular society. Such an attempt proved fruitless, and we realised that this kind of face-to-face associational activity does not appeal to many young people (Catto 2014). This generation does 'gather' online, however, so we turned to social media. We posted our call for respondents online and created a project Facebook page. The call was picked up on Twitter, including by British comedians Robin Ince and Josie Long, who both publicly discuss their own atheism, and this particularly helped recruitment. Thirty-seven young people aged between eighteen and twenty-six answered our call.

Respondents were asked to submit a personal profile, including whether they attended any kind of event or group in connection with their stance. Four presidents or past presidents of their student non-religious society participated, suggesting that there are some young people who combine both online and offline associational activity and that our call attracted at least respondents who are keen to assert their atheist identity publicly. We promised that all data would be anonymised in any presentation to protect individual identities: young atheist participants are designated here by the same initials as in our earlier work (Catto and Eccles 2013). Out of the thirty-seven respondents, twenty-four agreed to be interviewed by either Eccles or Catto, and meetings took place across England and Scotland. Four of the participants were in full-time paid occupations, and the rest were university students of subjects ranging across the arts, humanities and social and natural sciences, with four students having theology or religious studies as part or all of their degree course. We also attended some events and studied atheist material online, some of which had been mentioned in interviews. These generally lasted about an hour and were recorded and fully transcribed. We expected more male than female participants, because more men than women identify as atheist, but we were surprised to receive about equal numbers of responses. All participants were white and almost all were university-educated, which, by contrast, follows the statistical profile for this group in both the UK and US (Beit-Hallahmi 2007; Zuckerman 2007; Altemeyer 2010; Manning 2010; Pasquale 2010; Brown and Lynch 2012).

Eccles's 2014 self-funded project studied women identifying as atheist, largely recruited via a couple she had met at a humanist meeting, and thence by the snowball method. Ages ranged from thirty to mid-eighties; all were white and the majority tertiary educated, again supporting the finding that atheists tend to be more highly educated than the average population (Zuckerman 2007; Brown and Lynch 2012). Respondents were largely in teaching (see also Pasquale 2010: 50) or secretarial and general administrative workers. Again, interviews, which lasted rather longer for these older women, were recorded and transcribed. All names are pseudonyms.

There was no formal list of questions for either set of interviews. We felt it important that conversation should develop either from profile information supplied by the young atheists, or, for the older women, from an opening gambit of asking how they had reached their present identification. Stories were allowed to flow in an effort to ensure that respondents themselves were in charge of what they said (and did not say). Subjects discussed included previous (religious) affiliation(s), family background and socialisation, school and experiences growing up, attitudes towards religion, politics, ethical stances and community activism.

Inductive thematic analysis (Attride-Stirling 2001; Braun and Clarke 2006; Guest, MacQueen and Namey 2012; Riessman 2012) was employed for young atheist data, identifying themes through constant revisiting of the material. The process was supplemented by discussions with other researchers and feedback from the young participants through an online forum. Eccles used similar procedures for the data collected on older women but did not make use of any methods involving Internet technology. Both studies were small-scale and are illustrative rather than representative of whole populations. Atheists become 'visible' as atheists only in certain circumstances. Interviews gave us the opportunity to hear how and when such circumstances arose and note how many were remarkably similar in type.

Ritual encounters: contesting religious claims over public space

There are no buildings and very few material objects that could be deemed specifically atheist for our respondents. Visually, the only representation we encountered during our interviews was a hooded top emblazoned with a university's atheist society logo, worn by one respondent, a former president (Aston 2015, in particular 173–212, addresses atheist representation). Yet, we found that disbelief in G/god certainly seemed to have developed over time through embodied, emotional experiences for both sets of respondents. Many of their routine daily interactions may well be indistinguishable from anyone else's, but there are specific material contexts in which our respondents' 'lived' atheism comes to the fore.

Rather than only denying a belief in G/god, respondents did hold strong value commitments and positive beliefs that they associated with their non-religious identity. Narratives of their formation and the nature of their atheism were embedded in conversations with student flatmates, in the classroom, in relations with the school hierarchy as a parent, the workplace, encounters with neighbours and on social media. Such interplaying of sacred forms arose in the testimonies of some young atheists, who, despite their atheist stance, were interested in investigating forms of religion by attending church events with

Christian friends or meetings of their university Islamic society. This was partly in an attempt better to formulate their own position and evaluate what *they* held as sacred (which many struggled to do). Older women, by contrast, were often specifically and emphatically rejecting that form of religion that they had known (only too well) in the past for a new form of the non-religious sacred.

For some respondents, religious matters sometimes unexpectedly 'intrude' within an everyday space that they had always assumed to be secular. They sense a profanation of that particular secular sacred space when religion does rear its head. In an effort to defend its secular nature (not always successfully), they transform what was an everyday material space into a place of ritual encounter and contestation (Chidester and Linenthal 1995).

SM was a young atheist policeman, who differed from the rest of the sample in having children and not having attended university. His wife's family belonged to an evangelical conservative Protestant congregation, which he likened to Westboro Baptist Church in the US (Knott et al. 2013: 86). He recounted going with a friend to their church for the first time:

> I actually met the person who would later be my wife there. But only in the sense that 'X, this is Y', quick shake of hands and with her father who is one of the elders of the church. They call them elders instead of preachers or anything. But they were a very extremist church is the best way I can describe them. I've always thought of them as a cult really. It seems like that, yes, very in your face, evangelical with massive American evangelical choirs and preachers and that. It was held in a local hall in a school on a Sunday when there was no one else there and it wasn't structured at all. There was a band playing at the front with chairs loosely scattered about, people all over the place. A very strange place and just the preaching there and things made me start to question and think . . . I never really believed in God before that but that's when I really started to disbelieve in God.

SM was familiar and comfortable with the liberal Methodism of his father, which he witnessed in his local church, but here the mundane space of a secondary state school hall, normally used for routine activities, had been unexpectedly transformed into an unfamiliar, disorientating, apparently religious place, lacking structure and full of noise. Although disorientated, SM did not allow this episode to come between him and the woman who later became his wife, but he did not wish to visit the school hall again on a Sunday. Initially the couple simply lived together but then produced a child out of wedlock. SM and his partner ventured back to the hall for a service at this point, as a means of trying to reconnect with her family, who had cut themselves off in disgust. They were told they would 'burn in hell' for their 'sin of fornication', and no further communication took place. Both SM and his partner were completely devastated by this highly charged emotional encounter in the same school hall, at which point SM resolved to have nothing more to do with religion. Learning of the British Humanist Association (BHA) through online searches he became a member, assuming thereafter an atheist identity.

Zoe, a somewhat older atheist, married to a man also now atheist, was brought up without religion. The couple bought their small, semi-detached house on marrying, unaware at the time, it seems, that the nearest school was Christian faith-based. When their daughter Annabel was born, Zoe realised this could present problems, and she entered into a protracted battle with the local authority for her daughter to be admitted to a non-faith school further away, a battle which she lost. Consequently, Annabel now attends the local faith school, which turns out to be quite avowedly evangelical, holding a weekly hour-long assembly, conducted by the local vicar, with shorter assemblies by the head teacher on the other four days. Zoe has no problem with her daughter attending a morning assembly as such. State schools generally are expected to begin the day with an assembly of 'a broadly Christian character',[3] but there is considerable latitude in how this is interpreted by many head teachers. Zoe would have been happy with the interpretation of the head at the more distant school. Annabel appears to have absorbed a strong religious 'message' through the assemblies at the school to which she has been allocated, often repeating at home, 'Our god is a Christian God,' 'God made the Earth,' 'God lives in the sky.'

The battle with the local authority and the subsequent outcome have caused considerable distress to Zoe, who told Eccles that she has been treated for clinical depression as a result. She has finally secured permission for Annabel to be excused from the vicar's, as she sees it, proselytising assembly and takes her into school an hour later. Zoe showed Eccles a letter that she had written to the head teacher explaining her concerns, reflecting both the scientific rationalist and humanistic worldview (Mumford 2014) that she wishes to inculcate in her daughter. She asserts that Annabel's beliefs should be based 'on evidence, judgment and critical thinking' and believes that school should be a place 'for learning about facts using logic and reason'.

Another older participant had had her three children baptised simply to get them into the village faith-based school, which provided the better education at the time. In the end, a new head in the non-faith school improved standards, which meant she could comply with her own secular principles. Should this not have happened, she agreed that the sacredness of her children's welfare would have 'trumped' her own personal commitments. As already noted, individuals tend not to orient their lives around a single sacred form but are often influenced by the interplay of sacred forms and their multiplicity present in individual and social life (Lynch 2012).

Spaces of belonging

Given that the secularity of public spaces could not be taken for granted and could be threatened, younger respondents in particular sought out convivial spaces for interaction related to their atheism, either on or offline. While all the respondents we spoke to were firm in their atheist stance, few of the students interviewed had taken up any formal commitment to join a group (Bullivant 2008; Pasquale 2010: 44, 49, 79; Zuckerman 2012: 175). Some attended ad hoc events, such as Sceptics in the Pub[4] or Nine Lessons and Carols for Godless

People,[5] but on the whole they preferred to be atheists in their own way. However, as already noted earlier, a few were members of a student humanist or secular society, part of the National Federation of Atheist, Humanist and Secular Student Societies (AHS),[6] founded in November 2008 and now having thirty-two member societies across UK universities. Meeting in the pub appeared to be a common practice, as others have found (Engelke 2014). HM, a female history student, for example, thought it good to have a 'safe' space in the Humanist Society where atheists/humanists can express views comfortably, an opinion echoed by a male biology student at a university with a Christian foundation. HM did not feel her particular society was setting out to win hearts and minds, but that it was important that that space existed. She felt it would be much less important once she had left university but that it currently provided a useful place of retreat after interacting regularly with the religious.

The day scheduled for HM's interview with Eccles coincided with the group's weekly meeting in a nearby pub. At that meeting, to which Eccles was duly invited, HM and her fellow members were keen to stress that doing good was certainly not the preserve of religion but that we 'do good because we should' (Didyoung, Charles and Rowland 2013; Guenther 2014), a view fervently shared by pretty well all the people we spoke to.

Some of the older women did belong to a formal humanist group and had found a place of belonging, sharing space with similar people when others around might misunderstand or be critical or judgmental. It had also been more in retirement that many of the women had found the need for a face-to-face community and a 'safe' place to express their lack of belief in g/God. When they had been working, a number had been too busy juggling home and career to have much time to give to such activities. They had encountered religious worldviews among work colleagues and felt antagonistic to these views, albeit not always feeling able to express this 'out of political correctness'. As we have remarked elsewhere (Eccles and Catto 2015) about other older women who have become simply non-religious (as opposed to identifying as atheist), these respondents have reacted much more against past forms of religion being 'drummed into them' or 'indoctrinated' and so tended to express themselves rather more forcefully as being both anti-religion and explicitly atheist, unlike the younger people, who generally adopted a more tolerant stance. Being less media-savvy, older women are generally less likely to go online for their information or, even if they have done, find it insufficient for their (emotional) need to articulate and discuss their beliefs and values with sympathetic others.

Mediating atheism

Lynch (2012: 87) argues that all sacred forms are mediated, and, in this volume, Morgan advocates attention to mediation in a material approach to religion. Media enable communication about and interaction with sacred forms. Sacred meanings are not free-floating signifiers but materially mediated. This can be through material objects, spaces, institutional practices and even bodies, as we saw with the hooded top and the daily school assembly, for example. We could also add that one young atheist proudly proclaimed that he had had the opportunity to shake the hand of Richard Dawkins. However, here we focus on the narrower sense of print media, radio, television, the Internet and the ever-expanding world of mobile technologies. Atheist/secularist/humanist blogs, posts, discussion lists and websites are safe, secular sacred spaces, ideal then for the kind of embodied online associational (inter)activity favoured by most of the young respondents.

All the young atheists reported visiting atheist and agnostic websites or following atheists on social media.[7] Some, as has been noted, also attend 'safe' face-to-face humanist meetings. We also note with Lynch the increasing blurring of boundaries between public and social media, such as YouTube videos, which may initially be produced for consumption between a small group but have the potential to 'go viral'. As Zuckerman notes, advances in electronic media production mean the non-religious have far more means of reaching out to like-minded others than they ever did in the past (2012: 175). They need no longer feel isolated.

In the same vein as Morgan (2009) quoted earlier, Lynch (2012) sees identification with sacred forms as not simply an intellectual assent but an embodied, affective and aesthetic engagement with their mediation. Hence, media can generate a sense of community, as we found with some of our participants. SM was planning to set up a local face-to-face group of non-religious individuals in his neighbourhood, so they could hold events, such as Sceptics in the Pub, thus providing a welcome opportunity for interaction with local atheists as well as a form of entertainment. Nonetheless he greatly valued being part of the online humanist community.

Having found its website and read its worldview, a student of German decided she fitted perfectly into the BHA online community. The Internet proved useful for 'naming' the community, and reading the BHA website was affirming: she could call herself a humanist rather than only an atheist, defined by what she does not believe in (Bagg and Voas 2010: 93). She saw herself as believing in 'the non-existence of god', used Twitter a lot and admired Robin Ince as well as other left-leaning, non-religious comedians. She approved of the fact that 'there is a movement now. You've almost got faces to it' (Smith and Cimino 2012). Similarly, another young atheist had abandoned the idea of becoming a Pagan in favour of humanism, which she had learned about online. She had become a member of the BHA and valued the sense of belonging and identity, living, as she did, in a city much riven by sectarian strife.

For the older women, particularly those who are less Internet-savvy, print media, radio and television are more important for encountering sympathetic others. Public media representations of religion can be a powerful force, in that negative portrayals of religion reinforce negative perceptions (Taira, Poole and Knott 2012: 33). A number of negative perceptions were reported to us in interviews, culled almost wholly from watching particular British and American public media's portrayals of religion.

Knott, Poole and Taira note that Pope Benedict's visit to the UK in 2010 was first heralded in the media with some doubt and scepticism, in view of the cost in times of economic stringency and the various sexual abuse scandals associated with Catholic priests (2013: 155–171). There was also the pope's known antipathy to homosexuality, abortion and gay rights. However, the three authors report that the final verdict in the media was that the pope's visit had been a success, largely due to his perceived humility, his general apparent inoffensiveness, the sheer numbers who had turned out to greet him, his visit with the queen and his blessing of babies (Taira, Poole and Knott 2012: 160). This contrasts with the resentment felt by some of our participants that the *Protest the Pope* campaign, of which they had been part and which had had a visible presence at the processions held in various parts of the UK during the pope's visit,[8] was not shown on national television footage of the events. The atheist voice was heard only in more 'hidden' expressions, specifically catering to atheists, on the National Secular Society website, for example, and in much less prominent places in the press (http://www.secularism.org.uk/; Knott, Poole and Taira 2013: 161). There was shock that the public space of national media could not be taken for granted as secular/neutral.

A number of both younger and older participants had read and actually possessed a copy of Richard Dawkins's *The God Delusion* (2006). They were grateful to him for putting 'atheism on the map', as more than one said, bringing atheism as a belief out of the shadows (Smith and Cimino 2012). A number said they liked 'the arguments against the existence of G/god' which they could use. Several, however, disliked his militant stance as intolerant.

An older charities administrator said she was 'a great admirer, possibly because he's just articulating and reinforcing views that I hold'. She enthusiastically declared that she enjoyed 'Richard Dawkins, he cheers me up. If I'm feeling particularly down, I have a glass of wine and read Richard Dawkins or watch something on TV.' We might argue here, in fact, that Dawkins has become for this participant at least, a sacred text, much as Christians might find their Bible a form of comfort and encouragement in their particular worldview. Other than this participant, however, none seemed to prize particular atheist texts. They were useful to turn to for information and affirmation from time to time, admittedly, but other forms of media were resorted to much more often. Many people live hectic lives, and printed texts require sustained effort to get through. Much online material is much more quickly accessible. One young atheist, for example, told us that one of his daily rituals consisted of eating breakfast while googling the latest (atheist) news and reading his favourite bloggers.

Ritual and rites of passage

Assembling with friends and family for the kind of naming, wedding and funeral ceremonies overseen by humanist celebrants, as reported by Engelke (2014) and Aston (2015), constitutes another example of joining with like-minded others. Those who are non-religious are thereby enabled to have a personalised service specifically geared to their requirements. This appeals to those who have not found what they were looking for in other ceremonies for rites of passage, usually in traditional church services (Engelke 2014; Aston 2015). Young atheist RC had attended humanist wedding ceremonies in Scotland, where humanist weddings are legally recognised. She reported,

> I just remember it was nice because they were able to write their own vows and the celebrant was able to say what they wanted her to say and yeah, it wasn't the sort of formal type, kind of church wedding that people seem to dream about regardless of whether they're believers or not.

Of one particular ceremony, she said,

> They had drummers which was nice . . . yeah, it was a sort of procession, drummers and fire . . . I'm awful at describing things but swinging things with flames and a procession, so that was cool. I can't imagine that coming out of a church.

When asked what she thought happened at the end of life, she found that

> rather than sad or bad I found that almost exciting . . . that sounds really strange but to me it's refreshing and I don't need to worry about any comeuppance or any [quiet voice] divine retribution or just, you know, in this life, if I want to make the most of it and do what I want, do it on my terms.

Apart from RC, not many of our participants, either of the older or younger generation, had had much involvement with non-religious ceremonies for rites of passage, but the older women in particular were aware of their existence. One woman had been married in church just after the Second World War, and her children had been baptised, she told me, but they were born in the decade just after the war, so she had been unaware of humanism/atheism at that time. Marriage and infant baptism in churches were the common expectation of most couples at that time (Brown 2001, 2006).

Conclusion

Studies of materiality in 'sacred space' have previously tended to focus upon the form of religious buildings, rituals, shrines and spiritual landscapes. The work of Knott, Engelke, Aston and others is shifting focus towards everyday and secular spaces. To quote Morgan (this volume), 'taking materiality seriously means focusing our attention on the things and conditions that embody the relations that organise a [non]religious life-world.'

While at first glance atheism may seem a purely intellectual position, it is very much embodied and situated. Ordinary, everyday places and spaces, assumed to be normatively secular by our respondents, can, they discover, be contested by the 'intrusion' of the religious. Although they may live their lives indistinguishably from their fellow citizens much of the time, occasions arise when commitment to an atheist identity demands resistance to such 'intrusion'. They also seek spaces free from such intrusions where they can be confident that the secular is securely normative and which generate a sense of belonging with like-minded others (Morgan, this volume). Atheism is lived in these ritual encounters in which the human body, mind and emotions are implicated. As Lynch (2012: 128) argues, the power of sacred identifications is still a potent motivating force in modern social life, including among people who define themselves as non-religious.

Further research into non-religion starting from a material perspective is required, and we hope that this chapter has shown that such work would be feasible and worthwhile.

Notes

1 http://www.theguardian.com/commentisfree/2016/jan/20/no-religion-britons-atheism-christianity (accessed 17 March 2016).
2 We are grateful to all research participants for their contribution and the Jacobs Foundation for funding the Young Atheists Research Project. https://www.facebook.com/pages/The-Young-Atheists-Research-Project/123483571055246?sk=info.
3 According to the School Standards and Framework Act 1998 'each pupil in attendance at a community, foundation or voluntary school [in England and Wales] shall on each school day take part in an act of collective worship,' 'subject to the parental right of excusal or other special arrangements', and that act of collective worship will most likely be of a 'broadly Christian character' but can vary depending on the nature of the school: https://humanism.org.uk/education/parents/collective-worship-and-school-assemblies-your-rights/ (accessed 8 February 2015).
4 http://www.skeptic.org.uk/events/skeptics-in-the-pub (accessed 5 January 2015).
5 http://en.wikipedia.org/wiki/Nine_Lessons_and_Carols_for_Godless_People (accessed 5 January 2015).
6 http://ahsstudents.org.uk/ (accessed 5 January 2015).
7 Numerous sites/activities were mentioned to us by the YAs – for example following BHA, the humanist philosopher A. C. Grayling and humanist physician Ben Goldacre on Twitter; https://www.youtube.com/user/Thunderf00t; http://www.badscience.net/; https://www.youtube.com/user/AronRa; http://www.atheist-experience.com/; http://pennandteller.net/ (all accessed 4 September 2014).
8 http://www.secularism.org.uk/protest-the-pope-rally-sees-thou.html (accessed 4 September 2014).

References

Altemeyer, Bob. 2010. 'Atheism and Secularity in North America'. In *Atheism and Secularity: Volume 2: Global Expressions*, ed. Phil Zuckerman, 1–21. Santa Barbara, CA: Praeger.
Amarasingam, Amarnath. 2012. 'Introduction: What Is the New Atheism'. In *Religion and the New Atheism: A Critical Appraisal*, ed. Amarnath Amarasingam, 1–8. Chicago, IL: Haymarket.
Aston, Katie. 2012. 'Finding Space for Nonreligion? Further Possibilities for Spatial Analysis'. *The Religious Studies Project*, September 26. http://www.religiousstudiesproject.com/

2012/09/26/finding-space-for-nonreligion-further-possibilities-for-spatial-analysis-by-katie-aston/. Accessed 14/03/2016.

———. 2015. *Living Without God: Nonreligious Alternatives in the UK*. PhD, Department of Anthropology, Goldsmiths, University of London.

Attride-Stirling, Jennifer. 2001. 'Thematic Networks: An Analytic Tool for Qualitative Research'. *Qualitative Research* 1(3): 385–405.

Bagg, Samuel and David Voas. 2010. 'The Triumph of Indifference: Irreligion in British Society'. In *Atheism and Secularity: Volume 2: Global Expressions*, ed. Phil Zuckerman, 91–111. Santa Barbara, CA: Praeger.

Beit-Hallahmi, Benjamin. 2007. 'Atheists: A Psychological Profile'. In *The Cambridge Companion to Atheism*, ed. Michael Martin, 300–317. Cambridge: Cambridge University Press.

Braun, Virginia and Victoria Clarke. 2006. 'Using Thematic Analysis in Psychology'. *Qualitative Research in Psychology* 3: 77–101.

Brown, Callum G. 2001. *The Death of Christian Britain: Understanding Secularization 1800–2000*. London and New York: Routledge.

———. 2006. *Religion and Society in Twentieth-Century Britain*. Harlow: Pearson Education.

Brown, Callum G. and Gordon Lynch. 2012. 'Cultural Perspectives'. In *Religion and Change in Modern Britain*, eds. Linda Woodhead and Rebecca Catto, 329–351. London and New York: Routledge.

Bullivant, Stephen. 2008. 'Research Note: Sociology and the Study of Atheism'. *Journal of Contemporary Religion* 3(23): 363–368.

———. 2012. 'The New Atheism and Sociology: Why Here? Why Now? What Next?'. In *Religion and the New Atheism: A Critical Appraisal*, ed. Amarnath Amarasingam, 109–124. Chicago: Haymarket.

Catto, Rebecca. 2014. 'What Can We Say about Today's British Religious Young Person? Findings from the AHRC/ESRC Religion and Society Programme'. *Religion* 44(1): 1–27.

Catto, Rebecca and Janet B. Eccles. 2013. '(Dis)Believing and Belonging: Investigating the Narratives of Young British Atheists'. *Temenos: Nordic Journal of Comparative Religion* 49(1): 37–63.

Chidester, David and Edward Tabor Linenthal. 1995. *American Sacred Space*. Bloomington: Indiana University Press.

Cliteur, Paul. 2009. 'The Definition of Atheism'. *Journal of Religion and Society* 11: 1–23.

Connolly, William E. 2006. "Europe: A Minor Tradition". In *Powers of the Secular Modern: Talal Asad and His Interlocutors*, eds. David Scott and Charles Hirschkind, 75–92. Stanford, CA: Stanford University Press.

Crockett, Alasdair and David Voas. 2006. 'Generations of Decline: Religious Change in 20th-Century Britain'. *Journal for the Scientific Study of Religion* 45(4): 567–584.

Dawkins, Richard. 2006. *The God Delusion*. London: Transworld.

de Botton, Alain. 2012. *Religion for Atheists: A Non-believer's Guide to the Uses of Religion*. London: Penguin.

Didyoung, Justin, Eric Charles and Nicholas J. Rowland. 2013. 'Non-Theists Are No Less Moral Than Theists: Some Preliminary Results'. *Secularism and Nonreligion* 2: 1–20.

Eccles, Janet B. 2012. 'Changing "Emotional Regimes": Their Impact on Beliefs and Values in Some Older Women'. *Journal of Beliefs and Values: Studies in Religion and Education* 33(1): 11–21.

Eccles, Janet B. and Rebecca Catto. 2015. 'Espousing Apostasy and Feminism? Older and Younger British Female Apostates Compared'. *Secularism and Nonreligion* 4(5): 1–12.

Engelke, Matthew. 2014. 'Christianity and the Anthropology of Secular Humanism'. *Current Anthropology* 55(S10): S292–301.

Falconi, Ryan C. 2012. 'Is God a Hypothesis? The New Atheism, Contemporary Philosophy of Religion, and Philosophical Confusion'. In *Religion and the New Atheism: A Critical Appraisal*, ed. Amarnath Amarasingam, 203–224. Chicago, IL: Haymarket.

Gledhill, Ruth. 2012. 'Mirrors to the World'. In *Religion and the News*, eds. Jolyon Mitchell and Owen Gower, 89–98. Farnham and Burlington, VT: Ashgate.

Guenther, Katja M. 2014. 'Bounded by Disbelief: How Atheists in the United States Differentiate Themselves from Religious Believers'. *Journal of Contemporary Religion* 29(1): 1–16.

Guest, Greg, Kathleen M. MacQueen and Emily E. Namey. 2012. *Applied Thematic Analysis*. Thousand Oaks, CA: SAGE.

Harris, Sam. 2004. *The End of Faith: Religion, Terror and the Future of Reason*. New York: W.W. Norton.

Hitchens, Christopher. 2007. *God Is Not Great: The Case against Religion*. London: Atlantic.

Knott, Kim. 2005. *The Location of Religion: A Spatial Analysis*. London and Oakville, CT: Equinox.

———. 2010a. 'Religion, Space and Place: The Spatial Turn in Research on Religion'. *Religion and Society: Advances in Research* 1: 29–43.

———. 2010b. 'Theoretical and Methodological Resources for Breaking Open the Secular and Exploring the Boundary between Religion and Non-Religion'. *Historia Religionum* 2: 115–133.

———. 2011. 'Spatial Methods'. In *The Routledge Handbook of Research Methods in the Study of Religion*, eds. M. Stausberg and S. Engler, 491–501. London and New York: Routledge.

Knott, Kim, Elizabeth Poole and Teemu Taira. 2013. *Media Portrayals of Religion and the Secular Sacred*. Farnham and Burlington, VT: Ashgate.

Lee, Lois. 2012. 'Research Note: Talking about a Revolution: Terminology for the New Field of Non-Religion Studies'. *Journal of Contemporary Religion* 27(1): 129–139.

Lynch, Gordon. 2012. *The Sacred in the Modern World: A Cultural Sociological Approach*. Oxford: Oxford University Press.

Mahlamäki, Tiina. 2012. 'Religion and Atheism from a Gender Perspective'. *Approaching Religion* 2(1): 58–65.

Manning, Christel. 2010. "Atheism, Secularity, the Family, and Children". In *Atheism and Secularity: Volume 1: Issues, Concepts, and Definitions*, ed. Phil Zuckerman, 19–41. Santa Barbara, CA: Praeger.

McKearney, Patrick. 2010. *Religion and Ridicule in Contemporary British Stand-Up Comedy: Finding Rituals and Ethics in Unexpected Places*. M. Phil, Theology and Religious Studies, Cambridge.

Morgan, David. 2009. 'The Look of Sympathy: Religion, Visual Culture, and the Social Life of Feeling'. *Material Religion* 5(2): 132–155.

Mumford, Lorna. 2014. 'The Divergent Discourses of Scientific and Humanistic Atheism'. *NRSN Blog*, April 4. http://blog.nsrn.net/2014/04/04/the-divergent-discourses-of-scientific-and-humanistic-atheism/. Accessed 10/03/2016.

———. 2015. 'Living Non-Religious Identity in London'. In *Atheist Identities: Spaces and Social Contexts*, eds. Lori G. Beaman and Tomlins Steven, 153–170. Switzerland: Springer International.

Office for National Statistics. 2012. 'Religion in England and Wales 2011'. http://www.ons.gov.uk/peoplepopulationandcommunity/culturalidentity/religion/articles/religioninenglandandwales2011/2012-12-11. Accessed 10/03/2016.

Pasquale, Frank L. 2010. 'A Portrait of Secular Group Affiliates'. In *Atheism and Secularity: Volume 1: Issues, Concepts, and Definitions*, ed. Phil Zuckerman, 43–87. Santa Barbara, CA: Praeger.

Riessman, Catherine Kohler. 2012. 'Analysis of Personal Narratives'. In *The SAGE Handbook of Interview Research: The Complexity of the Craft, 2nd ed.*, eds. Jaber F. Gubrium, James A. Holstein, Amir B. Marvasti and Karyn D. McKinney, 367–380. Thousand Oaks, CA: SAGE.

Riis, Ole and Linda Woodhead. 2010. *A Sociology of Religious Emotion*. Oxford: Oxford University Press.

Smith, Buster and Richard Cimino. 2012. 'Atheisms Unbound: The Role of the New Media in the Formation of a Secularist Identity'. *Secularism and Nonreligion* 1: 17–31.

Stringer, Martin D. 2013. 'The Sounds of Silence: Searching for the Religious in Everyday Discourse'. In *Social Identities between the Sacred and the Secular*, eds. Abby Day, Giselle Vincett and Christopher R. Cotter, 161–171. Farnham and Burlington, VT: Ashgate.

Taira, Teemu, Elizabeth Poole and Kim Knott. 2012. 'Religion in the British Media Today'. In *Religion and the News*, eds. Jolyon Mitchell and Owen Gower, 31–43. Farnham and Burlington, VT: Ashgate.

Zuckerman, Philip. 2007. 'Atheism: Contemporary Numbers and Patterns'. In *The Cambridge Companion to Atheism*, ed. Michael Martin, 47–65. Cambridge: Cambridge University Press.

———. 2012. *Faith No More: Why People Reject Religion*. Oxford and New York: Oxford University Press.

Part 3
Circulation

10 Death in material and mental culture

Douglas J. Davies

Introduction

The universality of death makes it exceptionally valuable for studying the pervasive interplay of 'mental' and 'material' culture. The imaginative thought-worlds through which the very notion of 'life' has been conceived, categorised, and partnered with death parallel the pragmatic materiality of the human body whose terminal lifelessness prompts its disposal.

This chapter explores the interplay of thought and action surrounding death through selected key theories derived largely from social-cultural anthropology. From nineteenth-century ideas of animism through twentieth-century concern for ritual-symbolism to the twenty-first-century cognitive science of selfhood, this account includes notions of embodiment, human emotions, and identity pursued through brief comparative examples drawn from established religious traditions. Feeling and thinking are mutual dynamics of human identity, embedded in the notion of embodiment and its combined mental and material culture. These dynamics are reflected ahead in a cluster of mortality-linked phenomena: death, dying, the disposal of human bodies, memorialisation, and memory. The pervasive nature of death will ensure that wider issues of material culture, as in the case of icons of 'the dead', are deployed in the religious life of the living.

Embodiment and identity

When framed by the adaptive behaviour of our human response to the environment, the 'feeling-thinking' motif is expressed in a people's organisation of feelings towards and classification of the world. This motif loudly echoes the 'bio-cultural' description of today's dominant approach to human emotions (Davies 2011). Emile Durkheim's earlier sociological portrayal of the human being as *Homo duplex* is not dissimilar, interpreting a person as consisting in the intricate interplay of 'individual' and 'society'. For him, language and the classification of things provided by society were archetypical of the complex individual-society bond (Davies 2011: 26, 29, 187–190). From the cultural 'screens' of the cave paintings of pre-antiquity, through funerary remains evidenced by archaeology, to the contemporary architecture of human dwellings and the electronic technology of social media, society's influence upon the interplay of thought and feeling is dramatically evident, not least for death and memory.

'Material' and 'mental' culture are aligned through the creative and imitative capacities of human beings as social animals. It is as much through death-related phenomena as through any other aspect of life that people find an alignment, and sometimes a dissonance, between material and mental cultures. The intensification of thought, in memories, dreams, and emotions of grief occasioned by death, is frequently triggered by the material world of corpses, their containment, burial, cremation, or other funerary treatment. Furthermore, the experience of bereavement, which often prompts reflection on our own death, has led the great majority of societies to explore the idea of post-mortal existence in afterlife environments of underworld, paradise, or heaven, or in samsara-cycles of transmigrating souls. These imaginative thought-worlds are frequently sustained in ritual activity conducted in highly social liturgies and in domestic and individual devotion.

Tylor: animism, totemism, and embodied awareness

Historically and theoretically speaking the seminal anthropologist Sir Edward Burnett Tylor (1832–1917), foremost of nineteenth-century British creators of the discipline of anthropology, provides a foundation for discussing material and mental dimensions of death. His *Primitive Culture* of 1871 and its 1881 complement, *Anthropology, An Introduction to the Study of Man and Civilization*, presented a great deal of data belonging both to the realm of imaginative thought and to the domain of manually produced artefacts. Of the 1871 volume's 850 pages, three quarters are given over to the description of 'Animism', the 'groundwork of the Philosophy of Religion' which accounts for 'the deep-lying doctrine of Spiritual Beings' embracing both the 'souls of individual creatures, capable of continued existence after death' and of 'powerful deities' ([1871] 2010, Vol. 2: 385). As for the 1881 study, some quarter of its 440 pages is given over to pragmatic themes dealing with the 'arts of life' and 'of pleasure', all introduced by the pragmatic sense of 'the arts by which man defends and maintains himself, and holds rule over the world he lives in' ([1881] 1900: 182).

For Tylor the notion of 'soul-embodiment' aptly accounted for ideas of souls associated with objects or, as it were, for 'the real presence of a spiritual being in a material object' ([1871] 2010, Vol. 2: 151). Today's discussion of grief in terms of the popular notion of the continuing bonds between the living and their dead is presaged in his brief description of 'the mourner among ourselves' who goes to weep at a grave, showing how 'imagination keeps together the personality and the relics of the dead'. Many other examples, including Chinese ancestral tablets, also link thought and objects of mental and material culture ([1871] 2010, Vol. 2: 138–140). Tylor's work, whose historical importance for material and mental culture is not as academically familiar today as it might be, draws us to the deeply human experience of knowing life through objects.

While this indirectness of knowledge is an important issue that could be much pursued in philosophical and psychological terms, it suffices to say here that the very idea of 'life' as an abstract noun is, itself, strange. Our knowledge of 'life' comes not only through our sense of ourselves as 'living' but also through our sense of other 'living' things, of phenomena that strike us as possessing a distinctive quality. Some contemporary cognitive anthropologists and psychologists approach this in terms of 'animacy' (Boyer 2001: 105–154) and engage with it experimentally, but it still reflects the life force experienced in 'things' that Tylor considered as intrinsic to human nature.

Death, too, may be understood as an abstract noun whose significance changes as experience of dead 'things' increases, notably of individuals who have been closest to us. Consequently, death intensifies the 'thinking-feeling' dimension of our understanding, seldom stronger than in the case of the corpse. Here another of Tylor's notions is germane, that of the 'emotional tone' that combines with a 'bodily attitude' to generate its own form of 'gesture language' enabling a complexity to develop in social life ([1871] 2010, Vol. 1: 147–150, 211). Indeed, the emotional tonality fostered by the material culture of death highlights the significance of cemeteries and locations of memorial within any society, not just in terms of personal engagement as in visits to a cemetery but also in corporate acts of remembrance.

Interestingly, Tylor's *Primitive Culture* was published just a year before Charles Darwin's *The Expression of the Emotions in Man and Animals* of 1872, though Darwin's emotions work was grounded in research extending much further back, including his sixteen-point questionnaire of 1867 sent to many individuals across the world (1872: 15). Certainly each knew and appreciated the other's work: both were, of course, Fellows of the Royal Society. While Tylor's concern with death focused on the life force in the body or as the departed soul, Darwin's interest focused on what we might describe as the 'material culture' of the body itself. This included his description of the grief responses of the individual, with its considerable detail on the 'grief-muscles' that produce distinctive vertical ridges between the eyebrows. As with much else in life, Darwin thought that the capacity to exercise these muscles was subject to heredity, with some families possessing the ability much more than others (1872: 181–183).

Embodiment expands

Much more socially focused than Darwin, and more symbolically orientated than Tylor, twentieth-century anthropology aligned the body and social behaviour in ever more integrated ways. Marcel Mauss's brief French anthropology of 'body techniques' ([1935] 1979), along with Max Weber's ([1922] 1965) and, especially, Pierre Bourdieu's ([1972] 1977) theoretical enhancement of the notion of *habitus*, increasingly brought bodily behaviour to the fore in cultural studies. Claude Lévi-Strauss's notion of totemism (1962) contributed to this by the way he speaks of objects that are 'good to think', encouraging a view of objects as vehicles helping to formulate thoughts by allowing us to grasp ideas through the various relationships we perceive as existing between things. By the mid-twentieth century anthropological thought had become very alert to the way human bodies and cultural values pervaded each other, not least through symbolic ritual activity (Rappaport 1999). The corpse, gravestone, and the social fact of cemeteries, as well as certain objects that once belonged to the living, may each become a medium through which we can think of our dead, our relationships with them, and our own forthcoming demise. Here 'thinking' is a dynamic process with emotions prompted by memory.

This embodiment approach can also help in understanding issues of what might be called devotional epistemology – that is of how we 'know' what we know about the divine and the dynamics of piety both during 'ordinary' periods of life and when certain periods may intensify them within theological debates, practical action, and through unexpected events, such as sudden bereavement. The ritual world of liturgical performance, with its area of overlap between corporate action and private prayer, provides forms of emotions that conduce to a sense of the truth of things, a point long-established by Geertz's much debated cultural definition of religion as 'a system of symbols' establishing 'moods and motivations' that possess 'such an aura of factuality' that they 'seem uniquely realistic' ([1966] 1973: 4). While the unique realism occasioned by emotional engagement with symbols takes one form in large-scale religious traditions, its influence also pervades personal life, especially in secularised societies and among groups developing what are frequently seen as forms of 'non-religious' spirituality where death and its material manifestation also make their presence felt.

Theoretically speaking, Victor Turner's (1969) anthropological analysis of symbols complements Geertz's view of 'religion'. Turner's 'symbol' possesses ideological and sensory poles whose ritual deployment integrates them in ways valuable for considering the dead and mortuary rites. The ideological pole, for example, represents the cultural classification of 'the dead', 'the corpse', coffin, ashes, flowers, or memorial objects. This element offers scope for extensive cultural exegesis not only of formal philosophical and theological ideas but also of local and folk explanations of life. Here, too, historical analysis of how phenomena arrive at their present form can find its proper place. In terms of mortality, the sensory pole embraces the full gamut of experience created, alerted, or numbed through death, notably the complex kaleidoscope of grief. As with most cultural symbols, individuals encounter and use them in the company of others, especially when symbolic objects are used in the focused behaviour usually described as ritual. This is why it is often useful to speak of ritual-symbols, as a firm reminder of the social arena of deployment. This is not to say, however, that an individual's thought and feeling in connection with any particular symbol do not carry deeply individual and even idiosyncratic connotations that a person brings to or takes from a ritual event in which the more common features take public precedence. This private domain may well be especially active in memories of the dead and in objects and places of domestic and intimate relationships.

Corpse symbolism

Death, then, intensifies the 'thinking-feeling' dimension of our understanding. 'Death's' abstraction becomes more experiential as life proceeds and, most especially, as we lose those who have been closest to us. This is where the corpse, interpreted as a symbol – as something that participates in what it represents – becomes influential as a meeting place of our 'thinking and feeling'. Death becomes a material reality with strong mental impact. The corpse presents a universal symbol of both death and life as two existential elements standing as necessary complements to each other. In a technical, philosophical sense, each is the 'imaginary' of the other.

As for 'life' intuited as a form of animacy, this is nowhere as powerfully encountered as in a corpse, precisely because of life's absence. The world in which the deceased once participated is marked by movement. The very phrase 'the breath of life' is indicative both of 'breath' and of the movement of breathing. It is precisely the distinction between movement and stillness, and their corollaries of sound and silence, that marks the essential boundaries between life and death. The body, as material that moves, is the totem of vitality while, as material that ultimately lies still, it is also the primary totem of mortality. However, while stillness is a characteristic feature of the corpse, that body does not remain changeless. Not long after death it undergoes the stiffness of *rigor mortis* followed by relaxation of muscles; discolouration of the flesh occurs as blood collects under the force of gravity, and decay commences under the influence of the body's own bacteria; the exudation of fluids and the onset of smell present sensory data of death for the bio-cultural response of survivors, including the sense of the separation of the person who once was from the material that now is. External sources, including flies, their larvae, other insects, animals, and ultimately plants, complete the process.

Even so, a near-universal belief in life force or soul has served profound ends in providing an explanation for this 'person', who, despite decay, is now elsewhere, independent of the body. The practice shared by large segments of humanity of cremating or burying the same day as death, notably in Indian, Islamic, and Jewish traditions, has largely overcome the extended decay factor while enhancing the belief in an ongoing journey of the soul. This is evident in Islam where, in many contexts, the dead is not en-coffined but shrouded and buried in a grave that is so constructed as to allow the 'dead' to sit up when, shortly after burial, they are visited by angelic beings in a form of question-judgment that relates to their ongoing destiny. Rapidity of burial, including the material culture of grave-digging and structure, can be seen as part of a process of dying – preferably also accompanied by someone rehearsing key idioms of the declaration of faith that there is only one God and that Mohammad is God's prophet, words that the buried Muslim will need to rehearse during the angelic visitation. The role of prayers for 'dead' Muslims, to assist them in their post-mortem condition, which for most involves some real pain as 'life' or consciousness is finally withdrawn from them, reveals its own form of making merit for the dead, a theme developed ahead.

By sharp contrast to rapid funerals, the practice of retaining the dead while they decay and then subsequently treating the bones makes dissolution its own reality among the living. Robert Hertz's famous account of 'double-burial', or double processing of the 'wet' stage of decay and the 'dry' stage of dealing with the bones, showed how the ritual treatment of the dead transformed the dead person into an ancestral status (1905–6). Generations later Bloch (1971) demonstrated a similar transformation of the recently dead into the long-term dead in Madagascar, where immediate earth burial is followed by transferring bones to ancestral tombs out of which the remains are periodically retrieved, rewrapped, and replaced. The dead eventually progress into the very dust of the ancestral territory within which the kin-linked tombs are built.

Coffin containment

In these rites the corpse is often a dynamic aspect of material culture, albeit one with strong and transforming relationships with the living. In most developed societies the containment of the corpse within a container, in modern times that of a coffin, begins the process of removal of the dead from the living. The very familiarity of a coffin, or of the more elaborate casket of the United States, should not lead us to ignore its powerful role in the material culture of death. In terms of some of the undergirding themes of this volume the coffin offers a powerful example of a medium that reveals 'death' while often 'concealing' the dead, especially since the great majority of British funerals employ a closed coffin, with some exceptions, including Greek-Russian Orthodoxy. While coffins assumed a relatively traditional design over the later nineteenth and into the late twentieth century, with key manufacturers producing them for easy purchase by funeral directors, the early twenty-first century has witnessed the emergence of more individual designs, allowing a person to obtain a coffin expressing his or her hobby, sporting-leisure associations, and the like. Even reinforced cardboard containers have their place, not least as being especially suitable for family decoration with paint, collages, and so on. There is almost no end to the possibility of such design. Even in very traditional Finland, for example, by 2015 it is possible to have a small boat-shaped coffin available for interment. Similarly, the making of themed and highly original coffins is well known in contemporary Ghana. These examples reflect the important part played by the notion of 'production' in this volume.

Natural burial

A similar symbolic interplay of mental and material culture can be identified in the practice of what is, variously, described as natural, woodland, green, or ecological burial currently developing in the UK and beyond. Originating as a funeral innovation in the mid-1990s this has, by 2015, led to the very rapid creation of more than 250 or so sites in the UK where bodies are buried in contexts deemed 'natural', rather than in formal cemeteries with headstones or permanently visible markers of interments. Though marked, variously, on maps, electronically, or by satellite location, these plots are intended to be overgrown by grass, plants, and local vegetation. Motivations include a love of 'nature', the desire not to have a grave that has to be 'cared for', or to be located in a beautiful place. This practice seems to be informed by a preference for being amid 'living' things rather than in the serried ranks of gravestones above the 'dead'. Here, again, we encounter mental and material cultures combining in an anticipated identity of being placed in just such a life-dynamic natural place.

These sites were created for the burial of corpses, but their popularity has had the relatively unintended consequence of attracting people who wish to place cremated remains in them. The imaginative sense that fostered the diverse location of cremated remains will be discussed ahead, but it would seem that this same imagination has extended itself to innovative forms of relating the whole corpse to the earth, including the use of easily biodegradable 'coffins' woven from bamboo, willow, or the like.

Cremation and circulation of memory

Burial is one thing, cremation is another, yet the nature of coffins and their material culture remains significant in cremation. In contemporary European Union countries, for example, laws exist to control coffin-making materials and noxious gases released during cremation. Similarly, expensive mercury abatement filtering systems are prescribed for crematoria to account for the use of that metal in dental fillings. Here the mental culture of ecology intersects with the material components of corpse and coffin.

Ashes

Modern cremation, from its late nineteenth-century origin, had to devise ways of treating post-cremation remains. Some were interred in graves, but others were placed in urns deposited in newly architected columbaria – buildings replete with niche shelving. A classic example, at London's Golders Green Crematorium, holds urns of some variety, often inspired by classical antiquity and bearing the names and professions of many late nineteenth- and early twentieth-century cremations of the rich and relatively famous. To see them arranged in the niches after which the 'dove-cote' or columbarium took its name – again from classical Rome – is to see a distinctive form of cultural archive of innovative thinkers and cultural innovators. Nevertheless, these columbaria, static, monumental, and relatively costly, did not establish themselves in the rise of later British crematoria. Instead ashes were more likely to be placed within the lawns and gardens of crematoria, or perhaps buried in family graves alongside pre-existing coffin burials.

From the mid-1970s or so Britons began to take ashes to a wide diversity of locations, such as domestic gardens, holiday or sporting venues, or other significant places. This practice was not shared by most other Europeans, whose countries, until very recently, maintained sharp laws governing the use of ashes. Some English Premier League football clubs allowed ashes to be placed within their grounds, at least until the practice became a little too demanding. Associated venues then needed to be used, such as training grounds. Rivers where the deceased had fished, or mountains where they had walked, proved to be easier venues. It is very likely that hundreds of culturally significant places have had cremated remains discreetly located within them, enabling the material symbolism of the dead to be aligned with a greater variety of locations than ever before in British history. Metaphorically speaking, the dead were assisted in wandering far beyond churchyard, cemetery, or crematorium. This highly private and family-based activity is widely familiar to society at large, presenting a fascinating case of symbolic concealment and disclosure as part of the circulation of memory. Here we see the force of this volume's emphasis on circulation, played out at a micro level that, nevertheless, echoes the macro level of society at large.

Icons

Cremated remains are not only highly portable but also easily divisible, allowing for a single person's remains to be shared among family members or placed in several places that had been significant for the dead. This is both a modern and an ancient practice. After the death of the Buddha, for example, his cremated remains were placed in a variety of stupa monuments. Two and a half millennia later, the ashes of Mahatma Gandhi were placed in selected sites across India as the 'father' of the nation. So, too, in the 1970s and 1990s, Zhou Enlai's and Deng Xiaoping's remains were distributed in a China that was seeking to foster cremation (Davies 2005: xxiv).

These examples are reminiscent of Early and Medieval Christianity, when no church of any significance would be devoid of some body parts or personal items of saints and martyrs held as holy relics. In terms of mental and material culture, relics placed within or under an altar in the Catholic tradition offer prime symbols of the past and present community of faith. When the priest kisses the altar at the commencement of the Mass he clearly engages in that communal unity. In Orthodoxy, too, the role of relics and the dynamic ritual use of icons serve to bring the living into face-to-face relationship with the holy ones. The very nature of ecclesial icons highlights the radical interplay of mental and material culture.

The very word 'icon' has, interestingly, assumed considerable popularity in recent decades to describe both navigational aids on computer screens and typical celebrity figures in the media, but historically this symbolic form has engendered troubled periods within several religious traditions. These eras reflect the power of material culture to focus ideas through the bodies of the long-dead. Differences of abstract philosophical theology tend to become forcefully polemical when those ideas are aligned with physical objects, ritual, or architecture. This is a reminder of what was said earlier about the notion of totemism. When the human body is the medium of expression of an idea, then attitudes towards its representation become potentially problematic. If the 'idea' is somehow aligned with notions of 'truth' and the reception of truth then differences of opinion can become extremely fraught, as both history and the present day make dramatically clear.

Ancient Judaism is well known for its opposition to the making and use of material things that could be the focus of worship, defined as idolatry. This is included in the Ten Commandments, which prohibit making and worshipping any physical representation of anything that exists in the heavens, on earth, or in the seas (Exodus 20: 4). The explicit command not to make gods of gold or silver is paralleled with the command to kill and sacrifice animals on a rude altar made of earth (Genesis 20: 23–24). Engaging with God involved behaviour pairing life and death through sacrificed beasts, rather than through inanimate representations of life or death. The prohibition on physical representation of deity retained its force in Judaism, where the ritual focus on a spectrum of sacrificial offerings was retained until the Temple of Jerusalem was destroyed in 70 CE. The subsequent Jewish focus on congregational gatherings in synagogues, ritual observance within the home, and the observation of behavioural and dietary laws brought a diversity of material culture into play, not least the text of sacred scripture in the form of Torah scrolls.

Islam includes a similar avoidance of depiction of supernatural realities while possessing an enormous emphasis on the text of the *Qur'an* and further commitments to the stories and traditions known as *Hadith*. The power of literary traditions in creating and owning scripts, often curated and ritually performed by relatively elite groups of scribes and priests, allows for texts to be learned by heart and in that sense to foster a worldview in which mental and material culture cohere. To have learned a text that is believed to have a divine source, whether in divinely inscribed tablets as with Moses and the Ten Commandments, or as communicated through the angel Gabriel to Mohammad in the case of the Qur'an, and to be able to recite these bring a distinctive sense of identity to a community, not least to the millions of Muslims in Britain and beyond.

Those relatively few described by most observers as Islamic extremists, notably those categorised as the so-called Islamic State fighting for dominance as an Islamic caliphate in the Middle East, have engaged in the destruction of numerous pre-existing sacred buildings. This includes the ancient site of Palmyra, a UNESCO world heritage site whose renowned curator, the Syrian archaeologist Khaled Asaad, was beheaded as a 'director of idolatries' and 'as a spy' (Trew, Coghlan and Richardson 2015: 30–31). This very modern form of iconoclasm expresses the Islamic notion of non-representation of created things that might be worshipped. This theme of representation has also become relevant to the media-conscious world of contemporary communications, as when newspaper cartoons depict Mohammad and provoke violent responses from some Muslims. To put such representations in the form of satirical cartoons is defended by some cartoonists as an expression of freedom of speech, and read by some devotees as an inexcusable provocation that causes offence.

As for the emergence of what Christians call the New Testament, this, too, presented its own focused phenomenon of 'truth' manifest in the material culture of texts that portray the life and work of Jesus of Nazareth identified as a divine figure and of his Apostles. In the course of time the eighth- and ninth-century Orthodox Church experienced its own deeply contentious debates over paintings or icons of such 'biblical' and subsequent saintly figures. Heated controversy debated their value for retention or destruction, with the outcome favouring retention. This fostered a mode of spirituality affirming a quality of perceptive relationship with the painted and often impressively framed object, an outlook transcending any simple depiction of subject and object, and enhancing faith through a devotee's engagement with the divine through these sacred symbols. In keeping with the widely agreed notion of a symbol as something that participates in what it represents, devotees' relationships with icons of Christ, the Blessed Virgin Mary, and some saints bring a sense of engagement fostering active spiritual blessing. This is not a question of art appreciation, or simply looking at a painting, but of that painted representation bringing qualities of the one depicted to bear upon the person now attending to it. Actions of kissing, prostration, or other acknowledgement of icons, set within church or home or used liturgically, are acts of mutual relationship.

In theoretical terms some might see elements of Tylor's animism at work here, while others would focus theologically on the divine presence in and through a multiplicity of material things. Those who paint icons would speak of their own devotional attitudes while engaged in their work. This offers something of a phenomenological similarity to the careful practice of constructing physical statues of the Buddha, completed by the devotionally aware painting of the eyes, at which point a quality of realism or life is believed to come upon the 'statue'.

Such attitudes to devotional phenomena presaged the sixteenth-century Protestant Reformation concerning ritual and devotional practices. Reformers placed an intensified focus on biblical texts and their interpretation and expressed concern lest 'images' somehow detract from the divine truth enshrined in biblical texts appropriated through preaching, listening, and study. In terms of material culture, these debates involved church and church-state bureaucracies in competition for religious and secular power. In the Protestant-Catholic rifts of the Reformation the significance of material entities provided apt vehicles for much wider social-political-economic, let alone purely theological, debates.

Luther (1483–1546) was radically catalytic for shifts in European religion that would have worldwide consequences for the expression of mental and material cultures of religion. So too was Nanak (1469–1539) and what became Sikh tradition. Each was concerned with the thinking-feeling heart and the material contexts of piety. Guru Nanak's form of spirituality generated the Sikh movement in the late fifteenth century, and reveals a strong emphasis on interior rather than external religious phenomena. Pilgrimage is better viewed as a journey within one's own being, and genuine prayer is of the heart rather than of religious postures. While 'pilgrimages, penances, compassion, and almsgiving' may result in gaining some extremely small merit, it is hearing, believing, and loving the divine Name that allow a person to 'bathe and be made clean / In a place of pilgrimage within him' (Singh et al. 1960: 40). Over time, as with most religious traditions, Sikhs did come to ascribe significance to key places within their and their gurus' history, notably the building of the Golden Temple at Amritsar in the Punjab in the late sixteenth and early seventeenth centuries.

Merit: mental and material ritual

The concept of 'small merit' in Sikh scriptures reminds us of the very powerful phenomenon of merit-making in many religious traditions. Merit entails a close intersection of mental and material culture concerning the dead, their identity and destiny. Intensifying the role of reciprocity in community cohesion, the idea of merit comprises a kind of salvation-capital effective in relation with the divine, and often with post-mortem identity. Prayers, some ritual performances, and the payment for indulgences were significant in Medieval Christianity as means of assisting the 'dead' in their purgatorial afterlife. Much the same applies in some contemporary Christianity and notably in some Islamic prayers at the time of death, as intimated earlier. Protestant Reformation thought opposed such practices, as do many devotional forms of piety which stress divine love and the grace bestowed upon devotees. In post-Reformation Scotland all prayer was forbidden at funerals for some time to ensure there could be no merit-aligned prayers. This issue of merit and grace is rooted in the notion of status before the divine or, in other terms, is fundamentally concerned with individual identity and its destiny. In both Hinduism and Buddhism merit plays a significant part in the post-mortem transmigration of souls, including one's place in the traditional caste system.

Identity and sacrality

Identity, a complex notion open to numerous interpretations, affords a prime example of the interplay of thinking and feeling. Death brings its own challenge to identity, and religious traditions have developed different means of challenging death's apparent finality.

One thinker whose work enhances identity theory is Hans Mol (Mol 1976; Davies and Powell 2015). His theory of the sacralisation of identity argues that those things that confer a sense of identity upon a person are, in turn, viewed and treated with great respect. This mutuality of identity conferral on the one hand and ascribing of respect on the other has profound implications for material and mental cultures. In fact, it radically integrates them, for to speak of respect is, in fact, to invoke a spectrum of ascription. Things that contribute to my life habits I may simply 'like', as with a particular hairbrush or item of clothing. Other objects may carry strong sentimental significance for who I am, as in a ring that marks a relationship with another person or, perhaps, with an institution, or even some jewellery or object that once belonged to a deceased parent. These mini-totems are 'good for me to think', and help me to engage with who I am. The deep meaning they carry makes a loss of them significant. This becomes strongest of all in the 'loss' of someone I love and whose existence has contributed significantly to my own sense of identity. So, 'liking' something and 'loving' someone mark bands on a spectrum of identity conferral. In terms of religious devotees this spectrum can be extended to include the notion of 'worshipping' a divine figure, or perhaps even a religious principle and the material phenomena that enshrine that principle.

In the case of Christianity, for example, Jesus came to be the Lord whose death transcendence afforded identity to believers not only in terms of their life after death but also as contemporary participant members of a church whose rites, and even architecture, contributed to their present sense of identity and its eternal entailments. In terms of Mol's sacralisation of identity we could argue that the increasingly exalted status accorded to Jesus of Nazareth, culminating in creedal affirmations that he is one person of a threefold Godhead, was a reflection of the church community's sense of its own unique status. Jesus became increasingly exalted as the community became increasingly distinctive in its identity of salvation. Many consequences flow from this interpretation, including the fact that some groups make the 'church' itself a sacred institution through identity-alliance with Jesus and his first Apostles or, as with some later groups, through a renewed divine announcement to the world through a new prophet-leader.

Ritual creativity within such emergent institutions carries its own generative power to link mental and material culture. None, perhaps, is more obvious than the rise of the practice and doctrine of the Catholic Mass and the theology and centrality of the cross in Protestant domains.

The Christian use of bread and wine, within a rite evoking biblical narratives of Christ's sacrificial body and blood led, notably between the thirteenth and sixteenth centuries, to the development of a theology of transubstantiation. Its most influential pioneer, Thomas Aquinas (1225–1274), developed Aristotelian philosophical ideas in a theological direction. This brought to devotees the belief that the consecrated bread and wine was, intrinsically, and despite its obvious bread-like and wine-like appearance, the very body and blood of the Saviour. Liturgical accompaniments to this essentially miraculous act of the Holy Spirit intensified a symbolic process in which ideas of death, sacrifice, sin, grace, and divine mercy all combined in and through a doctrine of priesthood vested in a line traced back to Jesus's Apostles. The ringing of bells, genuflection, and the use of incense, as well as demarcated sacred spaces and objects, all further intensify the identity of a Christian believer as sinner saved through divine intent and ecclesial process. In Mol's terms the rite was accorded increasingly high status in alignment with the management of a devotee's spiritual identity and ultimate destiny. Material and mental cultures of faith cohered in acts of eating and drinking which, in theoretical terms, intensify the necessary processes of life's sustenance into sacred participation with the divine.

Part of the Protestant Reformation was linked to ideas that this elaboration of liturgy, not least in the role of priests as agents of mercy, and of various acts of payment for masses to assist the dead in the afterlife, detracted from the immediate intimacy of each individual's engagement with God, a concept expressed in the doctrine of the priesthood of all believers and in open access to the biblical text. Aligned with this reduced complexity of mental and material culture of salvation was a more fixed attention on the cross as the arena and culmination of Christ's work of salvation. The crucifix, a cross holding the body of Christ, which could easily portray what the ritual of the Mass enacted as a form of re-presentation of Christ's death, was abandoned for an 'empty' cross, or for an imagined cross encountered not in the material culture of worked objects but as the focus of preaching, praying, and hymnody. The bread and wine rites of many – but not all – Protestant churches took the form of remembering the death of Christ and not of bringing it into contemporary liturgical re-enactment, a distinction symbolised in some traditions by the use of 'ordinary' bread and non-fermented grape juice or even of water in place of wine. Such memorialisation exemplifies the phenomenon of mental culture. At the same time, it makes the narrative of the cross, notably in preaching, play a profound part in the emotional lives of believers, often linked with the identity-transformations described in conversions of the 'born-again' type. The symbolic practice of adult baptism itself offers a powerful sensory experience in the 'material culture' of water to symbolise in the fuller sense participation in the 'mental culture' of conversion.

Allure and the uncanny

The relational piety expressed in behaviour towards relics, icons, or the pivotal Christian rite of the Eucharist, with its variety of denominational descriptions as the Mass, Holy Communion, Lord's Supper, Sacrament Service, and the like, displays the creatively active mind – the mental culture of a person within a group – united with a material base for reflection and activation of contemporary emotion. This base itself consists in a complex interplay of liturgical objects, behavioural posture, the soundscape of hymns and silence, the emotional tonality of ritual language, an awareness of the flow of tradition, and, surrounding all this, the architecture of a familiar place of worship.

Here, the concept of the allure of such a situation is theoretically valuable. Lindsay Jones developed ideas of allurement in relation to religious architecture to describe the magnetic attraction, invitation, and sense of expectation surrounding one's hopes and desires enshrined in such a place (2000: 79). Something very similar was explored by de Certeau, Giard, and Mayol to describe a certain uncanniness that seems to surround distinctively enduring buildings within urban environments (1998: 133). These emotions are easily related to cemeteries and other memorial sites with which individuals engage. The notion of the uncanny had, of course, been much explored in a theological and philosophical fashion by Rudolph Otto in his famous *Idea of the Holy* with its account of experience of the divine as being that of a *mysterium tremendum et fascinans* ([1917] 1924). This forceful sense of enchantment by a mysterious source reflects something of the complexity of human emotions in relation to contexts of encountering the divine and, we could easily add, the dead. Whatever else might be said by way of religious belief in the self-existent nature of the dead, the memory of the departed can exert dramatically powerful influence through the dreams and in the reflections of the living.

More recently, some researchers have noted another form of strangely disturbing awareness prompted in human beings working with androids when these robots are not functioning or are, as it were, 'dead' – or when they do function, almost but not quite like humans. Described in terms of an 'uncanny valley' (MacDorman and Ishiguro 2006), this sense of challenged mimesis pinpoints the complex interplay of ideas of emotion, embodiment, and identity that draw human beings into relationship with each other. We have a 'theory of mind' that allows us to intuit that others have active thoughts as we do. Perhaps we might also have a 'theory of emotions' that, similarly, allows most of us to empathise with others. These theories prompt their own form of dissonance when met with such an android. Indeed, we might also posit something similar for the human response to a corpse that elicits some form of grief response (Davies 2015: 234–236). In theoretical terms these androids, and corpses too perhaps, hint not only at the issues of animacy and *habitus* already introduced earlier but also at the intrinsic complexity of human self-reflection and self-understanding that composes a sense of identity.

One intriguing context of such animacy may be found with specific reference to Buddhism and its artistic forms of the Buddha and other spiritually advanced persons. Here, framed by teachings of the transcendence of selfhood, these figures, in all their stillness, do not fall into the uncanny 'deadness' of unmoving androids. Perhaps this is because android 'existence' is, as yet, devoid of a grand narrative of relations with humans. Buddha figures, by contrast, possess an undisputable allure for devotees. Whatever dissonance they may possess due to their radical difference from the living is metamorphosed through ritual behaviour so that they are frequently regarded by devotees as a 'refuge, a beacon, and a template for creativity'; as 'art emanation bodies' they possess 'the power to transform' (Olinsky 1997: 15).

Conclusion

This chapter has depicted a wide variety of contextualised phenomena in which ideas of mental and material culture cohere in establishing human identity, notably in its engagement with death and death transcendence. The scholars and theories covered mark the importance of the body itself as the means in and through which ideas, values, and beliefs are manifest. The wider discussion of icons and iconoclasm has traced something of the entailment of identity construction in its more dispersed form of thinking 'through', or by means of, erstwhile physical objects. Animacy and 'totemism' have taken their place alongside theology in a brief anthropological consideration of death in material and mental culture, all within the wide phenomenon of circulation at a variety of interacting levels of individual and social action.

Works cited

Bloch, Maurice. 1971. *Placing the Dead*. Cambridge: Cambridge University Press.

Bourdieu, Pierre. (1972) 1977. *Outline of a Theory of Practice*. Cambridge: Cambridge University Press.

Boyer, Pascal. 2001. *Religion Explained*. London: Heinemann.

Certeau, Michel de, Luce Giard and Pierre Mayol. 1998. *The Practice of Everyday Life, Volume 2, Living and Cooking*. Minneapolis: Minneapolis University Press.

Darwin, Charles. 1872. *The Expression of the Emotions in Man and Animals*. London: John Murray.

Davies, Douglas J. 2005. 'Introduction'. In *The Encyclopedia of Cremation*, eds. Douglas J. Davies with Lewis H. Mates, xvii–xxv. New York: Routledge.

———. 2011. *Emotion, Identity and Religion: Hope, Reciprocity and Otherness*. Oxford: Oxford University Press.

———. 2015. *Mors Britannica: Lifestyle and Death-Style in British Religion*. Oxford: Oxford University Press.

Davies, Douglas J. and Adam J. Powell. 2015. *Sacred Selves, Sacred Settings: Reflecting Hans Mol*. Farnham: Ashgate.

Geertz, Clifford. [1966] 1973. 'Religion as a Cultural System'. In *Anthropological Approaches to the Study of Religion*, ed. Michael Banton, 1–46. London: Tavistock.

Hertz, Robert. 1905–6. 'A Contribution to the Study of the Collective Representation of Death'. In *Death and the Right Hand*, eds. R. Needham and C. Needham, 29–88. New York: Free Press.

Jones, Lindsay. 2000. *The Hermeneutics of Sacred Architecture: Experience, Interpretation, Comparison. Vol. 1*. Cambridge, MA: Harvard University Press.

Levi-Strauss, Claude. 1962. *Totemism*. London: Merlin Press.

MacDorman, Karl F. and Hiroshi Ishiguro. 2006. 'The Uncanny Advantage of Using Androids in Cognitive and Social Science Research'. *Interaction Studies* 7(3): 297–337.

Mauss, Marcel. (1935) 1979. 'Techniques of the Body'. In *Sociology and Psychology: Essays by Marcel Mauss*, ed. Ben Brewster, 95–123. London: Routledge and Kegan Paul.

Mol, Hans. 1976. *Identity and the Sacred*. Oxford: Basil Blackwell.

Olinsky, Frank. 1997. *Buddha Book*. San Francisco, CA: Chronicle Books.

Otto, Rudolph. (1917) 1924. *The Idea of the Holy*. Oxford: Oxford University Press.

Rappaport, Roy. 1999. *Ritual in the Making of Humanity*. Cambridge: Cambridge University Press.

Singh, Trilochan, Jodh Singh, Kapur Singh, Bawa Harkrishen Singh and Kushwant Singh. 1960. *The Sacred Writings of the Sikhs*. London: George Allen and Unwin.

Trew, Bel, Tom Coghlan and Alice Richardson. 2015. 'Isis Begins the Destruction of Palmyra'. *The Times*, August 25, pp. 30–31.

Turner, Victor. 1969. *The Ritual Process*. London: Routledge Kegan Paull.

Tylor, Edward Burnett. (1871) 2010. *Primitive Culture*. Cambridge: Cambridge University Press.
———. (1881) 1900. *Anthropology: An Introduction to the Study of Man and Civilization*. New York: D. Appleton.
Weber, Max. (1922) 1965. *The Sociology of Religion*. London: Methuen.

11 Religion materialised in the everyday

Young people's attitudes towards material expressions of religion

Elisabeth Arweck

Introduction

This chapter draws on both qualitative and quantitative data arising from the three-year project 'Young People's Attitudes towards Religious Diversity' (2009–2012), which was based in the Warwick Religions and Education Research Unit (WRERU) at the University of Warwick. (In order to avoid repeating the full title of the project throughout the chapter, I shall refer to it in its shorter form, as the 'Diversity Project'.) The Diversity Project sought to explore the attitudes of 13–16-year-old pupils across the United Kingdom towards religious diversity. Using data collected in focus group discussions and from a quantitative survey of almost 12,000 young people, the chapter reports perceptions and attitudes towards material expressions of religious belonging or adherence. The notion of 'material expression' is understood here in terms of any physical, tangible or embodied indication of lived religion, in this case including religious symbols (e.g. the cross for Christians, the *kara* for Sikhs), religious clothing (e.g. the turban for Sikhs, the *hijab*, *niqab* or *burka* for Muslims) and observance of particular requirements, such as dietary rules.

In this chapter, I draw on data from the Diversity Project to address two questions: how did young people relate to individuals' clothing in terms of what it suggests about religious belonging, and what did they think of fellow pupils wearing religious symbols in school? The qualitative data considered here were collected in schools in England and Wales, as these are the areas within the project where the author personally did fieldwork (see also ahead). The quantitative data considered here were collected in all the areas covered in the project.

This chapter first provides an overview of relevant literature. This is followed by an outline of the methods of data production and a detailed discussion of the data related to the research questions stated earlier. The data reveal a spectrum of views among the young people, ranging from general acceptance of religious dress to perceptions that clothes mark difference, reinforce religious identity and denote potential threat. The conclusion engages with some of the themes in David Morgan's chapter in this volume and considers young people's views in the light of the messages they receive from the media and the role of school in helping them put media reports in perspective. Space constraints preclude the inclusion of a description of the project, but see for example Arweck (2017).

Religious dress and symbols: a look at the literature

In the last two decades, the topic of 'material religion' has received increasing academic attention (e.g. Arweck and Keenan 2006; Vásquez 2011; Houtman and Meyer 2012). Materiality is intimately linked with the way religious faith manifests itself – for example in architecture, festivals, sacred spaces, artefacts, dance, ritual, music or dress. This range of topics – and the various aspects related to it – cuts across academic disciplines, thus stimulating research and thought not only in sociology and anthropology but also, for example, in law, geography, politics and education studies.

Among this wide-ranging literature is a sizeable amount of work specifically concerned with religious dress (e.g. Tarlo 1996; Arthur 1999, 2000; Keenan 2001; Lewis 2013), and within that is a body of work that has examined the wearing of the *hijab* or *burka* or *niqab* (e.g. Thomas 2006; Gurbuz and Gurbuz-Kucuksari 2009; Moors 2012; Ferrari and Pastorelli 2013; Brems 2014; Warburg, Johansen and Østergaard 2013; Koussens and Roy 2014).

The research in this field has grown substantially, not least because of controversies and debate in the public sphere about the wearing of religious dress and displaying of religious symbols, especially in public institutions, such as schools and courtrooms, and at the workplace. Such debates have considerable implications for policy and legislation. These developments are undoubtedly connected with the climate post-9/11, as wearing the *hijab* or *burka* has assumed highly sensitive political overtones since then.

Legal cases have contested arguments in favour of and against allowing religious dress and symbols to be worn or displayed in public places, testing legislation at the national and European level. These cases revolve around individual human rights and freedom of religion, the interpretation of existing legislation and issues around the separation of state and religion. National bans, for example, of religious dress and symbols in France (in 2004), of face veiling in the Netherlands (in 2005) and of the full-face veil in Belgium (in 2011), have given rise to a substantial body of literature looking at the legal aspects of these topics (some cited earlier), including publications with a specific focus on education (e.g. Molokotos-Liederman 2000; Hunter-Henin 2012), and work examining the different policies which European countries have adopted. There is also a sizeable literature that is concerned with individuals' perspectives on wearing religious dress and symbols (e.g. Gurbuz and Gurbuz-Kucuksari 2009) and non-wearers' perceptions (e.g. Moors 2012).

While there are no legal restrictions in the UK, controversies have at times flared up about religious dress and symbols in schools, often connected with reasons of health and safety, with young people not being permitted to wear headscarves or symbols like the *kara*. Schools are allowed to decide which dress code their pupils are to adhere to, and this has created cases where school regulations and individual preferences regarding dress and symbols have come into conflict. Where young people have contested the school's decision in court, each case has been ruled case by case, thus not necessarily resulting in a consistent approach.

The various issues around religious dress and symbols, which partly arise from the increasingly multicultural nature of Western societies, have implications for young people and religious education in schools. Schools include pupils from a range of religious backgrounds, which raises questions about how schools might deal with this diversity in practical and curriculum terms. It is thus not just a question of whether schools permit pupils to wear religious dress and symbols in school, but also how young people of both religious and non-religious backgrounds may be taught to relate to peers wearing religious dress and symbols. The Council of Europe's publication *Signposts* (Jackson 2014), on policy and practice in intercultural education, points to the European-wide relevance of such matters. The attitudes of young people towards others' religious dress and symbols reflect the various approaches taken in the respective national contexts across Europe, even if a majority of young people have been reported to be in favour of their peers being allowed to wear visible signs of religious belonging (Valk et al. 2009). Therefore, particular contexts are important regarding young people's attitudes to 'material religion'.

So far, only the European project REDCo (which led to the volume by Valk et al.) and the quantitative component of the Diversity Project at Warwick, which built on REDCo, have explored such attitudes. The Warwick project also sought to find out what factors influence such attitudes (see Francis et al., forthcoming).[1] In sum, while there is a sizeable literature on matters related to material religion, there is little to date on young people and their viewpoints on material religion in the multicultural societies in which they are growing up.

Following this brief outline of the literature on religious dress and symbols, I now turn to the methods used in the Diversity Project.

The qualitative phase

Given the exploratory nature of the project's ethnographic phase, we sought to elicit the key themes and issues young people identify with religious diversity and the variety of positions they adopt in response. Focus group discussions were chosen as the best tool to achieve this, realised in twenty-one[2] visits to secondary schools[3] across the four nations of the UK and London. London was considered a special case because of its size and its characteristic diversity, resulting from successive waves of immigration. The schools were chosen according to several criteria, such as pupil composition, geography, social context, type of school and access, with a view to including a wide range of schools. However, the research design did not aim for a representative sample.

Semi-structured schedules were used for the focus groups, with questions revolving around four main themes: faith background/identity, values, encounter with diversity and attitudes to diversity. Priority questions were identified in anticipation of the need to be flexible in the school contexts (e.g. in case of time constraints) and to ensure that the two researchers who shared the fieldwork gathered reasonably even data.

The focus groups were usually mixed in terms of gender, ethnic and social backgrounds and school classes and consisted on average of six pupils. Although we planned to separate pupils into religious and non-religious groups, according to their self-identifications, this did not happen in all cases. The organisation of the groups was in the hands of teachers, with whom we discussed selection criteria beforehand. The young people were generally willing, often eager, to participate. The focus groups generally took the place of a lesson, the length of which varied across schools (40–60 minutes). Each group was briefed about the project and the purpose of the discussion. Also, pupils were asked to confirm consent to participate and permission to record the discussions.[4] After data collection, the transcripts from each school were collated and analysed, with findings and extracts from the focus groups organised under thematic headings.[5]

This chapter draws on the perceptions of and attitudes to 'material religion' that young people articulated in the focus group discussions and on relevant questions in the survey. In the focus groups, none of the questions specifically asked about such topics, but related matters emerged in the discussions. Conversely, the questionnaire included direct questions about religiously significant clothing and symbols. As many direct quotes from the focus groups are included as space allows, as one of the project's objectives was to foreground the voices of young people. It needs to be stressed, however, that, due to the nature of focus groups, the findings derived from them are indicative rather than definitive or representative.

The quantitative phase

The quantitative phase aimed to obtain data from 2,000 pupils (aged 13–15 years[6]) in each of the five regions, using a questionnaire. The sample of 10,000 ensured reliable visibility of minorities. Completed questionnaires were provided by 11,725 pupils: 2,398 from England, 1,988 from Northern Ireland, 2,724 from Scotland, 2,319 from Wales and 2,296 from London. Roughly half the questionnaires were completed by pupils attending schools with a religious character and roughly half by pupils attending schools without a religious foundation.

The questionnaire was designed for self-completion, using mainly multiple-choice questions and Likert scaling on five points (agree strongly, agree, not certain, disagree, disagree strongly). Ten items explored young people's views on religious clothing and symbols in the major religion – for example 'Should Muslims be allowed to wear the headscarf/*burka*/*niqab* in school?' or 'Should Sikhs be allowed to wear the turban/*kara*/*kirpan* in school?'.

Quantitative data

Data from the quantitative survey are included here in order to provide some idea of what the broader picture looks like across the four nations of the UK and London (see Table 11.1). Table 11.1 shows that the majority of pupils are in

Table 11.1 Pupils' responses to questions about religious dress and symbols – for example 'Should Christians be allowed to wear the cross in school?'

Should pupils be allowed to wear the ...	Yes (%)	NC (%)	No (%)
Cross	63	25	12
Headscarf	58	24	18
Burka	49	27	24
Niqab	49	29	22
Turban	58	25	17
Kara	54	29	18
Kirpan	50	30	20
Star of David	59	26	15
Kippah/yarmulke	54	30	17
Bindi	55	28	17

Note: Yes = Sum of 'agree strongly' and 'agree' responses.
NC = Uncertain responses.
No = Sum of 'disagree strongly' and 'disagree' responses.
Percentages are rounded to whole numbers.

favour of their peers being allowed to wear religious dress or symbols in schools, with approval ranging from 49% (for the *burka* and *niqab*) to 63% (for the cross). It also shows that there are sizeable proportions who are 'not certain', ranging from 24% (for the headscarf) to 30% (for the *kirpan* and the *kippah/yarmulke*), although it is possible that 'not certain' denotes uncertainty about what some of the items are. The negative responses range from 24% (for the *burka*) to 12% (for the cross).

Regarding pupils' own stances, 52% who described themselves as having no religious faith said that Muslims should be allowed to wear the headscarf in school. The proportions rose to 87% among Muslim pupils and 78% among Hindu pupils. Further, 51% of pupils who described themselves as having no religious faith said that Sikhs should be allowed to wear the turban in school, with the proportions rising to 81% among Muslim pupils and to 80% among Hindu pupils. Finally, 54% of pupils who described themselves as having no religious faith said that Christians should be allowed to wear crosses in school, but the proportion rose to 75% among Muslim pupils and 78% among Hindu pupils.

Having drawn a broad-brushstroke picture of what the survey revealed about how young people relate to religious symbols and clothing across the four nations of the UK and London, I now present thumb sketches arising from the qualitative data.

Qualitative data

The qualitative data were analysed to explore how young people relate to the way individuals' clothes suggest religious belonging and how they perceive other aspects of appearance that denote religious belonging. Most of the aspects that young people touched on concerned Islam, which is perhaps not surprising given the continuing impact of 9/11 and 7/7, to which pupils explicitly or implicitly referred. Comments about other religions were triggered by controversies, such as the then current debate about whether Sikh religious symbols, such as the *kara*, should be worn in school (BBC News 2008). Also, most of the young people's comments referred to clothing (e.g. the *hijab*) and appearance (e.g. men wearing beards) rather than religious symbols.

The young people's views on the topic ranged quite widely, from general acceptance and learning such acceptance to clothes being labels, marking difference, reinforcing religious identity, occasionally expressing faith and being a barrier or potential threat. What they have in common is their dual perspective, combining the external with the internal or the public with the private. Each internal aspect entails political (in the wider sense of the word) or public aspects, when displayed in public or looked at from other people's perspectives; both interact with one another, thus resulting in interesting constellations of individual intention and others' perceptions.

Acceptance/normality

Some young people indicated that the expression of religious diversity in clothing and symbols was part of religious practice and everyday life in a multicultural society:

> It's like, if it's their religion, if it's part of their religion, they're allowed to wear it.
>
> (Y9/2,[7] male)[8]

> I think like in the multicultural society that we've got now, when you're little and you're going through town and you see somebody with a headscarf, it's normal, it's not out of the ordinary and so therefore you don't consider it and it's not something that you go 'why is [s]he wearing it?' It's just a fact of life that they are wearing it and as you grow older then you realise why they wear it.
>
> (Y9/Y10, female)

Most of the young people had become accustomed to this aspect of religious diversity in early childhood, even if it may have appeared strange and unfamiliar at first:

> In like nursery you have kids with headscarves on and you just kind of . . . it's just your lifestyle and you're just used to it.
>
> (Y8, female)

> Be true to your religion to a certain extent, going back to that thing where in the Qur'an, it says 'just cover your head'; it doesn't say, 'cover your face

and only show your eyes', because when I was small, I used to be scared of the women; when I was tiny, they walked past and I'd get scared, but now it's not that scary anymore because I'm bigger now obviously, but I don't always like a woman wearing something just to show her religion, it doesn't scare me any more.

(Y10/2, male)

A label

However, religious clothing could just be an accessory – or, when seen from outside, a kind of label or an act of labelling – if it was worn without the spiritual demeanour of which it was to be an expression, as the following pupil tried to convey:

Say if a Muslim wears a scarf or I get to fast and things, that's a moral thing like being vegetarian, but doing the washing and the praying at certain times of the day, I think most of that is just to make themselves feel better because they think that if they do those things they're a Muslim. Anyone could do that, I could put a scarf on and go and wash myself and pray to a god that I don't believe in, but it wouldn't make me a Muslim so I think that a lot of it is putting a label on people rather than actually believing.

(Y9/Y10, female)

This aspect demonstrates the close connection between public and private: individuals may have their own reasons for choosing to wear religiously significant dress, but others judge them by their appearance. In this sense, clothes make the (wo)man, but (wo)man also makes the clothes. Seen from a believer's point of view, dress is meant to reflect the inner (religious/spiritual) attitude of the person, but this may not always apply, as people may adhere to the outward signs of a faith, but not practise it otherwise, while the person looking at the individual assumes that dress denotes believer.

The differences between insider and outsider perspectives have given rise to some of the debate and controversy of these issues and to some of the academic literature. This may be particularly pertinent when religious dress and symbols are worn as fashion items:

Since like the media has come in like the fashion and all those kind of things, if you see the kind of clothes, in Islam women are meant to cover themselves, so it really declines religion because, if you put fashion into religion, it doesn't really match.

(Y11, male)

A pupil in a London school drew parallels between media influence and the decline of religion (i.e. the modest dress code in Islam), pointing out that the media's promotion of fashion brought fashion into religion. In that sense, the media dictated what was acceptable, created peer pressure and raised issues related to gender (again related to modest dress for women). This pointed to a general secularising effect:

> Yeah, you have to change your religion to match everyone's fashion . . . And the peer pressure that they're gonna face.
>
> (Y11, male)

> If you see girls or women not dressed as moderately [. . .] I think that it degrades them and I think that the Western society especially has become so . . . they aim to please the men in the world, I feel, because like singing groups for example or dancing groups, if you see the boys they're covered up and you're mainly looking at how they're dancing or how they're singing, but with women you're looking at what they're wearing, how their hair is, how their make up is, they're not really concentrating on anything else and I think that because religion is not [. . .] as big a thing in Western society.
>
> (Y11, female)

Thus geographical location was relevant in the way a given religious culture developed. For example Muslims who live in the West behave somewhat differently compared to Muslims in predominantly Muslim countries:

> I think that also it's different as in how Muslims act in the Western society and how they act somewhere else because I think that the boundaries are totally different as well; you're like able to walk around as you please, as long as you're decently covered, but in other countries, some Muslim countries, they want you to wear a headscarf, they want you to wear an *niqab*, they want you to wear a *jilbab*, so you're totally covered, but here especially women I think they have more freedom.
>
> (Y11, female)

> I think there's very orthodox methods of practising the religion as well as like less strict methods and I'd be the first to admit that I don't always pray but I do fast and I only have *halal* food and I obviously pray the Qur'an regularly, but it's maybe not as regular as some people do and maybe the fact that we're living in the Western world it's kind of adapting your religion as well as the culture of the country that you're living in so maybe I do some things, for example, like the way I dress or the fact that I don't wear a headscarf, which is probably not what my religion teaches, but I've adapted my religion to the way that I'm practising it in this country. Maybe if I was living somewhere else it would be different.
>
> (Y11, female)

There can be tension between modern Western culture and the tempting allure of fashion and the discipline of wearing the headscarf, as the following quote illustrates:

> Basically in our Qur'an it says 'wear a scarf'. Okay, it says 'girls should wear a scarf for modesty' and then a new fringe style comes out and you all get tempted and we believe that that's a devil that's tempting us and we've got the Qur'an so we can't move [. . . there are people who] say they're Muslims, they're obviously practising Muslims, but they wouldn't wear a scarf because it's in the twenty-first century. I said it to my parents once before 'get with the time [. . .] It's the twenty-first century, just let me curl my hair, whatever' and then they lead me free will and then you understand that 'Okay, it's your religion' and your religion, the whole test, is getting harder and harder until the day of judgement so you're going to have to fight it more so you still wear a scarf, what the Qur'an says, don't just think 'it's the twenty-first century, he'll be fine with it as long as I curl my hair'.
>
> (Y9/10, female)

Marking difference

Religious clothing and symbols thus represent markers of difference, when seen and understood from both within and without, even if for different reasons:

> You go home and at home it's your home, you'd have your parents, your siblings, but the things you do might be different, like what you eat or what clothes you wear and stuff like that, that's a difference, but in general what you do and how you do it is different.
>
> (Y9, female)

> I guess I feel different sometimes because I'm a Muslim [. . .] I was the only one who used to wear a scarf throughout the whole school, so you walk in and you just feel different straight away because everyone's looking at you, 'What are you wearing on your head?' and then you just get used to it and then you just think, 'I feel different' but then I feel good that I feel different because everyone used to be like that and then everyone thought I'd be like, 'Oh, no, I'm wearing a scarf, I'm gonna take it off' but then I thought, 'No, this gives me more reason to wear it so then everyone knows' so I can practise my religion openly and then they'd have to get used to it, instead of me turning to their way, they'll just have to get used to what I'm doing. I guess you do feel different but then I kind of like it that I feel different.
>
> (Y11, female)

> With my friend, if we see a non-Muslim girl, we sort of talk about the way she dresses and the way she acts and then with that we follow on and go and talk about our religion.
>
> (Y10, female)

> I try and like make myself different in that like I said I don't swear and I try and act not horrible but I would never say I wasn't a Christian, I would never hide my faith but I wouldn't go round and . . . I wear my cross and if people ask me questions I'll answer. I would never hide it but I'm not going round . . .
>
> (Y11, female)

Items of clothing or religious symbols were often the first things that sprang to young people's minds when thinking about different religions:

> Jewish people wear the hats and stuff like that. I don't really know what Buddhists do actually. Don't they wear orange suit things and go to some place? And Christians, you can have a cross and sometimes they go to church or some don't. Maybe Buddhism and [the] Jewish [religion have most in common], but in some ways . . . I don't know.
>
> (Y9, female)

Difference in religious dress could also arouse curiosity and interest in pupils who were eager to know about religious traditions they were not familiar with:

> When people say 'religion' to me, the first thing that comes to my mind is Christianity because it's what I know, but it's not something that I just want to know. I want to know about other religions. Like we had a teacher who came in who was actually Jewish and everyone was just so fascinated with his culture and the way he was and the way he dressed and stuff, it was just so fascinating.
>
> (Y8, female)

Being different in appearance could also be a challenge when others questioned or even teased about markers of difference, as a young woman recounted who changed from not wearing a scarf to wearing one:

> In year 7 when I first came there wasn't a lot of Asians that I knew so I started hanging around with atheists and then during year 8 about half-way I met [fellow pupil] so then we were both quite close [. . .] and then when I first started wearing my scarf then they said to me, 'Why are you wearing a scarf. Take it off, stop wearing a scarf,' but then I felt really weird like I thought, 'Oh, I should take it off. I don't think I look nice in my scarf,' and issues like that started coming up [. . .] but then obviously [fellow pupil] helped me and then I don't take off my scarf as much as I used to.
>
> (Y11, female)

Religious dress could be a marker of difference between generations: a female Muslim pupil in a London school commented at length on wearing the *hijab* (which she wore) and how it differed between countries and between generations – the reason why her mother wore a scarf differed from the reason this pupil wore it. She felt strongly that dress was an individual's choice and that there should be no discrimination because of it:

> In some countries they're not allowed to wear the *hijab* and it's like it's against the law [...] my mum doesn't wear a scarf like me, she wears it the way that she was brought up and most of her head's showing and I sometimes say, 'Mum, if you're gonna wear a scarf, you might as well cover your whole body, instead of just wearing it just because you're told to or you were brought up to,' and a lot of people are kind of like ... they question whether I'm forced to wear it or whether it's my own choice and I tell them, 'It's my choice.'
>
> (Y10, female)

This statement points to another topic emerging from the data: the tension between individual autonomy and the expectations of religious tradition and community. In this case, the young woman does not want people to see her wearing the *hijab* in relation to the religion she adheres to, but as individual preference. She thus claims autonomy over the need or expectation of conformity.

Another example of generational difference is a Sikh girl in a school in Preston who explained that her parents were quite relaxed about religion, while she chose to wear the five symbols of Sikhism ('the 5 Ks'):

> My dad isn't religious at all, like he'll go to temple every week but he sees more the culture, he doesn't really see the religion. [...] I've made more of an effort to make religion into my life [...] I wear my kara [...] I actually have the 5 Ks so I wear it out of choice, but for my religion there's nothing actually in the Guru Granth Sahib that says that you have to dress like this, you have to say this, you have to do this but it's all religious culture [...] if you live in England my parents aren't strict about how I dress and stuff so I wear the kara out of choice and I want people to know I'm Sikh because I'm proud of who I am and I do believe that religion is a big aspect of my life.
>
> (Y11, female)

This quote further illustrates the importance of context: this pupil's parents have adapted to the Western lifestyle, while she is asserting her religious identity in that very context (see also ahead).

Assertion of religious identity

If wearing religious dress and symbols is a matter of personal choice and a marker of difference, it may be also be motivated by political rather than spiritual or strictly personal dispositions. Some young people pointed out that the media's repeated stereotyping had a paradoxical effect in making some Muslims appear more Muslim than they had before, with the implication that the events of 9/11 were the point which divided the 'before' and 'after'. The effect was that Muslims who had not been that strictly observant before in practice and appearance ('they never used to act like Muslims') now made a point of being observant in obvious ways by wearing traditional clothes and growing beards. Such comments may suggest a radicalisation among 'ordinary' Muslims and/or a perceived need to emphasise and display Muslim-ness for all to see – in other words, appearance serves to underline difference and makes difference more visible. It could also be a mark of solidarity with the wider Muslim community.

> I'm a Muslim. You're probably wondering why I wear a scarf but the reason is to show who I am, I'm a Muslim, as many people know and many people are afraid . . . well, I know some people are afraid to show that they are Muslim so they don't wear a scarf and they don't go out in public wearing them, but I'm not afraid basically. I'm a Muslim and I'm proud.
>
> (Y11, female)

Some comments on this topic point to a certain sense of unease and/or ambivalence:

> I know a lot of people that they were Muslim, but they never used to act like Muslims; they used to do stuff that you're not meant to do and then all this kind of thing that was happening about 'Oh, Muslims are bad,' then that kind of built their religion up; like now I see them and they used to wear trousers and now they wear proper Islamic clothes and they've grown beards and stuff like that, so in a way it's good, but I think it's more bad than it is good.
>
> (Y10, male)

Reinforcement of one's identity

The notion of choice – whether, when and how to wear the *hijab*, for example – relates to individual expressions of identity. Thus outward symbols like a headscarf – or any other material item that symbolises one's religion – can strengthen one's faith (or religious identity), as they are a constant reminder of who or what one is:

> I also think when you have a material thing that symbolises your religion, it strengthens your faith. Like when you're constantly reminded by the scarf on your head that you're a Muslim, you feel it more strongly and . . . you feel the religion more and it strengthens your faith.
>
> (Y10, male)

An occasional public expression of faith

The element of choice and personal sense of identity could lead to wearing religious dress and symbols only occasionally in public, for very personal rather than conventional reasons, with the former privileging convenience (as perceived by the individual) over (communal) religious dress code:

> I'm a practising Muslim [...] but [...] I don't regularly pray. I do fast and I do abide by the food laws [...] For me, it's more the spiritual aspect of my faith that I'm kind of connected with [...] I do sometimes wear a headscarf, but I think my reasons are different to a lot of other people. For me it's more convenient as opposed to dressing modestly, which doesn't sound all that great, but I'm just being honest.
>
> (Y9/Y10, female)

This ties in with other research that has reported occasional wear of religious dress – for example for particular religious occasions, such as rites of passage or festivals (Warburg, Johansen and Østergaard 2013).

A barrier

When traditional dress codes were fully embraced – for example a Muslim woman wearing the *niqab* – this could present a barrier, as this pupil stated:

> But I would say the main thing is the way that they dress, for instance, like some people in Islam dress all in black with just eyes showing. [Interviewer: Would you say that's a barrier?] I would say yes, but ... [laughs].
>
> (Y9 female, Muslim)

Ironically, creating a barrier between the person wearing the *niqab* and 'the world' is of course the very purpose of the *niqab*, but this pupil's statement also points to some unease. It may have been prompted or influenced by public debates at that time about the all-concealing veil being a barrier to human interaction, precluding the face-to-face contact which is part of communication between people – at least in Western societies. The then Labour MP Jack Straw had voiced this concern in early October 2006, stating that wearing the *niqab* restricted his constituents' full participation in British society for that reason (Straw 2006).

Other public figures have since expressed similar concerns in this ongoing debate, with some suggesting a ban in schools and other public places, such as courtrooms (Swinford and Hope 2013). Some young people were aware that such a ban was in force in other countries (e.g. France and the Netherlands), although they did not give any examples or refer to the wider debate about the arguments for or against a ban. They were aware that religious dress and symbols could cause public controversy, as the case of the Sikh pupil in Wales demonstrated, or lend themselves to misinterpretation:

> One girl had a bracelet [kara] on, didn't she, and she got excluded from her school because it was her belief, so she didn't take it off.
>
> (Y9, male)

> Yeah, 'cause sometimes, like maybe if someone's carrying a blade, then people can mistake it for something else and complain about it.
>
> (Y9, male)

Potential threat and/or reason for discrimination

In particular situations or contexts, unease about people's appearance (regarding dress or other physical features) could turn to threat, again pointing to the change of perceptions as a result of 9/11 and 7/7. One pupil referred to the new climate, with people being easily judged by their appearance and treated accordingly:

> But [...] since the 2000s, everyone's a little bit more judgemental of people and everyone's judging by their appearance and everything, so if there's like Muslim people and they've got turbans and everything, everyone automatically thinks or assumes of what they think and it's hard for people to say what they *really* like want to say.
>
> (Y8, female)[9]

Young people admitted that some people's appearance triggered thoughts of possible terrorist threat, especially when combined with other things (e.g. backpack and *niqab*), even if they could check these and put them in perspective:

> [If I found myself in the situation on the underground] I wouldn't think about anything. Maybe I'd just have a quick thought that he's got a bomb, but that's only because we've been kind of programmed by the media and stuff to think that.
>
> (Y13, female)

> A lot of people would tell you, maybe they wouldn't say *now*, but if you talk, a lot of people go like, 'I was on a plane and I was really scared because a man was wearing a turban.' That's something that tends to happen a lot, or if you're at a train station and you see like a Muslim, people will start to immediately think, 'Oh, he's a suicide bomber.'
>
> (Y11, female)

> No [I wouldn't step back from every Muslim], but then, if they'd got a letter box – the scarf thing – where you can only see their eyes . . . [wearing

a full *burka*]. Say, they were wearing that and then they'd got a backpack as well . . . But say, I'm on a train, like, and then there's this person who's got one of them on and say they've got a backpack, I would think, 'Oh, my God'. I'd get off.

(Y10, male)

The way the media portrays some religions . . . for example like the 7/7 bombings, that if a person's got a beard, you gotta search them before they go into the tube station, before they go on to the plane. Not every Muslim is like that at all and [. . .] they're normal people, not terrorists all the time.

(Y11, female)

It's quite bad because, if you see especially a man, if you see a man that definitely isn't your religion because he's wearing different clothes and acting different, and then you see him acting suspicious, you automatically think, 'Oh, he's a terrorist,' so it is quite frightening how easily you can change your mind about something.

(Y11, female)

Conclusion

This chapter has interrogated quantitative and qualitative data from the 'Young People's Attitudes to Religious Diversity' project to explore young people's views and perceptions of religious dress and symbols. The quantitative data paint a broad-brushstroke picture, revealing, for example, that the majority are in favour of religious dress and symbols in school and that pupils attending schools with a religious character hold neither a more positive nor a less positive attitude in this regard, compared with pupils attending schools without a religious foundation (see also Francis et al., forthcoming). The qualitative data provide a more nuanced picture, but, given the nature of these data, the picture consists of snapshots. The two sets of data combined allow for some idea of how young people in the UK perceive religious dress and symbols.

Relating some of the discussed themes to Morgan's 'moments' of material analysis, it is clear that young people are able to place material religious objects (in this case dress and symbols) within a system of 'classification'. In other words, they know the function of such objects, both within the religious traditions to which they belong and within adherents' individual understanding(s). While they made no comments about the medium of such items, they spoke about the 'circulation' or deployment of dress and symbols, indicating, for example, that fashion had entered that arena, that their peers should be allowed to display religious symbols at school and that the events of 9/11 have had a visible impact.

Regarding Morgan's notion of 'reception', comments on dress, especially from young Muslim women, pointed to variations from original or designed intent, including (local) traditions, resulting in private or individual ways of appropriating, for example, the wearing of the headscarf. The ideological or cultural work involved still reproduces motifs (and motives) and symbols, which relate to a particular cultural *habitus* while also generating individual behaviour and practice. It is important to note that this kind of cultural work is done by both insiders and outsiders to a given tradition and that it also involves emotional work. It also links to the way young people construct their bodies, at times under the gaze of others, at other times concealed from that gaze. Such occasions may be determined by particular criteria (e.g. context, individual preference, convenience). How young people think about and approach their own and other people's wearing of dress and symbols also testifies to the evolving nature of culture, as they themselves pointed out in referring to the custom of previous generations, comparing what their (grand)parents did with what they do.

Overall, it is striking that young people show tolerance towards the display of religious belonging in their peers, with most referring to individuals' right to decide what they believe and practise and how to express their faith. The qualitative data also show that young people's attitudes are influenced by the media (in the wider sense), as they are exposed to stereotypical reporting and negative messages as well as reports about controversial issues related to religions. Such attitudes have an impact on the way they perceive others' appearance and the way they make their choices of wearing religious dress and symbols themselves, in some cases becoming deliberate markers of difference and a way of asserting religious identity. Given the public debate of controversial cases and the topicality of issues around Islam in the aftermath of 9/11, it is not surprising that these topics featured prominently in the focus groups. Thus, although there is general tolerance among the young people, there is also some confusion (about which item of dress denotes which religion) and unease.

Annelies Moors (2012: 294) points out that 'face veils evoke strong affective sensations.' While they have positive and aesthetic connotations for the wearer, they produce negative feelings for others, including discomfort and fear. Moors argues that such feelings do not just occur naturally, but are produced by affective language used in public discourse (Moors 2012: 294). This perspective goes some way to explain the effect of the media and public debates on the young people who took part in the project. However, this perspective also provides clues as to how the power of language could be harnessed in (religious and intercultural) education to equip young people with skills that allow them to analyse such discourses and their underlying assumptions and intentions.

The focus group discussions revealed that young people are in some ways quite media-savvy, being able to identify stereotypical portrayals and negative reporting, and that their direct experience of people from different religious and cultural backgrounds helped offset media messages and promoted greater understanding. The latter also depends on the geographical and social context in which young people grow up – how much chance they have of encountering the 'other'. In this respect, as in others, school can play an important role, both within and outside the classroom, to which some of the pupils' comments testify.

Acknowledgements

WRERU staff involved in this project gratefully acknowledge funding from the AHRC/ESRC Religion and Society Programme. We greatly appreciate the assistance of the staff of the schools visited and value the participation of the young people who took part in the discussion groups and completed the survey. We are also grateful to WRERU associate fellows and other colleagues (e.g. RE advisors, teachers, lecturers) who facilitated some school visits.

Notes

1 REDCo (Religion in Education: A Contribution to Dialogue or a Factor of Conflict in Transforming Societies of European Countries) was a European Commission Framework 6 project (2006–2009) involving nine universities, including the University of Warwick (for further details, see http://www2.warwick.ac.uk/fac/soc/ces/research/wreru/research/completed/redco/).
2 The research design foresaw fifteen school visits (three in each region) with three groups per school, but opportunities to extend this were taken up where possible.
3 Secondary (or high) school starts at age eleven or twelve in all four parts of the UK. At age sixteen (after the end of compulsory schooling), pupils either continue studying or seek employment. In England and Wales, pupils attend sixth form college, and then proceed with further training or university. There is no sixth form college in Scotland; pupils either leave to gain employment or study for 'Highers' (one year), followed by either 'Advanced Highers' (one year) or university. In Northern Ireland, pupils may stay to study Advanced Level (AS and A2 level) subjects (which qualifies them for university) or more vocational qualifications.
4 All aspects relating to the project were conducted following the ethics code of the University of Warwick and pertinent professional associations (e.g. British Sociological Association). Parental consent was not needed.
5 However, in one school, a technical glitch prevented the recording of all the discussions.
6 For technical reasons, the age range in this phase was slightly different.
7 The respective year groups translate into the following age ranges: Y9 13–14, Y10 14–15 and Y11 15–16.
8 While efforts were made to capture the (non-)religious backgrounds of pupils, it is not possible to match the recorded voices with the respective affiliations.
9 The reference in this quote (and others cited) to turbans as part of Muslim attire also shows the confusion between Muslims and Sikhs that has often happened in the aftermath of 9/11.

References

Arthur, Linda, ed. 1999. *Religion, Dress and the Body*. Oxford: Berg.
———. 2000. *Undressing Religion: Commitment and Conversion from a Cross-Cultural Perspective*. Oxford: Berg.
Arweck, Elisabeth, ed. 2017. *Attitudes to Religious Diversity: Young People's Perspectives*. Abingdon: Routledge.
Arweck, Elisabeth and William Keenan. 2006. *Materializing Religion: Expression, Performance and Ritual*. Aldershot: Ashgate.
BBC News. 2008. 'Sikh Girl Wins Bangle Law Battle'. 29 July. http://news.bbc.co.uk/2/hi/uk_news/wales/7529694.stm. Accessed 08/09/2016.
Brems, Eva, ed. 2014. *The Experiences of Face Veil Wearers in Europe and the Law*. Cambridge: Cambridge University Press.

Ferrari, Alessandro and Sabrina Pastorelli, eds. 2013. *The Burqa Affair across Europe: Between Public and Private Space*. Farnham: Ashgate.

Francis, Leslie, Andrew Village, Ursula McKenzie and Gemma Penny. Forthcoming. 'Freedom of Religion and Freedom of Religious Clothing and Symbols in School: Exploring the Impact of Church Schools in a Religiously Diverse Society'. In *The Legitimization of Civil Human Rights on the Grounds of Human Dignity and Religious Considerations: Empirical Research and Theoretical Reflections*, ed. Hans-Georg Ziebertz and Carl Sterkens. Leiden: Brill.

Gurbuz, Mustafa E. and Gulsum Gurbuz-Kucuksari. 2009. 'Between Sacred Codes and Secular Consumer Society: The Practice of Headscarf Adoption among American College Girls'. *Journal of Muslim Minority Affairs* 29(3): 387–399.

Houtman, Dick and Birgit Meyer. 2012. *Things: Religion and the Question of Materiality*. New York: Fordham University Press.

Hunter-Henin, Myriam, ed. 2012. *Law, Religious Freedoms and Education in Europe*. Farnham: Ashgate.

Jackson, Robert. 2014. *Signposts: Policy and Practice for Teaching about Religions and Non-Religious Worldviews in Intercultural Education*. Strasbourg: Council of Europe.

Keenan, William J.F., ed. 2001. *Dressed to Impress: Looking the Part*. Oxford: Berg.

Koussens, David and Olivier Roy, eds. 2014. *Quand la Burqa passe à l'ouest: Enjeux éthiques, politiques et juridiques*. Rennes: Presses universitaires de Rennes.

Lewis, Reina, ed. 2013. *Modest Fashion: Styling Bodies, Mediating Faith*. London: I.B. Tauris.

Molokotos-Liederman, Lina. 2000. 'Religious Diversity in Schools: The Muslim Headscarf Controversy and Beyond'. *Social Compass* 47(3): 367–381.

Moors, Annelies. 2012. 'The Affective Power of the Face Veil: Between Disgust and Fascination'. In *Things: Religion and the Question of Materiality*, eds. Dick Houtman and Birgit Meyer, 282–295. New York: Fordham University Press.

Straw, Jack. 2006. 'I Felt Uneasy Talking to Someone I Couldn't See'. *The Guardian*, 6 October. http://www.theguardian.com/commentisfree/2006/oct/06/politics.uk. Accessed 07/06/2016.

Swinford, Steven and Christopher Hope. 2013. 'Britain Needs "National Debate" about Banning Muslim Girls from Wearing Veils in Public'. *The Daily Telegraph*, 15 September. http://www.telegraph.co.uk/news/politics/10311469/Britain-needs-national-debate-about-banning-Muslim-girls-from-wearing-veils-in-public.html. Accessed 17/04/2015.

Tarlo, Emma. 1996. *Clothing Matters: Dress and Identity in India*. London: Hurst.

Thomas, Elaine R. 2006. 'Keeping Identity at a Distance: Explaining France's New Legal Restrictions on the Islamic Headscarf'. *Ethnic and Racial Studies* 29(2): 237–259.

Valk, Pille, Gerdien Bertram-Troost, M. Friederici and Céline Beraud, eds. 2009. *Teenagers' Perspectives on the Role of Religion in their Lives, Schools and Societies: A European Quantitative Study*. Münster: Waxmann.

Vásquez, Manuel. 2011. *More than Belief: A Materialist Theory of Religion*. New York: Oxford University Press.

Warburg, Margit, Birgitte Schepelern Johansen and Kate Østergaard. 2013. 'Counting Niqabs and Burqas in Denmark: Methodological Aspects of Quantifying Rare and Elusive Religious Sub-Cultures'. *Journal of Contemporary Religion* 28(1): 33–48.

12 Mobilising Mecca

Reassembling blessings at the museum

Steph Berns

Introduction

The emblem of Mecca, and the spiritual focus of Islam, is the *Ka`ba*, the cuboid edifice at the centre of the *Masjid al-Haram* (the Holy Sanctuary). Each day Muslims around the world turn to its direction (*qibla*) to pray, and once a year millions of pilgrims descend on the holy city to perform the pilgrimage known as Hajj. The Ka`ba's silk covers, which enshroud the cube, are annually replaced. The previous years' covers are then cut into pieces and presented as gifts to dignitaries or acquired by pilgrims as souvenirs (Porter 2015). However, one cover from the Ka`ba's door (the *sitara*), made in 2003, underwent a different fate. This textile travelled in one piece to London for the British Museum's 2012 exhibition on Hajj.[1] Away from the sacred setting of Mecca, the sitara was exhibited to new people, spaces and interpretations. It performed different functions: evoking memories, stimulating imaginations and prompting questions and discussions.

In this book, David Morgan highlights how circulation defines the 'social career of objects' as movement creates opportunities for new encounters, which can build (but also weaken) bonds between people, places, other objects and divine beings. Taking the sitara from Mecca to a museum certainly exposed it to new people and forms of engagement. However, visitors who recognised the sitara (from their travels or imaginings of Mecca) also experienced a shift. While some felt that the exhibited sitara held no salience away from its sacred home, others thought it brought Mecca closer by providing a sacred link to the holy city. To explore this further, I place the sitara at the centre of the analysis and call on a growing body of research within the study of 'material religion' (see Morgan 2005; Meyer 2008; Plate 2014). Central to this exploration is how the Museum facilitated encounters with the materially mediated divine. In other words, how was this object an active agent in visitors' engagements with religious and spiritual evocations? Moreover, how does this work in a place well beyond those consecrated by religious institutions? As I will explain, visitors' devotional experiences in non-consecrated public spaces draw on their past experiences of religious assemblages in sacred places. These museum-based encounters, therefore, demonstrate the potency and persistence of visitors' prior religious networks and the capacity for objects to evoke experiences that contravene the conventions of their new environment.

This chapter draws on my doctoral research into the religious dimensions of the museum visit. For this I interviewed and observed visitors to the 2012 exhibition 'Hajj: Journey to the Heart of Islam', noting the diverse ways Muslim visitors encountered and engaged with the objects.[2] This was not a question of moving from the sacred to the profane. On the contrary, the sitara, as a mobile entity within interconnected networks that exist both within physical and imagined places, remained connected to its place of (sacred) origin. Studies about museum exhibitions on Islam tend to centre on cross-cultural interactions and interfaith dialogue (e.g. Shatanawi 2012), By doing so, they reduce religion to a form of cultural identity and ignore religious experiences, such as sensing a sacred presence. This analysis differs in that I focus solely on encounters with visitors who shared a religious association with the exhibits and had the potential to experience an object-mediated presence of the divine. In the context of the 'Hajj' exhibition, I therefore draw exclusively on my interviews with Muslim visitors.

The exhibition and the pilgrimage

'Hajj: Journey to the Heart of Islam', the final instalment of the British Museum's trilogy of exhibitions exploring 'Spiritual Journeys', told the story of the 1,300-year-old pilgrimage from its medieval beginnings to the modern day. To provide a sense of journeying and a feel of the sacred destinations, the exhibition assembled the story of Hajj as a pilgrimage with sections on the preparations, the arrival, the rituals and, finally, the homecoming. Each section included a variety of exhibits, such as artefacts, photographs, film, audio and artworks. However, for many of the Muslim visitors I spoke to, it was the textiles that covered the Ka`ba that were most striking. 'The videos you can see anywhere,' a Muslim visitor told me. In contrast, the textiles from the Ka`ba, especially the complete (uncut) pieces, were special because of their inscriptions, their craftsmanship, their material, but mostly because of where the textiles came from and what they had touched.

So, how does an object in a museum provide a sense of an absent and holy site? To address this question, I will now explain how devotional experiences with objects from Mecca required not only the object's journey (from Mecca to the Museum) but also a continual flow of things and people. Moreover, these journeys (both real and imagined) called for objects to be present and absent and mobile and immobile. Central to this process was the ability for some objects to be imbued with blessings (*barakah*), which could then travel to new places and spread the blessings of Mecca.

Taking place at the British Museum, the exhibition attracted around 117,000 people, almost half of whom were Muslim, while 16% of the audience visited from overseas (MHM 2012).[3] As expected, many had performed the pilgrimage or were hoping to do so in the future. And so, like souvenirs, the exhibits helped to reconstruct the pilgrimage in one of two ways. For those who had performed the pilgrimage, the objects revived memories of their embodied, emotional and devotional experiences. For those visitors who aspired to go, the objects prompted imagined journeys (Coleman and Elsner 1995). For both sets of visitors, Mecca acted as the common node (Cooke and Lawrence 2005).

As the fifth pillar of Islam, Hajj is a requirement for all Muslims who are financially, physically and mentally able to perform the act. The main destination of the annual pilgrimage is Mecca, in Saudi Arabia, with rituals also taking place in a number of nearby locations. As non-Muslims cannot enter these sites, only Muslims can perform Hajj, which takes place during the month of *Dhul-Hijjah* (of the Muslim lunar year).[4] The *Qur'an* states that the Ka'ba was built by Prophet Adam, the first human, and was later rebuilt, under Allah's instruction, by Prophet Ibrahim and his son Isma'il. In the seventh century, Prophet Muhammad restored the shrine and performed the first pilgrimage to the site. The rites of Hajj retrace the prophets' footsteps as pilgrims seek purification and fulfil their religious duty.

The practice of covering the Ka'ba has a long history, which predates Islam (McGregor 2010). Said to protect the cube from desecration, the veil also serves to reinforce its sacrality by shielding the building from view (Eimen 2006). The largest section of the cover is the *kiswa*, which enshrouds the building. There are also a number of other fabric panels, including the *hizam* (belt), which runs round the entire cube, and the curtain-like panel that hangs over the door, called the sitara or *burqu'*. Made from silk, dyed black, the sitara is embroidered with gold and silver wire threads and decorated with supplications and Qur'anic verses. Since 1962 the sitara has been produced in Mecca's kiswa factory and replaced annually. Unlike most covers, which are cut up and given as gifts, the sitara that came to the British Museum was intact and on loan from the King Abdel Aziz Public Library, Saudi Arabia. Ahmad Turkistani, the Library's spokesperson, stated that this 'sitara will stand to symbolize the Holy Kaaba' (Alrashid 2012). But the sitara was more than a symbol. Having been in Mecca, the curtain served as an indexical trace of and a sacred connection to the sanctuary.

During my days observing, I frequently witnessed Muslim visitors exhibiting embodied signs of recognition on seeing the sitara (including pointing, expressions of admiration, such as 'wow', and conversations with companions). Many recognised the curtain from their own travels or from previously seen images. This was especially important, as the curtain, being at the beginning of the exhibition, lacked interpretation. Only visitors who knew of the Ka'ba were able to appreciate its religious significance at this early stage. By contrast, my non-Muslim interviewees seldom mentioned the curtain. In a focus group of visitors organised by an external research agency (MHM 2012), a non-Muslim visitor mentioned the absence of interpretation at the entrance of the exhibition, stating that she dismissed the sitara as 'decoration'. Similarly, Angela, a Methodist visitor (fifties), told me that she could appreciate the Ka'ba's textiles only as artworks on her first visit. However, after returning for a second time, she connected the pilgrims' accounts to the objects and could appreciate what the pilgrimage 'meant rather than just saying, "That's beautiful."' Angela's encounters with the Ka`ba's textiles were therefore mediated through the experiences of the pilgrims conveyed in videos, photographs and personal testimonies.[5] By contrast, and as I will explain, the sitara was able to mediate experiences of the divine for those visitors who understood how they and the object related to Mecca and the pilgrimage.

Disseminating Mecca

Focusing on an object that was made in Mecca, and then came to a museum in London, requires a wide lens that encompasses encounters inside and outside the Arabian city's borders. As Seán McLoughlin argues, studies of Hajj must go beyond the 'circumscribed, time-space location' of Mecca and look at the many journeys that flow in and out of the sacred centre both before and after the month of Dhul-Hijjah (2015: 42). For this reason, scholars such as Richard McGregor (2010) propose exploring the material culture of Hajj. Through such object-orientated analyses, McGregor argues, it will be possible to study how things participate in 'scattering' the location of the Ka`ba. This approach therefore supports notions that places are fluid (Pink 2009), as pilgrimages promote the dissemination of place (Coleman and Crang 2002).

The dissemination of Mecca is made possible by the portability of the rituals within Islam (Nasser 2005). For example Muslim prayer (*salat*) does not require a sacred place. So long as the praying Muslim faces Mecca, he or she can pray anywhere. Similarly, pilgrims and objects can bring blessings from places that are sacred to those that are not. These everyday rituals extend Mecca's sacredness and (aim to) draw Muslims to the sacred city – in prayer, in thought and, eventually, in person. These centrifugal and centripetal forces therefore inspire more pilgrims to journey to Mecca, who (on returning) put more objects into circulation.

Anthropologist Tim Ingold, using the metaphoric language of fabric, proposes that interactions are made possible through the connecting of threads. Envisioning a knot that is connected to an ever-expanding multitude of fibres, Ingold likens the connected cluster to Bruno Latour's concept of a star-shaped network 'with a center surrounded by many radiating lines, with all sorts of tiny conduits leading to and fro' (Latour 2005: 177). Applying this analogy to Mecca, as the centre, helps to visualise how pilgrims and objects participate in this process of disseminating the holy city beyond its geographic limits. While the dispersed actors (be they human or inanimate object) can offer some experiences of the pilgrimage, they cannot provide all of it. The souvenirs of Hajj, as partially impoverished (Stewart 1993), direct people's attention beyond themselves and towards Mecca. Hence, when threads become knotted to new assemblages (like an exhibition in London) they remain connected to their origin. How this connection is made explicit, however, commands more actors and more connections.

This movement, to and away from the centre, requires the immobility (and spatial fixity) of the Ka`ba and the mobility of pilgrims and objects. These comings and goings are crucial in maintaining the pilgrimage, and though the materials of Hajj may no longer physically exist together, they are held together as a stable albeit geographically dispersed assemblage.

In their writings about actor networks, Annemarie Mol and John Law (2001) propose that some stable networks can travel. To do so they must exist within two forms of space, one that is fixed (the network) and another that enables movement (Euclidian). Through the repetition and maintenance of the pilgrimage's rituals, the Hajj network (formed of people, things, places and the divine) has 'sufficient durability to circulate across far-reaching space-times' (Fenwick 2011: 103). Because of this, Latour proposes that the network can abandon 'the tyranny of distance' by 'flattening the landscape' (2005: 174). In this flattened network, Latour argues, action is transported by 'conduits' and 'vehicles' (2005: 174). And so, like telephones, conduits bring together physically remote elements.

Actor networks also provide ways to connect actors that are transcendental, imagined and earthly. Though Mecca may be understood as a 'transcendent center' (Metcalf 1996: 18) and 'the paradigmatic place on earth where the vertical axis connects with the horizontal' (Bennett 1998: 95), in 'networked space,' the heavens, like any other place, are made connectable through both material and immaterial means. Overcoming distance is pivotal for interactions involving sacred objects. It therefore takes indexical traces (rooted in the material) and the capacity to stimulate imaginings and memories of Mecca to draw objects into relation with places both present (the museum) and absent. Objects and pilgrims are therefore 'mutually implicated' in the processes of dissemination (Lury 1997: 77) and capable of effecting change in other actors, as part of heterogeneous networks (Latour 2005).

Connected blessings

One afternoon at the British Museum, a young father, Omar (twenties), entered the exhibition with his wife and young child. Looking up and down the sitara, Omar edged closer. His gaze finally fell on the 'Please do not touch' sign displayed near its base. Omar turned to his wife, who was standing behind him, and then turned to me. 'Can I touch it?' he asked. Before I could respond, he blurted, 'Shut your eyes!', and with his hand outstretched, Omar gently brushed the fabric with his palm. When he returned to his wife, I asked him why he wanted to touch. Omar, looking rather sheepish after his defiant act, fell silent. Instead, his wife, Zainub (twenties), replied, 'Because it's touched a holy place.' Zainub likened the curtain to a prayer mat her mother brought back from Mecca. This mat had touched the Ka`ba and so came to her as a gift imbued with divine blessings. In the same way that Zainub's mother was transformed by completing her Hajj (and can now be called a *hajjah*), the prayer mat was changed by its presence in the sacred city. Though the couple had not performed the pilgrimage, their experiences of receiving souvenirs meant that physical contact constituted an integral part of their shared understandings of how to interact with the objects of Hajj.[6] The rare opportunity to touch the sitara was too good to miss.

Similarly, Parveen, a British teenager who had also never been to Mecca, was keen to make physical contact with the sitara, though (in compliance to the sign) resisted. Again, I asked why. She explained, 'It actually makes me feel closer to God. It's been there – the House of God . . . so it'll feel as if you're touching a part of that mosque that's been blessed.' With physical contact prohibited, seeing constituted a form of touch, by drawing the onlooker into an intimate and embodied relation with the divine (Morgan 2007). This notion of seeing-as-touching is also common in Mecca, as many pilgrims cannot reach the Ka`ba for the crowds. Thus, standing before the sitara in the exhibition brought Parveen closer to the Holy Sanctuary and, by extension, closer to Allah.

In Islam, a site is made sacred through its association with the life of prophets, as 'something of their sanctity, blessing (barakah) or grace (*karamat*) is transferred to that place' (Bennett 1998: 93). It is, therefore, through a process of association that places become holy, and become imbued with barakah. In discussing the rites of Hajj, al-Batanuni (following his pilgrimage in 1901) explained that the stones and structures in Mecca 'are not sacred for their own sake, but because of their relation to something holy and respected' (in Lazarus-Yafeh 1981: 121). In its simplest terms, a blessed object 'makes you remember God and think of God' (Starrett 1995). Barakah, therefore, operates as a centrifugal force (Bille 2010) that extends God's blessings and grace.

Thus, Hajj plays a crucial role in generating, replenishing and disseminating blessed objects. Social anthropologist Azam Torab (2007) notes that the word 'barakah', when used as an intransitive verb, takes on a transformative quality as the objects become blessed and able to pass on these blessings. Barakah-imbued objects therefore share qualities with icons and relics, as they possess a kind of 'tangibilized contamination' (Belk et al. 1989) or 'holy radioactivity' (Finucane 1977: 26) that can flow along chains of places, people and things. Henceforth, Hajj souvenirs have the capacity to retain, transport and transmit the blessings of Mecca (Coleman and Elsner 1995).

In order to receive barakah, the recipient must believe in its transformative and transportable quality. It also requires an emotional and religious sense of being-in-touch with God (Bille 2010). Furthermore, as Susan Stewart (1993) concludes, the travelled object needs a supplementary narrative discourse to attach it to its origin. The 'flow' of barakah therefore relies on the thing itself and 'what we know, how we perceive and imagine the thing' (Hodder 2012: 32).

However, there is an inherent tension between the material and immaterial when barakah is applied to an object, as in the case of the Qur`an:

> The Qur`an offers a sense of "closeness" to God through remembrance of his words on the one hand. On the other hand, there is the theological

obligation not to worship the Qur'an as a *material* book in itself, despite its powerful Baraka.

(Bille 2010: 176)

I occasionally sensed this tension in my interviews. Zainub, for example, insisted that the act of touching things on pilgrimage was 'not religious'. This denial suggests at least two processes: first, the obscuring of material things within the practice of mediation between humans and the divine (Meyer 2010); and second, the strict prohibitions in Islam against worshipping material objects. These processes often led visitors to downplay the role of objects in their religiously orientated interactions or, as illustrated with Zainub, reject the presence of the divine in their material gestures. This subordination of material forms within religious practice reflects a broader struggle between the instinctive desire to touch things (in order to feel connected to a place, thing or being) and the perception (within the Abrahamic faiths) that religion is belief-centred and thereby framed in opposition to materiality (Meyer 2008).[7]

Barakah's capacity to act as a bridge between humans and the divine (Pinto 2013) can be experienced through touch, sight, smell or hearing (Torab 2007). The exhibition, therefore, held the potential to circulate blessings in a multitude of ways but also to highlight when a particular sensory experience was not provided. For example the scents of the Ka`ba continued to play a role in Sadia's (thirties) memories of Mecca as she received a piece of the kiswa on the last day of her Hajj in 2007:

> [My friend] handed me this little envelope ... When I opened it, in fact before I even opened it I smelt it because it's very highly perfumed with musk. And I knew instantly what it was. It was a piece of the cloth ... and I still have it to this day and it still smells.

This souvenir, as a symbolic reminder of the 'centre' (Kenny 2007), presented a conglomerate of qualities, as Sadia explained: 'It's spiritual, it's emotional ... it's a piece of the House of God.' As such, the absence of Mecca was not experienced as a loss, but as a surplus of signification (Stewart 1993). Moreover, its distinctive fragrance triggered memories that forged an olfactory link with Mecca and the divine (Ergin 2014). Sadia sought to make the same connection in the exhibition. 'I did have a little sniff,' she admitted, 'but I couldn't smell nothing.' The aromas of Mecca are highly regulated, as, in addition to the ritually scented textiles, pilgrims are prohibited from wearing certain perfumed products and instead use scented oils marketed specifically for use on Hajj. These scents were therefore remembered as Sadia and the sitara shared similar (Mecca-based) networks. As Sadia concluded, 'It's common ground for us, isn't it. Especially if you've been to the Holy Land yourself and you can relate to this stuff.'

For objects to function as barakah-imbued 'tangibilizing contaminants' (Belk et al. 1989), they must be sanctified through their participation in rituals and then move away in order to spread that sacredness to new places. Sociologist Celia Lury proposes that objects travel well when they 'retain their meaning across

210 *Steph Berns*

contexts and retain an authenticated relation to an original dwelling' (1997: 78). For that reason, determining the authenticity of an object, and its indexical and sacred connection, is crucial. At the exhibition, I often observed visitors questioning the authenticity of the sitara. Verification was provided by the label text, which stated that the curtain was made in the kiswa factory in Mecca.[8] 'That's the actual one,' one Muslim woman said twice, pointing to the label.

Questioning the legitimacy of the textile was a clear consequence of its Museum location. First-time visitors were particularly sceptical, being unaccustomed to the Museum's reluctance to display replicas. In Mecca one would never question the validity of the kiswa, as its very existence in that place serves as authentication. Likewise, the flow of pilgrims and their reverence for the pilgrimage and its sites also serve as forms of validation (Collins and Murphy 2010). In the Museum, visitors therefore negotiated the sitara's authenticity through different networks of relationships with places, people, institutions, things and texts (Jones 2010).

Fitting in or standing out

The sitara's change in location, from Mecca to the Museum, transformed its relationships to people, objects and places. Human and non-human actors were reshuffled into new assemblages, which formed new hierarchical structures. In these new arrangements, some objects took on more significant roles while others diminished.

In describing the ways people see religious materiality, Morgan proposes that the 'sacred gaze', which 'designates the particular configuration of ideas, attitudes, and customs that informs a religious act of seeing', works 'by concealing or minimizing one element in order to highlight another' (2005: 3). Pilgrims often act in ways that encourage respect and 'outward conformity to religious norms' (Coleman and Elsner 1995: 209). When nearing the Ka`ba pilgrims may therefore (attempt to) approach with head bowed and eyes lowered in order to heighten their experience and spiritual focus (McLoughlin 2015).

In addition, pilgrims are instructed to meditate on the divine, the prophets and their own faith as they circumambulate the Ka`ba. Thus, as the pilgrim approaches the sacred centre of the Holy Sanctuary, some elements appear as more significant, while others (such as the material components) become less so. In other words, as the pilgrim gets closer, the experience of God unfolds as a staggered revelation (Eimen 2006) and as 'concentric circles of increasing sacredness' (Plate 2014: 27). However, it is also the case that when God's presence feels more direct and immediate, the materials that mediate the encounter fade from view either in the experience itself or in its retelling (Meyer 2010).

For these reasons, a number of my interviewees explained that they were so consumed (spiritually and sensorially) by the rituals that little or no attention was paid to the building itself. For instance, Hena (thirties) explained,

> On Hajj what you're concentrating on is the very spiritual aspect and following the rituals. Whereas, obviously you do see the detail, but that's not

effectively what you're there for or you don't take in or appreciate that as much.

Tasmeen (fifties) concurred: 'On Hajj you're so engrossed with your own spiritual purification that sometimes you miss out on some details ... [and] the physical aspect of things, like looking at the cover.' Similarly, a Malaysian student in her twenties stated that she could not appreciate the textiles in Mecca as she was 'in the zone'. Finally, Masood (thirties) told me that while 'it was nice to see' the sitara in the exhibition and 'see the beauty of it', in Mecca he did not look at it, saying, 'You're just there for the experience ... You don't analyse.' It is likely that these visitors embarked on their pilgrimages with the intention and expectation to focus on prayer and their purification. These hopes, experiences and (identity-related) motivations (Falk 2009) then shaped their subsequent exhibition visit and retellings. As a result, the differences between Mecca and the Museum seemed more pronounced.

This provides an example of what Hodder calls 'fittedness' (2012). Simply put, some assemblages fit together better than others. The sitara in the Museum may work as an exhibit, but it fitted better in Mecca. There it slotted into place, blended with its neighbouring material actors and blurred with past and future assemblages. In contrast, the sitara's lack of fittedness in the Museum highlighted different qualities. In the exhibition, its size, artistry, materials and *thingness* were accentuated. It was also paraded as a star attraction for its rarity, exoticism and beauty. Away from Mecca, the sitara played a role that would be impossible in situ, where the network is too rigid. The Museum's star object therefore sat in contrast to the sitara's supporting role in Mecca, where it was one of many constituent elements.

Because of this, visitors who failed to consider or admire the Ka`ba's covers in Mecca could now, in the Museum, direct their attention to the curtain. Yet, a few of my informants felt that the covers held no salience away from Mecca. After hearing his companion speak passionately about the privilege of seeing the sitara, Zain (twenties) told me,

> This may sound cruel, but the kiswa is just a covering. I like the calligraphy and everything on it is amazing, but when I was actually on Hajj that was the last thing I actually concentrated on, so I don't have much recollection of what it looked like.

Zain also attributed his failure to appreciate the cover to the physical difficulties of performing the rituals among so many people. Most studies on the invisibility of religious things concern how religious objects or buildings are obscured within a landscape that is secular or dominated by a different faith (e.g. Kuppinger 2009; Kaell 2013). The sitara's lack of visibility in Mecca, experienced by Zain, was of a different kind. The curtain was simply overwhelmed and outperformed by other (material and immaterial) aspects of Hajj that were deemed more spiritually, emotionally and materially significant.

By contrast, Aasif (thirties) could appreciate the sitara in Mecca but not in the exhibition. He explained,

> I didn't even look at it, I was like, 'Oh, that's the door', and moved on ... It just can't do it justice ... There everything else looks beautiful and seeing it here holds no value ... What brings the kiswa value is the Ka`ba itself, not the cloth. It defeats the point. If there's no Ka`ba what's the point of the kiswa?

Barakah can flow only if the potential recipient understands and believes in its transformative quality and the object in question is sufficiently salient. Since the exhibited sitara held no value for Aasif independent of the Ka`ba, it could neither mobilise nor retain its sacred qualities.

Morgan proposes that a religious experience with an image requires a compact 'that sets out the conditions under which an image may deliver what the viewer expects from or seeks in it' (2005: 105). But if the 'viewer' does not agree to or is unaware of the compact, a religious experience is unlikely. By contrast, Tasmeen stated that she expected to feel 'spiritual' at the exhibition, as 'everything that is connected to Hajj and the Ka`ba and the Prophet' gave her that feeling. Tasmeen's prior ritual experiences and knowledge predisposed her to perceive certain forms of embodied, aesthetic and social interaction with the object-mediated divine. By the same measure, the knowledge and former experiences of visitors like Aasif and Zain prevented such object-divine encounters in the Museum.

The sitara's lack of fittedness in the Museum was also implicitly expressed by those who noted a sense of (object-mediated) sacredness. For example Zafar (forties), who had never performed Hajj, described 'a very spiritual feeling' on seeing the sitara, 'as if I was actually standing in front of the Ka`ba'. Similarly, Yasmin (fifties) said, 'It was just like I was there again ... when I was saying those words.' As suggested by their use of "*as if*" and "*it was like*," the women's engagements were always lacking and longing for the holy city.

Latour (2005) reminds us that transformation is an inevitable outcome of moving. The sitara in the Museum therefore hung differently to the one in Mecca, though it maintained an intrinsic link to its former location. Through this, the curtain shared a bond with every Muslim who prays and journeys to the city. Hodder (2012) refers to these attachments, which weave things and people into tightly woven relations, as dependencies. These dependencies can also be understood using Latour's notion of delegation, whereby objects take on the role of humans.

In the case of the Ka`ba, however, the building takes on the role of the divine. As 'the earthly counterpart to God's throne in heaven' (Esposito 2003: 165), the Ka`ba provides material form to Islam's sacred topography, linking the cosmic, local and supra-local realms (McLoughlin 2015). This is, Latour argues, 'because humans, nonhumans, and even angels are never sufficient in themselves' (writing as Johnson 1988: 305). And so, at the core of the pilgrimage there is a mutually dependent relationship between the divine and the material. But at a more local level, the sitara (and the exhibition) is dependent on the Hajj assemblage. As Hodder proposes, people give meaning to things 'because the things themselves are closely connected to other things in ways that draw humans in' (2012: 95). In other words, the sitara's meaning and ability to trigger memories and pass on barakah are accomplished through chains of dependencies between people, things and the divine. The sitara also depends on the Ka`ba to give it its sacred and physical stature. At the exhibition, the sitara was indebted to an entirely different set of 'things' (particularly for those unacquainted with Mecca) including labels, photographs and videos. Yet, even in the Museum, the curtain depended on its place of origin to give it religious and cultural meaning.

A different effect

At the exhibition the sitara became part of the Museum's network and party to new modes of engagement and perception. Art historian Sveltana Alpers describes this as 'the museum effect' – that is the 'tendency to isolate something from its world, to offer it up for attentive looking and thus transform it to art' (1991: 27). Though I contest the suggestion that the sitara was entirely isolated, as the curtain was within an exhibition on Hajj and still part of the pilgrimage's (transglobal) network, the museum conventions and environment (including the curtain's mounting on a gallery wall and its label) led some visitors to see the sitara through an aestheticising lens (Duncan 1995). Two Malaysian students (twenties) discussed the change in how they perceived the sitara in the Museum:

Safiah: When you're [in Mecca] the feeling is different because you know that those are Qur`anic writings and verses and you look it at . . . like, a sense of . . .
Komal: More in a prayer mood.
Safiah: Yeah . . . it's more like art here.

Tariq (late twenties) described a similar shift: 'The 'thing' can be the same, but the experience, the emotional attachment, the feeling of *there* – it's completely different.' The visitors' re-encounters with the sitara performed diametrically opposite actions. While their museum visits brought them physically closer to the curtain, its presence reinforced how distant (and different) their experiences were in Mecca. As visitor Isha (twenties) reflected, 'You're not in Mecca so there's only so far you can go.' However, most of my Muslim interviewees found that the 'museum effect' provided additional ways of engaging, allowing them to contemplate memories and imaginings of Hajj alongside appreciating the curtain's artistry, provenance and materiality. Visitors were therefore capable of both embracing and resisting the attempts of exhibition curators and designers to frame religious objects in ways that contravened their established religious habits of feeling and perception.

The 'museum effect' also provided some visitors with a much-appreciated change of pace, as they had more time to look at the curtain as an individual object, appreciate its craftsmanship, reflect on their own Hajj and meditate on the embroidered Qur'anic verses. Most pilgrims first physically encounter the Ka`ba when they perform the *tawaf* (the seven circumambulations).[9] During Hajj, the ritual is often crowded as pilgrims alternate between walking and prostrating around the black cube.[10] By contrast, most visitors at the exhibition were able to stop and look. Art historian James Elkins (2004) argues that to feel emotions in galleries requires time, patience and openness. At the exhibition, such experiences were aided by the (often unspoken) rules around museum etiquette, the spacing out of exhibits and the staggered ticketed entry. Ravi (thirties) who came with his nine-year-old son, explained,

> I've been to Mecca but it's so busy you never have a chance to go close to the Ka`ba or have enough time there to read the inscription on the cube itself . . . So being here in a static place, with not many people around, you get a chance to read it.

Nadia (forties), from Saudi Arabia, described a similar experience:

> I have taken moments to just see and reflect and read the actual script on the kiswa because during the Hajj you'll be very busy practicing and performing the Hajj itself so [today was] a good time to meditate and read.

For Ravi and Nadia, encountering the material components from their Hajj in more comfortable surroundings prompted memories of their struggles experienced on the pilgrimage. Moreover, it allowed them to appreciate the opportunity to read the embroidered passages from the Qur'an, which, by bearing the words of God, also emitted barakah (Starrett 1995). The affordances of the exhibition space therefore enabled different kinds of religious experiences in comparison to what most pilgrims feel on Hajj.

The curtain's placement in the Museum also gave visitors who had not performed Hajj the time to contemplate their pilgrimage. Describing the moment that he first saw the exhibited sitara, visitor Sadiq (sixties) told me,

> It strikes you. Perhaps it takes you there . . . For a little while, you just become totally oblivious of people, of things around and you're focused on that place, on that piece and where and whenever it was hanging – that place, going back in history. This was supposed to be the site of the first house of worship of God, even before the time of Ibrahim. So for that reason it takes you through a journey, I would say, almost like a spiritual journey. If you stand there in front and just let the thing take you.

Such a 'journey of the mind' is not passive (Eickelman and Piscatori 1990: xii). In order to appreciate the connections between objects, places and the divine, the (imagining) 'pilgrims' must exercise their imaginations (Uddin 2008). In other words, they must make the effort to know the pilgrimage and imagine themselves among its material components. In Sadiq's case this involved his experiences and memories of sacred places outside of the Museum along with *things* inside the exhibition, including the sound of the *adhan* (call to prayer) that was played at the entrance where the curtain hung. And so imagined pilgrimages are never purely immaterial, as they are always informed by the things the pilgrims encounter, whether those things are in museums or at consecrated pilgrimage sites.

To conclude

In this chapter, I have described how blessings flowed, imaginations wandered and minds travelled on Hajj and in the exhibition. Some of these movements happened across networks, which folded different times and places into the assemblage. Others happened across Euclidian space. 'Hajj demands its space and time,' and because of this Mecca, with its privileged access to the divine, needs to be at a geographic, temporal and spiritual distance (McCloud 1996: 65). As such, an exhibition about the Islamic pilgrimage cannot constitute the embodied rites (and nor did it aspire to). Instead the exhibition provided a sense of the sacred sites. Yet, by doing so, it reminded visitors how spatially specific the pilgrimage destinations are. Barakah operated differently. If, as Latour (2005) proposes, actions require conduits and vehicles, then barakah was the conduit and the objects were the vehicles, although even barakah, with its ability to bring the divine closer, pointed back to the sacred city as that which is out of reach.

The Muslim visitors' experiences described in this chapter drew on previous devotional encounters (from daily prayers to pilgrimage). These engagements illustrate a continuity in the ways the materially mediated divine was experienced, but also a precariousness as the visitors' engagements with the materially mediated divine were always open to new possibilities. These new kinds of hybrid experiences were therefore made possible by the distinctive assemblages of actors that occurred within the exhibition.

So was Mecca mobilised? The final conclusion must be 'in part' or, more specifically, as constituent parts. While some of these fragments moved away, as seen with the sitara and the pilgrims, others (like the Ka'ba) stayed in place. The objects that travelled therefore acted as pieces of and pointers to the Holy Sanctuary. Through this they disseminated blessings, spread callings and triggered memories, ensuring that the steady flow of pilgrims and objects continues year on year.

Notes

1 The exhibition ran from 26 January to 15 April 2012 and was curated by Venetia Porter.
2 To maintain the anonymity of my interviewees, pseudonyms are used throughout.

3 The British Museum, established in 1753, continues to aspire to a universal ambition, with collections representing the cultures of the world. As director Neil McGregor stated in 2010, it is a 'pre-imperial collection . . . now operating in a post-colonial world' (Rustin 2010).
4 Muslims can also perform *umrah* (the lesser pilgrimage) throughout the year. However, umrah does not fulfil the Hajj obligation for the fifth pillar.
5 Noted exhibits praised for conveying the emotions of seeing the Ka`ba included the diary of a schoolgirl (opened to the page she described seeing the Ka`ba as 'so majestic and awe-inspiring it is difficult to take your eyes off it') and an audio recording in which a male pilgrim recounted the moment his 'heart melted'.
6 As pilgrims perform the tawaf (the circumambulation of the Ka`ba), many try to touch, kiss or (if out of reach) salute the *barakah*-imbued Black Stone (*hajar al-aswad*), which is believed to be a relic of the original temple (Esposito 2003).
7 Within Europe, the influence of Protestantism also shaped the rationalist approach we now identify with the Enlightenment, which in turn came to define the ways we perceive 'secular' institutions, such as the British Museum.
8 The label gave the sitara's place and date of manufacture, materials and lender. It also noted (though with no translations) the inscriptions, which included Qur`anic verses, the name of the calligrapher and the Saudi king (at the time of its manufacture) alongside his title, 'Custodian of the Two Sanctuaries'.
9 The tawaf is said to symbolise the circling of angels in heaven (Uddin 2008).
10 Pilgrims may also perform the tawaf during quieter times during Hajj or umrah.

Works cited

Alpers, S. 1991. 'The Museum as a Way of Seeing'. In *Exhibiting Cultures: The Poetics and Politics of Museum Display*, eds. I. Karp and S.D. Karp, 25–32. London: Smithsonian Institution Press.
Alrashid, J. 2012. 'Sitara to the Door of Kaaba at British Museum'. *Arab News*, 19 January.
Belk, R.W., M. Wallendorf and J.F. Sherry. 1989. 'The Sacred and the Profane in Consumer Behavior: Theodicy on the Odyssey'. *Journal of Consumer Research* 16(1): 1–38.
Bennett, C. 1998. 'Islam.' In *Sacred Place*, eds. J. Holm and J. Bowker, 88–114. London: Continuum.
Bille, M. 2010. 'Seeking Providence through Things: The Word of God versus Black Cumin'. In *An Anthropology of Absence: Materializations of Transcendence and Loss*, eds. M. Bille, F. Hastrup and T.F. Sørensen, 167–184. London: Springer.
Coleman, S. and M. Crang, 2002. *Tourism: Between Place and Performance*. Oxford: Berghahn.
Coleman, S. and J. Elsner. 1995. *Pilgrimage: Past and Present in the World Religions*. Cambridge, MA: Harvard University Press.
Collins, N. and J. Murphy. 2010. 'The Hajj: An illustration of 360-Degree Authenticity'. In *Tourism in the Muslim World*, eds. N. Scott and J. Jafari, 321–330. Vol. 2. Bingley: Emerald.
Cooke, M. and B. Lawrence. 2005. 'Introduction'. In *Muslim Networks from Hajj to Hip Hop*, eds. M. Cooke and B. Lawrence, 1–29. Chapel Hill: University of North Carolina Press.
Duncan, C. 1995. *Civilizing Rituals: Inside Public Art Museums*. New York: Routledge.
Eickelman, D.F. and J.P. Piscatori. 1990. *Muslim Travellers: Pilgrimage, Migration, and the Religious Imagination*. Oxon: Routledge.
Eimen, A. 2006. *Museum and Mosque: The Shifting Identities of Modern Tehran*. Ann Arbor, MI: ProQuest.
Elkins, J. 2004. *Pictures & Tears: A History of People Who Have Cried in Front of Paintings*. New York: Routledge.

Ergin, N. 2014. 'The Fragrance of the Divine: Ottoman Incense Burners and Their Context'. *The Art Bulletin* 96(1): 70–97.

Esposito, J.L. 2003. *The Oxford Dictionary of Islam*. Oxford: Oxford University Press.

Falk, J.H. 2009. *Identity and the Museum Visitor Experience*. Walnut Creek: Left Coast Press.

Fenwick, T. 2011. 'Reading Educational Reform with Actor Network Theory: Fluid Spaces, Otherings, and Ambivalences'. *Educational Philosophy and Theory* 43: 114–134.

Finucane, R.C. 1977. *Miracles and Pilgrims: Popular Beliefs in Medieval England*. London: Dent.

Hodder, I. 2012. *Entangled: An Archaeology of the Relationships between Humans and Things*. Malden, MA: Wiley-Blackwell.

Johnson, J. 1988. 'Mixing Humans and Nonhumans Together: The Sociology of a Door-Closer'. *Social Problems* 35(3): 298–310.

Jones, S. 2010. 'Negotiating Authentic Objects and Authentic Selves beyond the Deconstruction of Authenticity'. *Journal of Material Culture* 15(2): 181–203.

Kaell, H. 2013. *Wayside Crosses – Objects That Reveal and Conceal*. Reverberations: New Directions in the Study of Prayer. http://forums.ssrc.org/ndsp/2013/09/25/wayside-crosses-objects-that-reveal-and-conceal/. Accessed 22/01/2015.

Kenny, E. 2007. 'Gifting Mecca: Importing Spiritual Capital to West Africa'. *Mobilities* 2(3): 363–381.

Kuppinger, P. 2009. 'Factories, Office Suites, Defunct and Marginal Spaces'. In *Re-Shaping Cities: How Global Mobility Transforms Architecture and Urban Form*, eds. M. Guggenheim and O. Söderström, 83–99. London: Routledge.

Latour, B. 2005. *Reassembling the Social: An Introduction to Actor-Network-Theory*. Oxford: Oxford University Press.

Law, J. and A. Mol. 2001. 'Situating Technoscience: An Inquiry into Spatialities'. *Environment and Planning D: Society and Space* 19(5): 609–621.

Lazarus-Yafeh, H. 1981. *Some Religious Aspects of Islam: A Collection of Articles*. Brill: Leiden.

Lury, C. 1997. 'The Objects of Travel'. In *Touring Cultures: Transformations of Travel and Theory*, eds. C. Rojek and J. Urry, 75–95. New York: Routledge.

McCloud, A.B. 1996. '"This Is a Muslim Home": Signs of Difference in the African-American Row House'. In *Making Muslim Space in North America and Europe*, ed. B.D. Metcalf, 65–73. Berkeley: University of California Press.

McGregor, R. 2010. 'Dressing the Ka`ba from Cairo: The Aesthetics of Pilgrimage to Mecca'. In *Religion and Material Culture: The Matter of Belief*, ed. D. Morgan, 247–261. London: Routledge.

McLoughlin, S. 2015. 'Pilgrimage, Performativity, and British Muslims: Scripted and Unscripted Accounts of the Hajj and Umra'. In *Hajj: Global Interactions through Pilgrimage*, eds. L. Mois and M. Buitelaar, 41–64. Leiden: Sidestone Press.

Metcalf, B.D. 1996. 'Introduction'. In *Making Muslim Space in North America and Europe*, ed. Barbara Metcalf, 1–29. Berkeley: University of California Press.

Meyer, B. 2008. 'Materializing Religion'. *Material Religion: The Journal of Objects, Art and Belief* 4(2): 227.

———. 2010. 'The Indispensability of Form.' *The Immanent Frame*, 10 November. http://blogs.ssrc.org/tif/2010/11/10/indispensability-of-form/. Accessed 07–06–2016.

MHM. 2012. *Bridging Cultures, Sharing Experiences an Evaluation of Hajj: Journey to the Heart of Islam at the British Museum, July 2012 (Draft)*. London: MHM.

Morgan, D. 2005. *The Sacred Gaze: Religious Visual Culture in Theory and Practice*. Berkeley: University of California Press.

———. 2007. 'Exhibition Review: The Critical View'. *Material Religion* 3(1): 135–142.

Nasser, N. 2005. 'Expressions of Muslim Identity in Architecture and Urbanism in Birmingham, UK'. *Islam and Christian–Muslim Relations* 16(1): 61–78.

Pink, S. 2009. *Doing Sensory Ethnography*. London: SAGE.

Pinto, P.G. 2013. 'Knowledge and Miracles: Modes of Charisma in Syrian Sufism'. In *The Anthropology of Religious Charisma: Ecstasies and Institutions*, ed. C. Lindholm, 59–80. New York: Palgrave-Macmillan.

Plate, S.B. 2014. *A History of Religion in 5 1/2 Objects: Bringing the Spiritual to Its Senses*. Boston, MA: Beacon Press.

Porter, V. 2015. 'Gifts, Souvenirs, and the Hajj'. In *Hajj: Global Interactions through Pilgrimage*, eds. L. Mois and M. Buitelaar, 95–112. Leiden: Sidestone Press.

Rustin, S. 2010. 'The Greatest Exhibition You Could Have'. *The Guardian*, 2 January. https://www.theguardian.com/culture/2010/jan/02/neil-macgregor-british-museum-history. Accessed 07/06/2016.

Shatanawi, M. 2012. 'Engaging Islam: Working with Muslim Communities in a Multicultural Society'. *Curator: The Museum Journal* 55(1): 65–79.

Starrett, G. 1995. 'The Political Economy of Religious Commodities in Cairo'. *American Anthropologist* 97(1): 51–68.

Stewart, S. 1993. *On Longing: Narratives of the Miniature, the Gigantic, the Souvenir, the Collection*. Durham, NC: Duke University Press.

Torab, A. 2007. *Performing Islam: Gender and Ritual in Islam*. Leiden: Brill.

Uddin, A.T. 2008. 'The Hajj and Pluralism'. *The Review of Faith & International Affairs* 6(4): 43–47.

13 Matter challenging words

From 'angel talisman' to 'prayer ornament'

Terhi Utriainen

Introduction

Angels – traditional Christian figures that every now and then descend among humans – can be circulated to become present, materialised and embodied today in many creative and intriguing ways. Angel practices documented in my ethnographic material collected among Finnish women include healings, meditations, angel card reading, photographing angels and angel visitations.[1] These sometimes involve clearly framed rituals, such as angel healing, visitation and meditation. However, some of these practices are much more vague, momentary and fleeting. Despite being intimate meetings with the extraordinary, they are very much embedded in the everyday profane life that they seek to affect (Luhrmann 2004; Utriainen 2013a, 2014a). An example of these often quite quotidian lived religion (Orsi 2005; McGuire 2008) practices can be found in an interview with one young mother, who told that she often imagined herself dressing her children in a blue or pink protective overall provided by the archangel Michael before sending them to school in the morning and that she purified her home of negative vibrations with the energy of angels. Another example would be how (bird) feathers, which one can find practically anywhere, have come to be interpreted as a manifestation of an angelic sign that something good will happen soon. In many ways – more or less material – everyday life can become 'touched by an angel.'

Angel practices are reflections of how some people in a secularised and pluralising (but culturally still Lutheran) society, such as Finland, clearly seem to be seeking and enacting new variations of substance, experience and practice in contradistinction to what mainline religiosity has offered as the default option (on religious change in Finland, see Kääriäinen, Niemelä and Ketola 2005; Nynäs, Illman and Martikainen 2015). Most of those engaging in angel practices – the clear majority of whom seem to be women – are members of the Evangelical Lutheran Church of Finland, but have found these new practices outside the church context to be attractive and, in many ways, helpful in their lives (on women's religion in Finland over time, see Utriainen and Salmesvuori 2014). It would appear that an increasing number of people in Finland are not completely content with the traditional version of vicarious religion (e.g. Bruce and Voas 2010) and the relatively passive practitioner role it offers laypeople as merely listening subjects and receivers of rituals enacted for and in front of them by a pastor. Instead, many seem to want to act and practise in different and often quite concrete ways, in order to thus feel the presence of the transcendent/otherworld within the immanent (Haastettu kirkko 2012: 35–46; Ketola, Martikainen and Salomäki 2014).

One example of this in the Lutheran Church of Finland would be the popularity of the so-called St Thomas Mass, which combines ritual elements from various Christian cultural models and invites participants to take part in several active roles in and around the service. Another example that takes place within and in the margins of the church is different versions of charismatic meetings, including the service called 'Healing Rooms,' which brings active Christians together in concrete and practical worship and provides them with a variety of actor roles to choose from. Furthermore, many people – both outside and also very much inside the church – have become drawn towards forms of alternative spirituality that they find more holistically engaging than standard Lutheran practices. Both Western and Eastern alternative practices and networks are welcomed, in that they provide new combinations of commitment and freedom, as well as emotional intensity. One thing that seems to count in these alternatives is a sense of doing and practising in often concrete and multifaceted ways that suit the practitioner's personality and style. This does not, however, mean doing things only individually, but also in many ways and varying degrees of collaboration with others (Hovi 2012; Ahonen 2014; Ketola, Martikainen and Salomäki 2014).

It could perhaps be said that the most important religious practice in many forms of Protestantism, and very much so in the Lutheran tradition, has been the combination of word, text and listening. Indeed, words and listening are so important to traditional Protestant religion that in the anthropology of Christianity, Protestantism has been characterised by its distinct and highly emphasised language ideology or, wider still, semiotic ideology (Keane 2007: 16–21). This is a historical and normative way of understanding language and its key role in achieving transcendence and salvation, which not only privileges language itself over other material sign systems and forms of divine mediation, but also valorises the content of a word or text over its form, texture and social performance. This ideology also poses moral guidelines for a particular way of conceiving of agency – that is who and what is to act and make things happen (Keane 2007: 59–82; Robbins 2012: 15–18).

Many people, however, find an appeal in variegated ways of doing and feeling instead of or in addition to relating to words. The mediation of otherworldly power has become more openly diffuse and pluralistic, and material is being used in ways that are not orientated to and focused on language (Utriainen et al. 2015). Furthermore, in this somewhat novel mode of practice – which Linda Woodhead and Rebecca Catto (2012) call the new post-Reformation style of religion – both outside and inside Christianity, *material and sensory pluralism and hybridity* become important, as well as the experiences of sacrality and enchantment that this pluralism can bring. This pluralism and enchantment may be further accompanied by new forms of subjectivity and agency in comparison to the traditional Lutheran listener of words.[2]

Sensational forms and enchanted matters of concern

The anthropologist Birgit Meyer (2006, 2008) asks scholars to pay closer attention to the ways in which culture-specific material and 'sensational forms' (such as many kinds of images, sounds and tangible artefacts, as well as the accompanying rituals and senses they engage with) mediate between the immanent and the transcendent. This mediation can take place both vertically and horizontally, often in dynamic, complex and delicately power-laden social contexts. Moreover, she claims that these sensational forms, as carriers and mediators of religion, become attractive and potentially incorporated in the subjects in compelling ways – ways that can also bring considerable and even unexpected changes in people's lives. More than many other scholars, Meyer puts special emphasis on the power of the specific *aesthetics* in these materials and processes of engagement. Aesthetics should here be understood in a broad way that comprises all possible forms of experiencing beauty and pleasure, as well as their counterparts.

Vernacular and lived religion is, of course, often noted as highlighting this material side and element of religion much more than some official and normative religions (Ammerman 2008; McGuire 2008; Bowman and Valk 2012; Whitehead 2014). What Meyer's notion of sensational forms adds to this is, above all, the importance of the particular concrete and also often mixed, hybrid engagements between human senses and non-human matter. This hybridity connects sensational forms to the dynamic of powers that can become lived as religious, magical or enchanted and that may sometimes become socially, culturally and politically very sensitive (at least this is the way I read her predicament). These material practices and sensational forms are often – in private lives and sometimes in the public sphere – involved in complex, dynamic and mutually interacting power plays of concealing and revealing (see Meyer and Pals 2003). These power plays may in many regards bring different religions or religious and secular enchantments together into a mixed representational economy (Keane 2007: 18–19).

Sometimes interesting instances of sensational forms appear in fleeting moments and quite small material practices or rituals. In the case of my research, they are not always found in the interview accounts themselves, but are documented in field notes from (sometimes participant) observation of several kinds of angel events. While anthropology can be described as studying moments (Siikala 1997: 46) (i.e. carefully chosen moments when something important happens), a researcher inspired by actor-network theory might add that we should try to identify and focus on *moments of gathering* (coming together) of the various actors and actants that together make agency and create difference, in order to analyse how these gatherings become composed (Latour 2005; see also Piette 2003; Orsi 2005; Harvey 2012; Lassander 2012). Bruno Latour (2004) also writes that, besides gatherings and associations, we should focus on 'matters of concern' instead of 'matters of fact' – that is matters that matter, that are of importance and that change something in the contexts and lives studied (even if that change may be only for a short moment). In my ethnography, an 'angel that happens' is approached as an example of such moments of difference and gathering. I approach these as sensational forms that are also socially, temporally and materially mediated and located matters of concern.

Instances in which an angel happens can be conceived of as an open and dynamic form or mode of 'religioning,' a specific mode which I call *enchantment* (Nye 2000: 467). In this context, enchantment is understood as an activity, a mode of gathering or creating associations that allows or brings together a variety of things, including the extraordinary or 'something other,' in order to allow some important difference, such as healing or a 'touch of magic' (Utriainen 2013b). Enchantment – or re-enchantment – in modernity has often been linked to the special mediating power and allure of popular culture, such as entertainment and art (e.g. film), as well as to alternative healing and well-being practices (e.g. Partridge 2004; Elkins and Morgan 2007). In her ethnography, Jone Salomonsen (2002) uses the term 'enchanted' to define the particular kind of spiritually inspired and enacted feminism of witches in San Francisco. Sometimes – particularly when emphasis is placed on special attempted outcomes or *effects* – enchantment may be further described as 'magic' (Meyer and Pals 2003).

In the following, I attempt to identify and disassemble some examples of *enchanted moments and sensational forms in which an angel happens*. My guideline in understanding enchantment has been the already classic perspective of Jane Bennett: 'To be enchanted is to be struck and shaken by the extraordinary that lives amid the familiar and the everyday' (2001: 5). Bennett also notes that enchantment is not always a spontaneous happening; it can also be fostered through deliberate action. Enchantment engages bigger or smaller alterity or transcendence ('the extraordinary'), either as a surprise or as something desired, summoned and invited (see Luckman 1990; Csordas 2004; Utriainen 2013a). In my case, an exemplary small and intimate enchantment is the 'touch of an angel,' which can be said to make considerable and delicate cultural work (see Morgan, this volume) through women's creative activity.

Old tradition circulated by new practices

My chapter draws on observations concerning the intricacy of material practices and accompanying words in one contemporary locus of intersection between Christian and what is often called 'alternative' spiritual practices and beliefs. It brings together and circulates elements from different religions and their practice and language, and it takes place in intersections between 'the religious' and 'the secular.' Thus it is related to the issue of religious plurality (simplifying things, one might even describe this as religion of the word meeting religion of matter). On the surface, the example of making an angel talisman, which is discussed in greater detail ahead, is merely about one enchanting or even entertaining micro-ritual that took place among a handful of Finnish women one winter evening. However, when investigated more closely, it can be shown as bringing together and touching upon many serious and significant issues, both on the level of personal lives and changes in society, as well as some problems that belong to the field of agency and religious authority (and how to deal with the latter). We might also argue that this spiritual practice, which is both merely entertaining and aestheticised in a particular way, comprises aspects of what Martin Stringer (2008) calls 'coping religion,' in that it opens towards serious, everyday lived life matters of concern.

Today angel practices are quite popular, particularly among women (e.g. Gardella 2007; Draper and Baker 2010; Walter 2011, 2016; Gilhus 2012; Uibu 2013). Most of them (according to my survey, N = 263; 73.8%)[3] are members of the Evangelical Lutheran Church of Finland,[4] who are also to varying degrees open to more esoteric and alternative spirituality, especially various forms of healing provided by it. However, not only women are interested in these practices. Recently different media, in particular women's magazines but also occasionally the news media, are reporting on them in relatively positive tones (Utriainen 2013b). In December 2013, two influential women – the bishop of Helsinki and the president of the Social Democratic Party – announced in the headlines of the tabloid *Ilta-Sanomat*, 'We believe in angels' (2015). In the interview itself, when asked if angels have appeared to her personally, the bishop answered in these words: 'For me, angels are ambassadors of God's goodness, angels are invisible. Angels are in the service of the goodness of God. I don't need to know more than this.' The president of the Social Democratic Party answered that 'I believe in the care and guidance by God that people can experience. Angels are symbols of this.' Interestingly, both women thus embrace angels (as may also be expected because of the context of the holiday season), but also take some distance from the possibility of their materialisation as spirits.

Furthermore, the actors of and around the Lutheran Church of Finland have noticed this new attraction and, consequently, have started to pay closer attention to the new forms of circulating the traditional figure of angel. This attention is taking the form of some corrective measures; for example Lutheran (male) theologians and Christian writers have been reminding ordinary people about how angels should and should not be understood in Christianity and Lutheran thinking – that is metaphorically and not as independent spirits (e.g. Seppälä 2003; Kuula 2011; Miettinen 2012). Another indication of this growing interest is that scholars (myself included) are invited to talk about this new form of spirituality in seminars (Utriainen 2014b came out of one such seminar organised by the Church Research Institute).

The attention given by the Church to angel practices and practitioners is understandable, since the people involved represent an important segment of its members. They are women 30–70 years old, who are not altogether satisfied with what the church has to offer for them personally (even if, at the same time, they may highly value the social work done by the church) and who want, as they often say, 'something more,' or something different in their personal spiritual lives. In the interviews, some of these women also state that they have hesitated about continuing their church membership, because their beliefs – and also, in some cases, concrete experiences about the way in which they want to think, feel and practise – do not get a positive response from church employees and are often considered to not be Christian in the right way. One of them noted how she thinks that the church should open its doors to angel spirituality:

> I think that the church would do wisely if it opened up to angels and the fact that people will be able to grasp spirituality through angels. It is much easier to approach angels than, for instance, Jesus – let alone God, who is such a high and remote notion for a human being to understand.
> (IF mgt 2011–011)

I might summarise that angel practices (together with many other spiritual practices, of course) have become for certain people something that either complements what the church offers or provides an attractive and plausible alternative to it. This situation might be compared to the approaches of complementary and alternative medicine (CAM) in relation to mainstream medicine. In terms of religious change and continuity, an issue may be whether these practices should become interpreted as complementary (like many charismatic trends and movements are understood to be) or alternative and exclusive to the official Christian institutions and the wider society. The outcome remains to be seen.

What is important in my treatise here is that these new practices and their sensational forms take place in a complex and pluralistic social world where traditional religious forms (like the Protestant word and language ideology) also still very much exist as models and reference points. As already mentioned, most of the informants were members of the Lutheran Church and connected in some ways at least to its cultural, social or spiritual influence. Indeed, one explanation behind the popularity of belief in angels may well be the fact that angels are a traditional – and for many also a beloved and nostalgic – Christian motif, which is now increasingly being circulated into the pantheon of alternative spirits and gods. For example in a focus group interview, three women who clearly and explicitly identified themselves as Lutheran discussed that if it was not for angels, they might not have been drawn to alternative spirituality in the first place. However, since an angel was for them a safe and traditional figure from their childhood (in particular, guardian angels have been very popular in children's religious culture and education in homes and Sunday schools), these three women had taken part in an 'angel visitation.' This is a ritual practice in the form of a chain letter that circulated on the Internet. In an angel visitation, one invited angels to visit one's home for a few days, during which time one would concentrate on one's wishes for the future. What is new in these practices is not so much the figure of an angel in itself, which is part of the Lutheran imagination and chain of memory, but some of the (occasionally 'magical') ways in which it is communicated and integrated in the present culture.

Making a talisman and surrounding matters of concern

Belief in angels can be further contextualised by the practice of making an angel talisman – or 'amulet' as it was also called – a jewel in the shape of an angel made to include a prayer or request. This practice of making a talisman, an intimate mode of production, was learned during an angel healing course that was organised during the winter of 2011–2012 in the home of a female teacher and healer in Helsinki. The course took place over two long weekends with more than a month's pause in between, allowing participants to do individual homework. A diploma of 'angel healer' was given to those who not only participated in the meetings and exercises but also passed exams that included, for example, the traditional Christian angel hierarchies alongside the Indian energy system of chakras. The diploma can be seen as a credential in the field of a pluralising and potentially competing spiritual market, as Marion Bowman (1999) has shown: with the diploma, one can prove (in a specific social world) that one has learned to contact the otherworld.

Angel healing can be practised in several ways. It can, for instance, be administered to oneself or to another person, by means of face-to-face contact or as a remote healing. In the version that I observed closely, the healer invokes angels one by one to come and spread their healing energies. The healer acts as a human channel for these energies, and the basic ritual gesture is rhythmically opening and closing one's arms to mimic the wings of the angels over the body of the person being healed. The different energies of the angels can be visualised as different colours. Any sensation or mental image experienced is noted and can be interpreted as a healing sign or message. The six female participants who took part in the course were also taught other techniques of making contact, such as meditation and creating a talisman (see Utriainen forthcoming).

The making of angel talismans was structured and guided by the teacher. It started by thinking about the content of one's request or prayer (i.e. what it was that one wanted to ask or say to an angel). This was followed by learning to write the letters and words of one's request in the special alphabet of angel language, following the model provided by the teacher, first in normal-sized letters on a larger sheet of paper and then in very tiny size on a small piece of thin, white silk paper. Language was thus anything but unimportant; however, not only the content of the words but also all the specific forms and material aspects mattered. After this, the small paper was folded into a tight parcel in a neat way. This was followed by choosing from the teacher's collection an approximately three-centimetre-tall angel talisman made of stained glass in the colour of one's liking (with the colour indicating a specific angel with its particular energy). The folded paper was then attached behind the talisman. The participants were instructed in how to maintain and recharge the power of the talisman over time by placing the talisman in a special place (in this case, inside a hollow lantern).

Sitting around a table on a darkening winter day, the women engaged in this exercise mostly in deep silence and concentration, carefully listening to the instructions of the teacher. The talismans, when ready, were given to everyone to keep. I still have mine at home with the prayer attached to it. We were also told that it was not necessary for the talisman to be made with a stained-glass figure, but that the prayer could also be attached, for example, to an angel card, which could be kept in one's purse or handbag – or, alternatively, put in one's car – for everyday protection and guidance.

After this exercise, the group talked. The discussion ranged from the enjoyable details of making the talisman (e.g. the beauty and strangeness of the special angel language and how and why one was drawn to a particular colour) to larger issues, such as how to earn a living and organise one's life. While some of the participants of the course were actively planning on starting their own angel healing, life-coaching small businesses or including angel healing methods in an already existent healing practice (this was why some participated in the course, which included a fee), one of them began to seriously consider the possibility of including angel practices in her work as a counsellor of young people in a Lutheran congregation. This woman found making the talisman to be a charming practice that might also have potential appeal in a church context. The teacher reacted to her plan in a very supportive way and considered it a real innovation. However, she also gave her a piece of advice that in that setting it might be better to talk in terms of a 'prayer ornament' instead of an 'angel talisman.'

This advice and the accompanying set of terms ('talisman' versus 'ornament') were immediately understood and acknowledged by all the women in the group, even with some shared hilarity. The women laughed and nodded; someone said, 'Of course!' Everyone seemed to recognise that the words reflected an important issue, potentially pointing to such categories as paganism and magic on one hand and Christianity and faith on the other. The terms 'talisman' and 'ornament' also highlighted an understanding of the ambiguous and sometimes critical relationship between material practices and words in a religious context. These women, raised in a Lutheran culture, thus had a shared understanding of the paramount importance of (correct, legitimate and authorised) words for Lutheranism. In this case, Lutheranism was defined indirectly and more tacitly than argumentatively; nonetheless, it was characterised quite spontaneously and unanimously by taking words – possibly not only the particular words of 'talisman' versus 'ornament' but also words in the larger and more far-reaching sense of carriers and condensations of sincerity, belief and dogma – extremely seriously. It is interesting that the women seemed to simultaneously think that today's Lutheran Church in Finland might be potentially open to new kinds of innovative material practices, provided that they were accompanied by well-chosen and correct verbalisations.

Words referring to anything even potentially associated with 'magic' are suspect in a Lutheran context. This is the case even if 'magic' has always been an intimate other of Protestantism and often practised in everyday activities.

Matter challenging words 227

Practices related to 'magic' – in the sense of emphasis on human agency and initiative in the communication with the divine, as well as in the sense of the instrumental use of a material practice such as prayer – have been scrutinised with suspicion. This tension has also surrounded the idea and figure of an angel for centuries after the Reformation. A strong belief in and vivid experiences of angels have often been seen as a result of heretical influences (e.g. Sulavik 2006a, 2006b). On the other hand, many Protestant churches are currently struggling to provide new practices in order to attract passive members; for instance yoga and dance have been given space in the Lutheran Church in Finland (although it could be argued that yoga and dance can perhaps be understood in a non-magical and purely expressive way, compared to talismans).

What I find interesting is that this small group of women, in their process of learning angel practices to change something in their lives, seemed quite perceptive about this delicate issue and were resourcefully – and not without a certain hilarity and sense of irony – together preparing to meet the challenge. There was a common understanding that although angels are part of Christian Lutheran belief and tradition, there are rules about how they should be approached in the Lutheran space. This *sensitivity to the importance of materiality on one hand and language and words on the other* is an example of very subtle and yet practical reflexive knowledge about the delicate and shifting limits of possible and credible agency in different religious contexts – that is knowledge of what makes a difference in a particular setting. This kind of reflexivity may be taken as a token of religious dynamism and plurality.

Meeting of matter and words

Thus, the ritual practice of making an angel talisman also describes a situation in which a novel and (for the practitioners in the documented example, at least) appealing material practice with sensational form and corresponding conceptions of agency meets the old, very familiar religion of childhood in the form of a traditional motif. In the traditional Lutheran system, certainly angels can be prayed to and contacted, but as some theologians emphasise in their contemporary writing, they should not be addressed too directly or in a summoning or commanding way, since angels act only in accordance with God's wishes and not when and how people want them to. One theologian wrote on the website of the Lutheran Church on St Michael's day in 2011 that '[angels] follow a certain order in a chain of command which leads up all the way to God.' Furthermore, he continued, 'angels are not private entrepreneurs who run their own errands – except for, perhaps, fallen angels' (Kuula 2011). In this way, even the figure of the fallen (dark) angel is included in this Lutheran corrective.

Also, angels should preferably be understood as metaphors rather than as spirits (Seppälä 2003; Miettinen 2012). A critical issue is that, according to official Lutheran dogma, the role of humans – and angels as well – is considerably more submissive than some people today would like it to be (to the extent that with the emphasis on the multiplicity of angels and their many effective powers, the role of God becomes less clear and active, thus stretching the limit of monotheism). In the contemporary practices that I encountered, the idea of human agency was indeed sometimes very strong, while the practice itself was explicitly material and also, to different degrees and in innovative but potentially challenging ways, 'magical' (in the sense of seeking direct efficacy). The level of 'magic' varied greatly, however. Sometimes angels were invoked to help in finding a parking place or lost object, but at other times they were merely asked to listen to one's worries.

A challenge for the women in the talisman-making was that the traditional Lutheran regime was considered to be very tightly bound to the importance of words. The use of right words – words that were not understood to bear magical connotations – was often considered a serious religious matter for the Lutheran faith. If the women wanted to remain in good standing with the tradition, they could not simply ignore this, but had to take it into account. We might even say that the women were tacitly aware of the Lutheran language ideology. Perhaps this awareness was not active and conscious (they might not have said they had it, if asked directly), but unconscious and embodied in their Lutheran cultural memory and habitus, which were learned already in childhood (cf. Kupari 2015). Interestingly, the case also shows how these angel practitioners – as a group of women engaging in (what was for them a new) embodied spiritual pedagogy (Shilling and Mellor 2007; Mellor and Shilling 2010), learning to talk a new kind of language and together appropriating new material and imaginary things that they could integrate in their everyday lives – were preparing to meet the challenges posed by the traditional religious institution and respond to it in a creative way, as well as with a good sense of humour.

A noteworthy perspective on the issue of how such spiritual practices may be perceived from the other side – that is from the viewpoint of the church – was provided during a relatively early stage of my project when I was invited to speak about angel spirituality at a seminar organised by the Research Network for the Study of New Religions in Finland (USVA) and Church Research Institute in Finland. One highly positioned administrator of the Lutheran Church in the audience reacted to my presentation with keen interest. He responded that the church would be wise to 'baptise' angel practices and rituals, suggesting that the church could perhaps include some of these in the churchly setting if people wanted them. My reply to him was that the idea sounded interesting and that some of my interviewees would warmly welcome it. However, the practices might also include other ideas that are not easily compatible with church belief and dogma, and some of these ideas might be so important for people that they would perhaps not be willing to compromise them. Aside from everyday enchantments, one can point to the frequently mentioned belief in reincarnation, as well as the idea that angels and other spirits may be approached in matters both large and small, from finding a parking place to communicating with the dead. Material practices, words and ideas exist in a dynamic and sometimes complex set of interactions and interdependence.

Angels as volatile, intimate and shared sensational forms

In the accounts and observations of my interviewees, angels can be circulated and mediated via variegated forms and practices, as well as sometimes through very concrete material objects, such as a talisman or a feather. The mediated angels are very diverse in how they appear and what they can mean, which can also change from one context to another. They are sometimes intimate personal spirits and at other times messengers between humans and divinity or an aspect of cosmic energy; they can also be understood as one's inner voice or as figures of speech, symbols or metaphors (e.g. of God's grace, friendship, intuition, goodness or light). For instance, Siân Reid similarly describes how her Canadian pagan research participants understood the many aspects of the Goddess in a dynamic way:

> Some believe that divinity is personal, some an aspect of one's own higher self, some that all the various divine personalities are expressions of one ineffable divine force, some in a true and competitive polytheism. Practitioners will describe their relationship to the divine and their beliefs about its nature differently, at different times and different contexts.
>
> (2008: 125)

Angels can in many ways and through different practices be seen, heard or felt on the skin (e.g. the 'touch of an angel' during a healing ritual or in the course of everyday life in the form of a breeze). They may become known, imagined or visualised in the mind during meditation, as well as featured in the words guiding the meditation. Materialising as balls of light ('orbs'), angels can also be photographed and captured in digital pictures, as was recounted to me by three separate interviewees; these images were then sometimes circulated on the Internet. Candles can be used in order to prepare the energy of the air for the arrival of angels. Sometimes angels are not seen by the practitioner herself, but instead become visible in the mind's eye through other people's visions and accounts (both as read in popular books and as recounted by friends); angels can even be communicated with through pets, such as cats and dogs, as I was told a couple of times (Utriainen 2013a). As very powerful and extraordinary angel moments are often materialised in some ways, as well as shared with others, they exist and become meaningful in social networks and via both horizontal and vertical relationships (see Day 2012; Walter 2016). Realising angels thus often describes shared rather than solely individual matters of concern and agency. This relationality of concern and agency was also evident in the depiction of the making of the talismans. To further stress my point, the following provides an ethnographic example of together making an angel 'happen' in a very concrete way.

During one angel evening, there was a newcomer who told the other participants that she did not know if she knew or felt angels in any way, but that of late she had nevertheless developed a strong interest in them. Very soon thereafter, the empty place beside her on the couch became occupied by an angel. How did this happen? First, the hostess of the evening took note of this empty seat and said that she was quite sure she had just seen somebody sitting in it and that it must have been an angel, since all the other seats were occupied, and only this one – a very good seat – was vacant. One by one, the other participants started to give support to this, either through words, smiles or by nodding their heads – that is by visible and audible signs of affirmation. In this way, they accepted the invitation of the hostess to see an angel on the couch and supported its being there. Thus, the angelic presence became commonly shared situational knowledge (which did not lack a degree of friendly social pressure). In this case, the very sensational form of angelic difference (the presence of an angel on the couch) was a product of collective making: a communicative, embodied act of enchantment around an empty seat. This example describes the power of a sensational form that is simultaneously in many delicate ways material, imaginary, intimate and social.

Conclusion

Despite a certain amount of laughter at the moment of translating 'angel talisman' into 'prayer ornament,' that moment (like others briefly discussed here) revealed important matters of concern. These matters show the richness of cultural work that circulating a traditional religious image can achieve. The sensational and aesthetic form of composing an angel talisman in the context of an angel healing course was – for some of the women more than others – about how to care for oneself and significant others, how to create meaningful work and income, and how to reorganise and relate to one's life again in a rapidly changing and unpredictable world. The issue of the increasing unpredictability of both work and the personal life was also a frequent topic in the interviews; many women recounted that the presence of angels was a big help in getting through difficult moments and phases. The talisman-making process also involved learning to be open about issues in one's private life in a new social network in order to find new perspectives and openings together. In many ways, the group worked as a peer-support network, jointly creating moments of intimate transcendence and solving problems. These moments of transcendence were not solely escapist and entertaining, but also firmly rooted in harsh everyday realities.

The example of the making of an angel talisman also shows interesting dynamics related to religion today, revealing how two different sensational forms – a language-orientated one and a more material one – meet, entangle and become negotiated. In moments in which the Protestant language ideology and its mostly metaphorical idea of an angel meet a new sensational form, such as an angel talisman, there is also a meeting of different concepts and practices of agency. The agency involved in talisman-making is hybrid, in that it mixes the human, the extraordinary and material enchantment (even 'magic') in ways that for some may compromise the Protestant idea of transcendent God and the manner in which the human subject should relate to that idea. And yet the women studied here were very much attracted and persuaded by this enchanting hybridity.

Through a glimpse of this kind of meeting and the potential tension of ideologies and practices, perhaps this example can also provide a point of reflection, like a raindrop can reflect its surroundings, on some more general issues and the kinds of expectations that people may have for religion/spirituality today as a resource and inspiration in everyday life. This example may also serve as a reminder about the potential spiritual importance and meaningfulness of matter. Lastly, I hope that focus on the angel talisman has also shown the ethnographic richness and potential of even the smallest material objects and moments.

Notes

1 This research is part of a larger project, Post-Secular Culture and a Changing Religious Landscape in Finland (PCCR), in Åbo Akademi University (2010–2014). The material consists of interviews, observations, a survey and media material. The interviews are kept at the Cultural Archive at Åbo Akademi University.
2 While many anthropologists of Christianity observe processes in which people turn from traditional religions to Christianity (e.g. Keane 2007; Robbins 2012), my observation concerns a case in which people from Christian backgrounds and culture become drawn to different degrees to alternative religious ideas and practices.
3 The survey was conducted at a lecture event by the Irish writer and angel-healer Lorna Byrne organised in Helsinki in 2011. The number of the audience was approximately 1,000 (94% of them being women). The survey material has been analysed by Elisa Mikkola in her master's thesis (Mikkola 2014).
4 In 2011, 77.2% of the population of Finland belonged to the Evangelical Lutheran Church.

Works cited

Ahonen, Johanna. 2014. 'Finnish Women's Turn toward India: Negotiations between Lutheran Christianity and Indian Spirituality'. In *Finnish Women Making Religion: Between Ancestors and Angels*, eds. Terhi Utriainen and Päivi Salmesvuori, 217–235. New York: Palgrave McMillan,

Ammerman, Nancy, ed. 2008. *Everyday Religion: Observing Modern Religious Lives*. Oxford: Oxford University Press.

Bennett, Jane. 2001. *The Enchantment of Modern Life: Attachments, Crossings, and Ethics*. Princeton, NJ: Princeton University Press.

Bowman, Marion. 1999. 'Healing in the Spiritual Marketplace: Consumers, Courses and Credentialism'. *Social Compass* 46(2): 181–189.

Bowman, Marion and Ülo Valk, eds. 2012. *Vernacular Religion in Everyday Life: Expressions of Belief*. Sheffield: Equinox.

Bruce, Steve and David Voas. 2010. 'Vicarious Religion: An Examination and Critique'. *Journal of Contemporary Religion* 25(2): 243–259.

Csordas, Thomas. 2004. 'Asymptote of the Ineffable: Embodiment, Alterity, and the Theory of Religion'. *Current Anthropology* 45(2): 163–185.

Day, Abby. 2012. 'Extraordinary Relationality: Ancestor Veneration in Late-Modern Euro-American Society'. *Nordic Journal of Religion and Society* 25(2): 169–181.

Draper, Scott and Joseph Baker. 2010. 'Angelic Belief as American Folk Religion'. *Sociological Forum* 26(3): 623–643.
Elkins, James and David Morgan. 2007. *Re-Enchantment (The Art Seminar)*. London: Routledge.
Gardella, Peter. 2007. *American Angels: Useful Spirits in the Material World*. Lawrence: University Press of Kansas.
Gilhus, Ingvild Sælid. 2012. 'Angels in Norway: Religious Border-Crossers and Border-Markers'. In *Vernacular Religion in Everyday Life: Expressions of Belief*, eds. Marion Bowman and Ülo Valk, 230–245. Sheffield: Equinox.
Haastettu kirkko. Suomen evankelis-luterilainen kirkko vuosina 2008–2011 (2012). Kirkon tutkimuskeskuksen julkaisuja 115.
Harvey, Graham. 2012. 'Things Act: Casual Indigenous Statements about the Performance of Object-Persons'. In *Vernacular Religion in Everyday Life: Expressions of Belief*, eds. Marion Bowman and Ülo Valk, 194–210. Sheffield: Equinox.
Hovi, Tuija. 2014. 'Servants and Agents: Gender Roles in Neocharismatic Christianity'. In *Finnish Women Making Religion: Between Ancestors and Angels*, ed. Terhi Utriainen and Päivi Salmesvuori, 177–193. New York: Palgrave McMillan.
Ilta-Sanomat. 2013. Uskomme enkeleihin. Suvi Kerttula. 12 December.
Kääriäinen, Kimmo, Kati Niemelä and Kimmo Ketola. 2005. *Religion in Finland: Decline, Change and Transformation of Finnish Religiosity*. Tampere: Church Research Institute.
Keane, Webb. 2007. *Christian Moderns: Freedom & Fetish in the Mission Encounter*. Berkeley: University of California Press.
Ketola, Kimmo, Tuomas Martikainen and Hanna Salomäki. 2014. 'New Communities of Worship: Continuities and Mutations among Religious Organizations in Finland'. *Social Compass* 61(2): 153–171.
Kupari, Helena. 2015. *Lifelong Religion as Habitus: Religious Practice among Displaced Karelian Orthodox Women in Finland*. Leiden: Brill.
Kuula, Kari, 2011. 'Mikkelinpäivä: Enkeleillä on kahdet kasvot'. http://evl.fi/EVLUutiset. nsf/Documents/20F97EDC1A8F71CFC225791000314D35?OpenDocument&lang=FI. Accessed 07/08/2015.
Lassander, Mika. 2012. 'Grappling with Liquid Modernity: Investigating Post-Secular Religion'. In *Post-Secular Society*, eds. Peter Nynäs, Mika Lassander and Terhi Utriainen, 239–267. New Brunswick: Transaction.
Latour, Bruno. 2004. 'Why Has Critique Run Out of Steam? From Matters of Fact to Matters of Concern'. *Critical Inquiry* 30(2): 225–248.
———. 2005. *Re-Assembling the Social: An Introduction to Actor-Network Theory*. Oxford: Oxford University Press.
Luckmann, Thomas. 1990. 'Shrinking Transcendence, Expanding Religion?' *Sociological Analysis* 50(2): 127–138.
Luhrmann, Tanya. 2004. 'Metakinesis: How God Becomes Intimate in Contemporary U.S. Christianity'. *American Anthropologist* 106(3): 518–528.
McGuire, Meredith. 2008. *Lived Religion: Faith and Practice in Everyday Life*. Oxford: Oxford University Press.
Mellor, Philip and Chris Shilling. 2010. 'Body Pedagogics and the Religious Habitus: A New Direction for the Sociological Study of Religion'. *Religion* 41(1): 27–38.
Meyer, Birgit. 2006. *Religious Sensations: Why Media, Aesthetics and Power Matter in the Study of Contemporary Religion*. Amsterdam: vrije Universiteit.
———. 2008. 'Media and the Senses in the Making of Religious Experience: An Introduction'. *Material Religion* 4(2): 124–135.

Meyer, Birgit and Peter Pals, eds. 2003. *Magic and Modernity: Interfaces of Revelation and Concealment*. Stanford, CA: Stanford University Press.
Miettinen, Esko. 2012. *Enkelit – taivaalliset auttajat*. Helsinki: Kirjapaja.
Mikkola, Elisa. 2014. *Apu on aina lähellä – Lorna Byrnen tilaisuuteen osallistuneiden enkelinäkemyksestä ja henkisyydestä*. Unpublished master's thesis. University of Helsinki.
Nye, Mallory. 2000. 'Religion, Post-Religionism and Religioning: Religious Studies and Contemporary Cultural Debates'. *Method & Theory in the Study of Religions* 12(1): 447–476.
Nynäs, Peter, Ruth Illman and Tuomas Martikainen. 2015. *On the Outskirts of 'the Church': Diversity, Fluidities and New Spaces of Religion in Finland*. Nordic Studies in Religion and Culture. Berlin: Lit Verlag.
Orsi, Robert. 2005. *Between Heaven and Earth: The Religious Worlds People Make and the Scholars Who Study Them*. Princeton, NJ: Princeton University Press.
Partridge, Christopher. 2004. *The Re-Enchantment of the West: Alternative Spiritualities, Sacralization, Popular Culture and Occulture*. London: T&T Clark International.
Piette, Albert. 2003. *Le Fait Religieux: Une Théorie de la Religion Ordinaire*. Paris: Economica.
Reid, Siân. 2008. 'The Soul of Soulless Conditions: Paganism, Goddess Religion and Witchcraft in Canada'. In *Women and Religion in the West: Challenging Secularization*, eds. Kristin Aune, Sonya Sharma and Giselle Vincett, 119–132. Hampshire: Ashgate.
Robbins, Joel. 2012. 'Transcendence and the Anthropology of Christianity: Language, Change, and Individualism'. *Suomen Antropologi: Journal of the Finnish Anthropological Society* 37(2): 5–23.
Salomonsen, Jone. 2002. *Enchanted Feminism: The Reclaiming Witches of San Francisco*. London: Routledge.
Seppälä, Olli. 2003. *Taivaallinen sanansaattaja*. Helsinki: Kirjapaja.
Shilling, Chris and Philip Mellor. 2007. 'Cultures of Embodied Experience: Technology, Religion and Body Pedagogics'. *The Sociological Review* 55(3): 531–549.
Siikala, Anna-Leena. 1997. 'Toisiinsa virtaavat maailmat'. In *Kaukaa haettua: Kirjoituksia antropologisesta kenttätyöstä*, eds. Anna-Maria Viljanen and Minna Lahti, 46–68. Helsinki: Suomen antropologinen seura.
Stringer, M.D. 2008. *Contemporary Western Ethnography and the Definition of Religion*. London: Continuum.
Sulavik, Andrew T. 2006a. 'An Annotated Bibliography on Protestant Theological Writings on Angels in Post-Reformation Thought from 1565 to 1739'. *Reformation and Renaissance Review* 8(2): 224–246.
———. 2007b. 'Protestant Theological Writings on Angels in Post-Reformation Thought from 1565 to 1739'. *Reformation and Renaissance Review* 8(2): 210–223.
Uibu, Marko. 2013. 'Creating Meanings and Supportive Networks on the Spiritual Internet Forum "The Nest of Angels"'. *Journal of Ethnology and Folkloristics* 6(2): 69–86.
Utriainen, Terhi. 2013a. 'Doing Things with Angels: Agency, Alterity and Practices of Enchantment'. In *New Age Spirituality: Rethinking Religion*, eds. Steven J. Suttcliffe and Ingvild Sælid Gilhus, 242–255. Durham: Acumen.
———. 2013b. 'Uskontotaidetta ja enkelinsiipiä: kaksi tapausta suomalaisissa naistenlehdissä'. *Media & Viestintä* 2: 40–52.
———. 2014a. 'Angels, Agency and Emotions: Global Religion for Women in Finland?' In *Finnish Women Making Religion: Between Ancestors and Angels*, eds. Terhi Utriainen and Päivi Salmesvuori, 237–254. New York: Palgrave McMillan.
———. 2014b. 'Enkeliuskon lumo'. *Kiistelty usko*. Tampere: Kirkon tutkimuskeskuksen verkkojulkaisuja 36: 34–42. http://sakasti.evl.fi/julkaisut.nsf/4D19C3DF942C29C7C2257 CD20026F74A/$FILE/verkkojulkaisu36.pdf. Accessed 7.8.2015.

———. Forthcoming. 'Healing Enchantment: How Does Angel Healing Work?' In *Spirit and Mind: Mental Health at the Intersection of Religion and Psychiatry*, eds. Helen Basu, Ronald Littlewood and Arne Steinforth. London: LIT Verlag.

Utriainen, Terhi, Linda Annunen, Nana Blomqvist and Måns Broo. 2015. 'Materialities, Bodies and Practices in Lived Religion'. In *On the Outskirts of 'the Church': Diversity, Fluidities and New Spaces of Religion in Finland*, eds. Peter Nynäs, Ruth Illman and Tuomas Martikainen, 95–110. Nordic Studies in Religion and Culture. Berlin: Lit Verlag.

Utriainen, Terhi and Päivi Salmesvuori, eds. 2014. *Finnish Women Making Religion: Between Ancestors and Angels*. New York: Palgrave McMillan.

Walter, Tony. 2011. 'Angels Not Souls: Popular Religion in the Online Mourning for British Celebrity Jane Goody'. *Religion* 41(1): 29–51.

———. 2016. 'The Dead Who Become Angels: Bereavement and Vernacular Religion'. *Omega: Journal of Death and Dying* 73(1): 3–28.

Whitehead, Amy. 2014. *Religious Statues and Personhood: Testing the Role of Materiality*. London: Bloomsbury Academic.

Woodhead, Linda and Rebecca Catto. 2012. *Religion and Change in Modern Britain*. London: Routledge.

Afterword
Materiality, lived religion, and the challenges of "going back to the things themselves"

Manuel Vásquez

In the influential Lived Religion in America, Robert Orsi called for a "materialist phenomenology" of religion (1997:8). He added the adjective "materialist" to move beyond the traditional appropriation of phenomenology in religious studies. This appropriation, of which Mircea Eliade (1959) was the most influential exponent, saw religion in essentialist terms, as the irreducible experience of *homo religiosus*, an ahistorical self whose relation to the sacred was shaped by archetypal forms. As such, although Eliade always sought to include in his analyses as many hierophanies – that is, spatio-temporal and material expressions of the sacred – as possible, he saw materiality as simply the medium for the historical manifestation of a deeper, more ontological, and trans-historical reality. In other words, traditional phenomenology did not grapple with the full implications of the inescapability of material mediation (Keane 2007).[1] It did not focus on the practices by which specific embodied individuals embedded in particular sociocultural and ecological contexts come to have real and efficacious experiences they deem religious. Scholars such as Russell McCutcheon (1997) and Tim Fitzgerald (2000) have rightly criticised traditional phenomenologies of religion for insulating religion from the sociopolitical contexts in which it operates, thereby "manufacturing" and legitimising the autonomy and authority of the discipline vis-à-vis naturalistic approaches in the social and natural sciences. In the wake of these critiques, phenomenology had to be rebuilt from the ground up, recovering our being-in-the-world in the fullest sense, as carnal beings living with, among, and through material agents, human and non-human.

While there have always been strands of scholarship in religion deeply interested in materiality, as the works of William Christian (1981), Peter Brown (1988), Carolyn Bynum (1987, 1995, 2011), and Colleen McDannell (1995) show, it is only in the last five years or so that we can speak of a materialist turn in religious studies. In his insightful chapter in this volume, David Morgan rightly points to the fact that the earliest works advancing the turn towards materiality tended to be heavily informed by theory, "applying abstract reasoning to non-material evidences, such as literary sources or philosophical debates." This theory-ladenness was justified by the attempt to ground the turn epistemologically, in particular to clear the space from the conceptual clutter that various forms of somatophobic idealisms and dualisms had created, allowing for the emergence of alternative frameworks and approaches that would allow us to explore materiality in all its dynamism and abundance. Nevertheless, Morgan is also correct in warning against the danger of engaging in excessive and one-sided metaphysical flights that may paradoxically end up ignoring the very same materiality these seminal works wanted to foreground, reproducing in many ways the textualism of traditional approaches to religion.

As the subfield has matured, several edited volumes have appeared, demonstrating empirically the implications of the turn towards materiality.[2] These volumes have brought to the fore the myriad of events, experiences, affects, practices, things, landscapes, and non-human agents that traditional phenomenology ignored, denigrated, or excluded from the legitimate scholarly study of religion. The strength of these volumes lies not only in the textured nature of the case studies but also in demonstrating the richness and multifarious potency of material religion, even in the contemporary world, a world that was supposed to be dominated by secular modernity. They are good expressions of Morgan's call to make materiality evidential, or to put it in good old phenomenological language: "to go back to the things themselves!" (Husserl 2001: 168).

As Morgan's chapter demonstrates in his discussion of religious objects and concepts like affordance, techniques of the body, habitus, and hexis, the next task is not only to continue to expand the empirical content of the turn to materiality, but also to develop fruitful cross-fertilisations of theory and facts that can allow for robust comparative analyses of materiality in different contexts. In other words, we need methodological tools that can make the analysis of material religion as sophisticated as the traditional study of texts, doctrines, and cosmologies. It seems to me that one of the major strengths of the essays in this collection is the fact that the authors operate precisely at that "meso-level," where the practice of theoretical reflection encounters the disciplined examination of particular material saliences. Building creatively on Morgan's suggestion to focus on the trajectory of things deemed religious, from production to use, the authors in this volume show that matter is best approached not as a brute given that human praxis transforms and animates by imbuing it with meaning, but as a process that involves contested-yet-relatively-stabilised networks of relations in which the various elements of the assemblage afford and/or constrain each other in specific ways.

Marion Bowman's chapter on candles is a good case in point. She shows that candles are "performative objects," which express "a range of purposes, meanings and emotions" of the communities that produce, circulate, and consume them. Thus, candles may materialise experiences of and longing for unity, diversity, healing, and/or inner spiritual enlightenment. They may literally enshrine what Yi-Fu Tuan (1974) called "topophilia," the visceral sense for and attachment to the energies of a place, as in the case of the Glastonbury Candles, which are made with local herbs. However, the candles' multiple valences are not unlimited: they are afforded and constrained by the nature of the materials – for example their durability and portability.

I would also like to suggest that another cross-cutting dimension that makes this collection cohesive and compelling as a paragon for study of material religion is the resolute effort by the various authors to study materiality in everyday life, to concentrate on "the way in which object[s] participate in making and sustaining a life-world." Whether it is blessed food among Jalarām Bāpā's devotees (Wood), music among British Muslims (Morris), the bodies of dead relatives and friends (Davies), relics and gestures (Carroll), dress (Arweck), artworks (Harvey), or talismans (Utriainen), the authors make a concerted effort to study how religious materiality is lived. Here they stand on the shoulders of the long-established "La Religion Vécue" school of French sociology, which always endeavoured to expand the study of religion beyond the literate elites, who, as Max Weber had proposed, articulate a rationalised and codified religion as a way to buttress orthodoxy. Pioneering works like Gabriel Le Bras's *Introduction à l'Histoire de la Pratique Religieuse en France* (1945), Henri Godin and Yvan Daniel's *La France, pays de mission* (1943), and Carlo Ginzburg's *The Cheese and the Worms* (1976), echoed and magnified by scholars such as Danièle Hervieu-Léger, Meredith McGuire, David Hall, Leigh Schmidt, and Orsi himself, shifted their focus to the study of vernacular beliefs, practices, and devotions of common persons, as they go about their daily lives, encountering existential predicaments through the spiritual and material resources at hand. As Orsi puts it, a lived religion approach

> insist[s] that something called "religion" cannot be separated from the other practices of everyday life, from the ways that human beings work on the landscape, for example, or dispose of corpses, or arrange for the security of their offspring. Nor can "religion" be separated from the material circumstances in which specific instances of religious imagination and behavior arise and to which they respond.
>
> (1997: 6–7)

The effort to approach materiality as a central dimension of lived religion, which this volume exemplifies, means that religion has to be studied not just in explicitly religious institutions, but also in spaces that modernity had designated as secular. Indeed, the study of lived religion points to the creative work of practitioners at the local level, blending media, times, spaces, and notions of individual and collective identity that modernity sought to keep separate. The recognition of these "hybrid cultures" informs, for example, Hutchings's piece on digital Bibles and online memorials, Nita's study of a climate camp and the Council of Beings, and Arweck's examination of young people's attitudes towards religion materialised in dress. These pieces show that to study materiality within lived religion is to concentrate on the way in which people negotiate the porous boundaries between the virtual and the physical, the local and the global, science and religion, the private and the public, individuality and tradition, outsider and insider status. This negotiation may result, often simultaneously, in a hardening of barriers to interaction (Arweck) and in the production of "new syncretic values" and practices of belonging and place-making (Nita). Such a negotiation is mediated by diverse forms of materiality. The horizons opened by the lived religion approach can even accommodate the illuminating work of Eccles and Catto on the "lived non-religiousness" of British atheists.

It seems to me, then, that this volume demonstrates that study of religious materiality is greatly enhanced by the skilful use of qualitative and quantitative field methods that enable us to map out the dynamics of production, dissemination, and use of various religious objects, as well as the interaction of these dynamics with other social, cultural, and ecological processes. Ethnographic and ethno-historical methods, in combination with critical geography and ecological psychology, seem particularly well suited to recover vernacular knowledges, popular practices, and subaltern voices. The materialist turn, thus, requires careful attention to and detailed analysis of the form and content of religious objects, and we can draw from disciplines such as archaeology, art history, media studies, and architecture, which have already developed powerful tools to approach them evidentially.[3] But, if the task is to follow the "social life of (religious) things," to adapt Arjun Appadurai's felicitous trope, this painstaking analysis of materials and styles must be accompanied and complemented by an equally robust examination of the "deployments" (Morgan, this volume) of the objects, the ways they are imbricated with other agents in the production of religious efficacy, an imbrication that often involves dynamics such as domination, resistance, and commodification. In that sense, the materialist turn is a truly interdisciplinary endeavour that seeks to bring into rigorous-yet-non-reductive focus everything from philosophical and theological discussions about the nature of matter to ethnographic studies of ritual practices and objects in particular communities, from surveys of attitudes towards materialised religion or of religious judgment (following Bourdieu's methodology in his monumental *Distinction*) to neurophenomenological investigations into meditation, prayer, or sacred dance, from explorations of digital religion to consideration of the ways in which institutions, like museums (Berns, this volume), global culture industries, or the neoliberal capitalist state, facilitate or hinder "encounters with the materially mediated divine" in the society of origin or in the diaspora.

Just as we need to be disciplinarily capacious, our focus also needs to widen to include not just relics and icons but also sacred spaces and environments – mountains, rivers, groves, forests, caves, rock formations, pilgrimage roads – as well as non-human animals and things, such as the window of a bank building or a tile on a subway station wall, which enable the presencing of the uncanny, like an apparition of the Virgin Mary.[4] All of these landscapes, beings, and things, together with the gods, goddesses, and spirits they "world," are instances of "the many non-human actors who circulate within a given network: agents who make their presence felt by sharing the labor required to gather, attach, move, motivate or bind their fellow actors together into a social aggregate" (Day 2010: 278).[5] This evidential multiplicity will require theoretical flexibility and a strategic methodological pluralism.

What we need is a fully "vascularised" study of religion. In physiology, the term "vascularised" is used to describe living tissues, whose relative vitality, robustness, and complexity are generated and sustained by a myriad of vessels that enable multiple flows to and from these tissues. Generally, living tissues show greater development as the vessels that supply them proliferate and ramify. Science studies scholar Bruno Latour (1999) and other actor-network theorists have borrowed the term to advocate for richer accounts of the social world that approach it as the stabilised-yet-contested outcome of the collaboration of heterogeneous actants, including a "multiplication of non-humans" (Latour 1993: 135), assembled by intersecting networks.[6] The essays in this volume succeed admirably in showing how the materialist turn "expand[s] our vocabulary and analysis," as Harvey (this volume) writes.

This success, however, raises the daunting challenge of how to capture in the fullest and most rigorous manner the complexity, diversity, and generativity of religious materiality. Here we must recognise the paradoxes of our own scholarly mediations of material mediation in religion. What are the affordances and constraints of the written word, even when accompanied by lavish illustrations, in re-presenting the liveliness of religious matter? What are the kinds of alternative knowledges, forms of scholarship, and mixed-hybrid-performative media needed to produce richer, more vivid accounts of the dynamism of religious materiality and to continue expanding our conversation about religion? Does the study of the things in motion, embedded in multiple scales, part and parcel of dense and shifting networks of relation, necessitate the rethinking of the academic regime of value in the humanities, which is anchored on the authoritative materiality of the monograph produced by the heroic efforts of the sovereign, "buffered" single author? Can the vascularised study of "vibrant matter" (Bennett 2010) usher in a new truly collaborative and cross-disciplinary scholarly habitus?

Notes

1 As Tim Hutchings and Joanne McKenzie point out in their introduction, the flight from materiality is a constitutive feature of modernity, part of its effort to construct a "buffered" self, a rational, unified, and sovereign self that is immune to natural and supernatural "forces [that] could cross a porous boundary and shape our lives, psychic and physical" (Taylor 2008). The construction of this self required the disenchantment of matter, the denial of its agency vis-à-vis a vulnerable, porous self, and the disembodiment of the self, since the body is the surface that affords that vulnerability.
2 For example see Morgan (2009), Houtman and Meyer (2012), Plate (2014), Promey (2014), and Pintchman and Dempsey (2015).
3 See for example Meskell (2005), Tilley et al. (2006), Dudley (2010), and Tolia-Kelley and Rose (2012).
4 For examples of this widening materialist focus, see Haberman (2013), Kent (2013), Kohn (2013), Maddrell, Terry and Gale (2015), and Shaffer (2015). On the Marian apparitions, globalisation, and materiality, see Vásquez and Marquardt (2000).
5 I borrow the term "worlding" from Heidegger, who used to explore the processes whereby the embodied and emplaced self (*Dasein*) comes to experience the things among which it is thrown as a meaningful life-world.

6 On the concept of network in the study of religious materiality, see Day (2010), Morgan (2014), and Vásquez (2008). For a good empirical illustration, see Neelis (2011).

Works Cited

Appadurai, Arjun, ed. 1986. *The Social Life of Things: Commodities in Cultural Perspective*. Cambridge: Cambridge University Press.

Bennett, Jane. 2010. *Vibrant Matter: A Political Ecology of Things*. Durham, NC: Duke University Press.

Brown, Peter. 1988. *The Body and Society: Men, Women, and Sexual Renunciation in Early Christianity*. New York: Columbia University Press.

Bynum, Carolyn. 1987. *Holy Feast and Holy Fast: The Religious Significance of Food to Medieval Women*. Berkeley: University of California Press.

———. 1995. *The Resurrection of the Body in Western Christianity, 200–1336*. New York: Columbia University Press.

———. 2011. *Christian Materiality: An Essay on Religion in Late Medieval Europe*. London: Zone Books.

Christian, William. 1981. *Local Religion in Sixteenth Century Spain*. Princeton, NJ: Princeton University Press.

Day, Matthew. 2010. 'How to Keep It Real.' *Method and Theory in the Study of Religion* 22: 272–282.

Dudley, Sandra, ed. 2010. *Museum Materialities: Objects, Engagements, Interpretations*. New York: Routledge.

Eliade, Mircea. 1959. *The Sacred and the Profane: The Nature of Religion*. Orlando, FL: Harcourt.

Fitzgerald, Timothy. 2000. *The Ideology of Religious Studies*. New York: Oxford University Press.

Haberman, David, 2013. *People Trees: Worships of Trees in Northern India*. New York: Oxford University Press.

Houtman, Dick and Birgit Meyer, eds. 2012. *Things: Religion and the Question of Materiality*. New York: Fordham University Press.

Husserl, Edmund. 2001. *Logical Investigations*. 2 vols. London: Routledge.

Keane, Webb. 2007. *Christian Moderns: Freedom and Fetish in the Mission Encounter*. Berkeley: University of California Press.

Kent, Eliza F. 2013. *Sacred Groves and Local Gods: Religion and Environmentalism in South India*. New York: Oxford University Press.

Kohn, Eduardo. 2013. *How Forest Think: Toward an Anthropology beyond the Human*. Berkeley: University of California Press.

Latour, Bruno. 1993. *We Have Never Been Modern*. Cambridge, MA: Harvard University Press.

———. 1999. *Pandora's Hope: Essays on the Reality of Science Studies*. Cambridge, MA: Harvard University Press.

Maddrell, Avril, Terry Alan and Tim Gale, eds. 2015. *Sacred Mobilities: Journeys of Belief and Belonging*. New York: Ashgate.

McCutcheon, Russell. 1997. *Manufacturing Religion: The Discourse on Sui Generis Religion and the Politics of Nostalgia*. New York: Oxford University Press.

McDannell, Colleen. 1995. *Material Christianity: Religion and Popular Culture in America*. New Heaven, CT: Yale University Press.

Meskell, Lynn. 2005. *Archaeologies of Materiality*. Malden, MA: Blackwell.

Morgan, David, ed. 2009. *Religion and Material Culture: The Matter of Belief*. New York: Routledge.

———. 2014. 'The Ecology of Images: Seeing and the Study of Religion.' *Religion and Society: Advances in Research* 5, 83–105.

Neelis, Jason. 2011. *Early Buddhist Transmission and Trade Networks.* Leiden: Brill.

Orsi, Robert. 1997. 'Everyday Miracles: The Study of Lived Religion.' In *Lived Religion in America: Toward a History of Practice*, 3–21. Princeton, NJ: Princeton University Press.

Pintchman, Tracy and Corine Dempsey, eds. 2015. *Sacred Matters: Material Religion in South Asian Traditions.* Albany: State University of New York Press.

Plate, S. Brent. 2014. *A History of Religion in 5 1/2 Objects: Bringing the Spiritual to its Senses.* Boston, MA: Beacon.

Promey, Sally, ed. 2014. *Sensational Religion: Sensory Culture in Material Practice.* New Heaven, CT: Yale University Press.

Shaffer, Donovan. 2015. *Religious Affects: Animality, Evolution, and Power.* Durham, NC: Duke University Press.

Taylor, Charles. 2008. 'A Secular Age: Buffered and Porous Selves.' Post on *Immanent Frame*. http://blogs.ssrc.org/tif/2008/09/02/buffered-and-porous-selves/.Accessed 11/05/2016.

Tilley, Christopher, Webb Keane, Susanne Küchler, Patricia Spyer and Mike Rawlands, eds. 2006. *Handbook of Material Culture.* London: SAGE.

Tolia-Kelley, Divya and Gillian Rose, eds. 2012. *Visuality/Materiality: Images, Objects and Practices.* New York: Ashgate.

Tuan, Yi-Fu. 1974. *Topophilia: A Study of Environmental Perception, Attitudes, and Values.* Inglewood, NJ: Prentice-Hall.

Vásquez, Manuel A. 2008. 'Studying Religion in Motion: A Networks Approach.' *Method and Theory in the Study of Religion* 20: 151–184.

Vásquez, Manuel A. and Marie F. Marquardt. 2000. 'Globalizing the Rainbow Madonna: Old-Time Religion in the Present Age.' *Theory, Culture & Society* 17(4): 119–143.

Index

aesthetics 90, 212–13, 221, 223
affordance 24, 31, 36
afterlife 170, 173
agency 220, 221, 228, 230; of objects 203
altar 144, 148–9
alternative spirituality 220, 222–4
Altieri, Pia 108
amulet 222, 225–7, 229–30
ancestor 110, 111
angels 219, 222–4; angel photographs 229; angels and Lutheranism 223–4, 227–8; angels in Islam 173, 177; angel visitations 219, 224, 229–30; *see also* amulet; healing
animacy 170, 173, 182, 183
animism 103, 113, 169, 170, 178
Aquinas, Thomas 180
architecture 170, 177, 180, 186; *see also* places of worship
archive 25, 95, 175
Aristotle 29
authentication 123, 210
authenticity 28, 76, 87, 109
authority 3–4, 139, 223; gatekeepers 136

belief 35, 43, 63, 180, 224; denial of 151, 155; education and 157, 198; expressions of 70, 144, 158, 224, 228; relativism of 40; religion as 5–6, 89, 103–4, 107, 209; *see also* embodiment and belief
blessing: in Islam (*Barakah*) 204, 208–9, 213–15; from and through objects 27, 126–8; from and through people 40, 121, 129; *see also* Jalarambapa, miracles and blessings of
body: constructed under gaze of others 200; and gestures 128, 171, 209, 225; relationship with soul 42, 122–5, 128, 131, 170, 173; as relic 1–2, 119–20, 122, 126, 176; *see also* embodiment
boundaries 4, 83, 139–41, 173, 237
Bourdieu, Pierre 29, 71, 171, 238

brands and branding 3, 9, 39, 73, 75; *see also* consumer culture and lifestyle; trade and commerce
Brown, Bill 24
Buddha 176, 178, 182
burial 96, 170, 175; coffin 1–3, 172, 174; natural 174–5

candles 35–6, 41–2, 95, 136, 229; as cause of damage 28; meaning of 36, 44–5, 48, 236; placement of 40, 45, 144
Catholicism 23, 40, 42, 119, 176; hostility to 2, 7, 160, 178
cemeteries 171–2, 182
ceremony 39, 57, 110, 161
Christianity: charismatic 220, 224; Church of England 2; Eastern Orthodox 120, 174, 176, 178; evangelical 6, 91, 156–7; Lutheran and Evangelical Lutheran 220, 223–4, 226–7; *see also* Catholicism; Protestantism
circulation 9, 15, 27–30, 41, 175, 206
classification 8, 15, 24
Clement of Alexandria 123–4
climate change 133; activism 133, 138–41; green Christians 139, 144; green movement 133, 138
clothing 15, 29; in Christianity 124, 126; in Hinduism, as gift 60–1; in Islam 76, 155, 185–6; 188–9, 192, 195–9; in Judaism 189; religious, attitudes to 185, 193–9; in Sikhism 61, 185–6, 188–90, 195, 198
Colonialism 7, 105, 141
colours, symbolism of 39
community identity 39, 69, 72, 139, 185
conflict, religious 2–3, 7, 37, 45, 177, 185
consumer culture and lifestyle 23, 73–8, 81, 106, 140; *see also* brands and branding; trade and commerce
cremation 170, 175; and disposal of ashes 175–6

damage 22, 23, 28
Darwin, Charles 171
Dawkins, Richard 151, 159, 160
death: bereavement 95, 170–2; corpse 1–3, 170, 172–4; *see also* body, as relic; burial; memorials
design 15, 22, 76–7, 93, 174; conservatism in design 26, 90, 94, 97, 174
digital: anthropology 90; internet, perceptions of 86; internet and music distribution 81–2; materiality of digital media 86, 89–90; social media 37, 91, 155, 159; websites 37, 74, 87, 91, 159, 227; *see also* space, virtual
distribution 54, 74–5, 78
Durkheim, Emile 169

Echchaibi, Nabil 74, 78
education and religion 186–7
education as religious pedagogy 70, 79–80; *see also* proselytism
Eliade, Mircea 138, 235
embodiment 29, 86, 115, 169–72, 205, 230; and belief 6, 14, 152, 155, 228, 235
emotion 6, 48, 200, 209, 220; communication of 70, 94; and conflict 153, 156; and rationality 152; and ritual 36, 56, 172, 182; *see also* death, bereavement
enchantment 222, 228–9
Engelke, Matthew 4, 6, 7, 49, 158
ethics and morality 52, 56, 63, 68, 75

fabric 125, 131; *see also* Mecca, *sitara*
feminism 222
festivals 40, 42, 52, 139, 186
fetish 105–8
flame, symbolism of 41, 42, 44, 45
food 110; divine and human consumption of 57, 62; fasting 70, 138, 191, 192, 197; *halal* 74, 192; production of 55–7; *see also* gift, as charity; ISKCON and food; Jalarambapa, miracles and blessings of
Foucault, Michel 129–30
function 15, 22, 24, 36, 89

Geertz, Clifford 172
Gell, Alfred 129–30
gift 27, 112–13; as charity or service 52, 54, 58–9, 61; *see also* proselytism, gift as
Glassie, Henry 35
Glastonbury 37–42
grief *see* death, bereavement

habitus 28–9, 76, 171, 200, 228, 239
Halal industry 73–4; *see also* food, *halal*

Hallowell, Irving 112–14
healing 39, 219, 225
Heidegger, Martin 122
Hine, Christine 86
humanity: human-non-human relations 5, 105, 137–8, 210, 221; nature of 86, 124, 127, 170; other-than-human persons 49, 106, 113; service to humanity 59; *see also* agency

icons 176–8, 208
identity: after death 179; change of 28, 86, 137, 181; construction of 5, 74, 169, 180; non-religious 154, 162; regional 3; religious 63, 68, 134–5, 141, 190, 195–7
idolatry 177
immateriality 6, 14, 30, 86, 90, 128, 208
Ingold, Tim 104, 108, 109, 122, 127, 206
intention, of maker or producer 5, 15, 22, 69, 105, 199
intention, of user or performer 36, 56, 69
interfaith relations 37, 62, 70, 71, 204
internet *see* digital
ISKCON and food 58–9, 62
Islam: beliefs and values 68, 70, 72, 173, 203; diversity and individuality 72; hostility or ambivalence to 190, 196, 197; Prophet Mohammed 177–8, 205, 212; prophets 205, 214; *see also* clothing, in Islam; *Halal* industry; Islam and music; Mecca; pilgrimage, *hajj*; Qur'an
Islam and music: fandom 81, 83; genres of 67–8; hip hop 71, 73, 75–6; instrumentation, restrictions on 75, 79; studios and production companies 80; *see also* Islam

Jalarambapa 52, 56; miracles and blessings of 53, 55–6, 60, 61; stories of 53
Jesus 42, 43, 142, 180–1, 224; *see also* statue, of Jesus and Sacred Heart

Latour, Bruno 7, 107, 135, 206, 212, 239; law and legislation 133, 175, 186, 195; life-world 15, 30, 48, 237; lived atheism 153, 155; lived religion 36, 105, 185, 219, 237; *see also* vernacular religion
Lynch, Gordon 152–3, 158, 159

Maffesoli, Michel 29
manufacture 8, 15, 23, 39; of technology 95, 97, 107
manufacturer 15, 22, 174, 205
masks 107, 108

Index

materiality, definition of 6, 88, 89
material religion, definition of 4–6
Mauss, Marcel 29, 171
Mecca 203, 206, 213, 215; *Ka'ba* 204, 205, 210, 212, 214; Mecca Cola 73; *sitara* 203, 205, 209–11, 213; *see also* pilgrimage, *hajj*
media, representations of religion in 140, 177, 200, 223; and Islam 191, 196, 198; Pope Benedict's visit to the UK 160
mediate, mediation 5, 87–8, 126, 158, 221, 238
memorials 93–6, 171–2, 175
memory 93, 203, 209, 213–15, 228; of the dead 36, 48, 94–6, 172, 175, 182
Meyer, Birgit 4, 6, 29, 87, 209, 221
migration 23, 53, 187
modernity 4, 7, 103, 107, 236
Mol, Hans 179
Morgan, David 4–5, 6, 8–9, 152, 210, 235
multiculturalism 187, 190
museums 27, 87, 108–9, 114; aestheticising effect 114, 213–14; British Museum 9, 203–4, 210–13
music 185; *see also* Islam and music

narrative *see* Jalarambapa, stories of
nature, natural 40, 107, 134, 144; *see also* burial, natural
non-religion 94, 151, 209; atheist 138, 151–3, 155, 162, 194; humanist 154, 156, 158

Olsson, Tord 106
Orsi, Robert 7, 235
Otto, Rudolph 182

Pels, Peter 104
performativity, performance 36, 48, 69, 97, 105
personhood 107, 110, 113–15, 129, 169, 182
pilgrimage 54, 120, 179; *Hajj* 70, 203–15; *see also* Glastonbury; saints, St. Cuthbert
places of worship: Christian 2, 5, 42, 120, 143, 220; Hindu 52, 57; shrines, in home 52, 95; *see also* candles; Mecca; space, sacred; statue
Plate, S. Brent 4–6, 88, 210
prayer: to angels 225–6; Catholic 25, 28, 44–6, 87, 179; Eastern Orthodox 120, 122–3; Green Christian 141; Islamic 69, 173, 192, 197, 206, 213
Primiano, Leonard 35, 49, 105
production *see* manufacture
proselytism 92; gift as 59, 93

Protestantism: and alternative spirituality 220, 227; Protestant Reformation 4, 178, 179, 181, 220, 227; and words 7, 220, 228

Qur'an 70, 177, 190, 192–3, 205, 208–9; Qur'anic decoration 205, 213–14; Qur'anic recitation 69

Rajdev, Saubhagyachand 53, 55
reception 15, 28
reincarnation and transmigration 170, 228
relationality: with the dead 45, 93, 111, 172, 176; with the divine 208, 213, 229; with the living 47, 91, 92, 113, 141, 229; with other cultures 114; with place and planet 134–6, 147, 152; with things 104–5, 109, 178
relics: in Catholic Christianity 1–2, 42, 119, 176; in Orthodox Christianity 119–23, 125, 176; *see also* body, as relic; clothing; saints, Virgin Mary
religion, definition of 30, 172
remediation 15, 25, 88
representation 104, 143, 155, 177–8; *see also* media, representations of religion in
ritual: and belief 6, 104, 170, 172, 177, 178; communion, Eucharist, Mass 104, 128, 141–2, 144, 176, 180–1; and language 107; liturgy 6, 16, 104, 120, 170–2, 181; material religion as study of 4; and memory 96, 98, 174, 206; and non-religion 153; and objects 36, 42, 104, 145, 147, 223; and protest or conflict 147, 155, 211; rites of passage 160–1, 197; ritual purity 56, 62; and space 135–8, 141

sacredness 4, 30, 152–3; sacred food 63; sacred objects 108, 126–7, 152; *see also* space, sacred; text, as sacred
saints: St. Anthony 45; St. Cuthbert 1–4, 5, 8–9; Virgin Mary 40, 125, 178; *see also* Jalarambapa
secular 42, 143, 178, 192, 222, 236–7; *see also* space, secular
shamanism 112
Sikhism 62, 178–9, 195; *see also* clothing, in Sikhism
space 5, 37, 94, 139–41, 152, 203, 207; sacred 37, 40, 47, 133–6, 138, 141–2, 146–9; secular 42, 156–8, 162; virtual 86, 96, 154
statue: Hindu 57; of Jesus and Sacred Heart 16–21, 25–8; manufacture of 23–4; of St. Anthony 45–7

symbols 178; and cultural reproduction 28; and identity 74, 141, 143, 176, 185–6, 229; and ritual 44, 98, 104, 113; and study of religion 6, 172

taste and kitsch 23, 28–9, 93
technology 26, 86, 90, 95
text: as focus for religious studies 5, 14, 70, 236; as material object 2, 6, 89, 92, 160; as sacred 91–3, 160, 177–8, 225; *see also* Qur'an
things: classification of 24–5, 122; definition of 103, 122; material religion as study of 4–5, 35; relations between 90, 109, 114, 172, 208–9, 213
tolerance 2, 41, 158, 200
totemism 177, 180, 183
touch, physical 16, 28, 89, 207; as blessing 120, 126, 204, 222; as cause of damage 28, 204
trade and commerce: collectibles 27; cost, financial 8, 16, 23–4, 42, 60, 93, 175; financial difficulty 82; religious shops and companies 9, 23, 26, 39, 47, 73; *see also* brands and branding; consumer culture and lifestyle; *Halal* industry
Turner, Victor 135, 139, 172
Tylor, Edward Burnett 170, 178

Universities and Colleges Christian Fellowship 92

Vasquez, Manuel 7, 105, 115, 186
vernacular religion 35, 105, 221, 237–8
vicarious religion 219
Virtus 119–20, 123, 131

water, use in ritual 39–40, 57, 144, 181
Weber, Max 171, 237

youth 70, 90, 154, 157, 185–7, 195, 200; *see also* education and religion
Yusuf, Sami 67, 71–2, 79

Printed in the United States
By Bookmasters